Psychosocial Therapy

Treatment Approaches in the Human Services

FRANCIS J. TURNER, EDITOR

PSYCHOSOCIAL THERAPY

Francis J. Turner

The Free Press
A Division of Macmillan Publishing Co., Inc.
NEW YORK

Collier Macmillan Publishers
LONDON

The Free Press
A Division of Macmillan Publishing Co., Inc.
866 Third Avenue, New York, N.Y. 10022

Collier Macmillan Canada, Ltd.

Library of Congress Catalog Card Number: 77-90456

Printed in the United States of America

printing number

1   2   3   4   5   6   7   8   9   10

Library of Congress Cataloging in Publication Data

Turner, Francis Joseph
    Psychosocial therapy.

    (Treatment approaches in the human services)
    Bibliography: p.
    Includes index.
    1. Psychotherapy. 2. Psychiatric social work.
I. Title. II. Series. [DNLM: 1. Socioenviron-
mental therapy. WM428 T946p]
RC480.5.T79   616.8'914   77-90456
ISBN 0-02-932720-2

To My Father

"When good men die their goodness does not perish, but lives though they are gone."

Euripides

Contents

Series Introduction

"Treatment Approaches in the Human Services" is the first series of professional texts to be prepared to cover a broad spectrum of approaches to social work practice. It is understandable that the editor and authors of this endeavor should be enthusiastic about its quality and prospects. But it is equally understandable that caution and prudence temper our enthusiasm. There is a presumptuousness in attempting to be on the leading edge of thinking and aspiring to break new ground, and our professional experience urges us to be restrained.

The first suggestion for this series came from the editorial staff of The Free Press in the spring of 1975. At that time, the early responses to *Social Work Treatment** were available. It was clear from these responses that, useful as that book appeared to be, there was a wish and a need for more detail on each of the various thought systems covered, especially as regards their direct practice implications. These comments led to a proposal from The Free Press that a series be developed that would expand the content of the individual chapters of *Social Work Treatment* into full-length books with the objective of providing a richer and fuller exposition of each system. This idea is still germane to the series, but with the emergence of new thought systems and

*Francis J. Turner, ed., *Social Work Treatment* (New York: Free Press, 1974).

theories it has moved beyond the notion of expanding the chapters in the original collection. New thinking in the helping professions, the diversity of new demands, and the complexity of these demands have increased beyond the expectations of even the harbingers of the knowledge explosion of the early 1970s. No profession can or should stand still, and thus no professional literature can be static. It is our hope that this series will stay continuously current as it takes account of new ideas emerging from practice.

By design, this series is oriented to social work. But it is not designed for social workers alone; it is also intended to be useful to our colleagues in other professions. The point has frequently been made that much of the conceptual base of social work practice has been borrowed and that social work has made few original contributions to other professions. This is no longer true. A principal assumption of this series is that social work must now accept the responsibility for making available to other professions its rich accumulation of theoretical concepts and therapeutic strategies.

This responsibility to share does not presume that professions with a healing and human-development commitment are moving to some commonality of identity and structure. In the next decade we are probably going to see clearer rather than more obscure professional identities and more rather than less precise professional boundaries, derived not from different knowledge bases but from differential use of shared knowledge. If this prediction is valid, it follows that each profession must develop increased and enriched ways of making available to other professions its own expanding knowledge of the human condition.

Although the books in this series are written from the viewpoint of the clinician, they will be useful for the student-professional, the senior scholar, and the teacher of professionals as well. On the principle that no dynamic profession can tolerate division among its practitioners, theory builders, and teachers, each book is intended to be a bridging resource between practice and theory development. In directing this series to colleagues whose principal targets of practice are individuals, families, and groups, we take the other essential fields of practice as given. Thus the community-development, social action, policy, research, and service-delivery roles of the helping professions are not addressed specifically in these books.

One of the risks of living and practicing in an environment characterized by pluralism in professions, practice styles, and theoretical orientations is that one may easily become doctrinaire in defending a particular perspective. Useful and important as is ongoing debate that leads to clarification of similarities and differences, overlaps and gaps in thought systems and theories, the authors of these books have been asked to minimize this function. That is, they are to analyze the conceptual base of their particular topic, identify its theoretical origins, explain and describe its operationalization in practice, but avoid polemics in behalf of "their" system. Inevitably, some material of this type is needed for comparisons, but the aim is to make the books explicative rather than argumentative.

Although the series has a clear focus and explicit objectives, there is also a strong commitment that it be marked with a quality of development and evolution. We hope that we will be responsive to changes in psychotherapeutic practice and to the needs of colleagues in practice and thus be ready to alter the format of subsequent books as may be necessary.

In a similar way, the ultimate number of books in the series has been left open. In view of current practice in the late 1970s, it is possible to identify a large number of influential thought systems that need to be addressed. We can only presume that additional perspectives will emerge in the future. These will be addressed as the series continues, as will new developments or reformulations of existing practice perspectives.

The practice of psychotherapy and the wide spectrum of activities that it encompasses is a risky and uncertain endeavor. At one time we were concerned because we knew so little; now we are concerned to use fully the rich progress that has been made in research, practice, and conceptualization. Clearly, we are just beginning a new era of human knowledge and improved clinical approaches and methods. This series is dedicated to this task in the humble hope that it will contribute to man's concern for his fellows.

Francis J. Turner

Preface

In the past decade we have observed a growing use of the term "psychosocial" in the professional literature of the human services. Although the term was used originally in a descriptive way to convey a bridging concept between psychological and sociological concepts, it now increasingly conveys a distinct orientation to psychotherapy.

Because of social work's historical commitment to and responsibility for man in interaction with his significant milieu, it is understandable that social workers have given particular attention to this form of practice. Indeed, it is the thesis of this book that social work, particularly the work of Florence Hollis, has made the major contribution to the development of psychosocial therapy as a distinctive practice style.

As a practice system in its own right, psychosocial therapy has drawn heavily from earlier therapeutic theories, particularly psychoanalytic theory and later the reformulations of ego psychology. What makes it especially useful for social work is its commitment to a broader and more diverse understanding of psychological man and his social functioning than was provided by earlier thinking. In an era when practice is being influenced by a wide spectrum of thought systems, this openness to new ideas from many disciplines and the willingness to incorporate them have made the psychosocial orientation of increasing value to all the helping systems—not only social work but also psychiatry, psychology, and education.

Psychosocial therapy is attractive to many practitioners, especially experienced practitioners, because of its fundamentally optimistic perception of human potential. It thus serves as a counterpoise to the negativistic attitude that can easily develop as one views the reality of the human condition as it is met in practice. Man's basic dependency and concomitant anxiety are recognized and respected, but so too are his powerfully positive qualities of curiosity and searching and his aggressive wish to achieve.

In the effort to help clients achieve their full potential within their own value frameworks, the therapeutic relationship is a powerful medium. His awareness of its power helps the psychosocial therapist to appreciate the conscious and unconscious influences of other relationships in the client's life and to use these as therapeutic resources. Thus, a strong theme of this book is that therapy is a complex activity requiring understanding and utilization of a broad range of thought systems, treatment methods, and environmentally oriented skills.

Throughout this book, use of the word "theory" is minimal. It is quite evident that at this point in its development the psychosocial system cannot fully qualify as a theory. Rather, it is probably somewhere between an orientation to practice and an emerging theory. This caution against overstating the tested conceptual base of the system is important for the exciting yet formidable empirical tasks that still lie ahead.

Much work is needed to specify and operationalize the principal concepts of psychosocial therapy and to develop and test the linkages between them. Further work is also needed to develop a diagnostic system and to interconnect the differential use of techniques, resources and methodologies with diagnosis. A theme of this book is that these next steps will probably be taken through many small, well-designed, interrelated experiments and research studies, not by the *grande étude* that seeks to be the definitive word.

As a part of The Free Press series on *Treatment Approaches in the Human Services,* this book seeks to provide a further resource to students and practitioners that will contribute to the enrichment of current practice and the development of future therapeutic techniques.

Acknowledgments

The process of writing a book is both a lonely, draining intellectual activity and a richly shared social experience. At its completion an author wishes to acknowledge all the persons involved in these two facets of its production. But this is a formidable challenge!

From the conceptual perspective I find it difficult to be precise. With each passing year I become aware that the sources of new ideas are multitudinous, complex and interactive; hence the impossibility of specificity. Certainly my teachers, students, colleagues and clients have influenced this book and to them I am grateful.

On the social side it is easier to be specific. In this instance the foresight, encouragement and support of The Free Press and its staff, especially Gladys Topkis, have played a facilitating role. The assistance and interest of several graduate students have been helpful and enriching. The patience and skill of the several typists have been welcomed. The continuing support of Joanne has been necessary. The enthusiasm of my assistants, Francis, Sarah, and Anne Marie, has been essential. Lastly, the reality of a new swimming pool has been a strong motivation. I am thankful to all.

Chapter 1

The Historical and Conceptual Development of Psychosocial Therapy

Among the many thought systems that are currently influencing the varied forms of psychotherapeutic and counseling endeavors, psychosocial therapy is rapidly achieving a prominent position. Although the term psychosocial, or various derivations of it, can be found in the literature of several disciplines going back over three decades and the ideas underlying the term can be traced back to the late nineteenth century, it is only in the early 1960s that psychosocial therapy emerged as a distinct approach to clinical practice. This took place with the publication in 1964 of the first edition of Florence Hollis's *Casework: A Psychosocial Therapy*.[1]

Hollis's choice of title for her landmark book on the practice of clinical social work was particularly significant and opportune. The book appeared at a time when several important inter- and intraprofessional issues were being debated. The first of these, which had predominated in the 1950s, dealt with whether the practice of casework, the clinical component of social work, was or was not a form of psychotherapy. Although this debate has long since been resolved in the affirmative, at the time it was a critical issue. Then, as now, social work had a powerful interest in

1

being recognized as one of the professions that practiced psychotherapy. This was especially so at the time because the mental health movement was enjoying strong public support. Thus to be a practitioner of psychotherapy conferred high status. But at the same time that this interprofessional struggle was under way, a parallel dialogue was taking place among social workers themselves. With the increased interest in psychotherapy as a cross-disciplinary activity, some social workers began to oppose the idea that casework and psychotherapy could be seen as coterminous. It was feared that such a perception might undermine and eventually destroy appreciation of the unique contribution of social work among the helping professions. This was seen as a serious risk to the identity and hard-won status of social workers: the possibility that our functions would be absorbed into the role of other professions.

Thus Hollis's book was most timely. Although it was perhaps not realized then, the conceptual thrust of the book, as reflected in its title, spoke to both of these prior questions. First, it clearly took a position that placed the skills and knowledge of the social worker within the psychotherapeutic arena. At the same time it made a strong case for the autonomous role of the social worker among the psychotherapists. The foundation of this autonomy was to be a *psychosocial* approach to practice, the theoretical basis on which the book was written.

Psychosocial theory starts from the premise that a proper understanding of man that will lead to responsible and demonstrably effective intervention requires that a balanced position be taken between man as a psychological entity and man as a social entity. Thus people are to be understood as products of the interaction among their biogenetic endowment, the effects of significant relationships, the impact of life experiences, and their participation in societal, cultural, and current events. Clearly this perception of man was not a discovery of the early 1960s, nor was it the contribution of any one person. It reflected a tradition in both social work and other professions extending over seventy years. What was unique about the Hollis book was that it presented the psychosocial approach clearly and comprehensively as a unique theoretical basis for practice.

The stance toward practice presented in Hollis's book proved to be an important contribution to another intraprofessional dispute of this period. As the casework–psychotherapy question was being debated between professions, another issue took on prominence, an issue that has proved to be a more critical and a more extensive one. This question, debated throughout the 1960s and only just beginning to diminish in intensity, concerns the relative importance of the therapeutic activities of social work and its social action or community development activities and responsibilities. The issue emerged in the form of a challenge from within to the position of dominance that casework had enjoyed in social work for decades. The practice of social work was seen as reducible to a dichotomy, albeit a complex and many-faceted one. During this period of intraprofessional struggle casework was soundly criticized. The critics challenged its importance, relevance, usefulness and effectiveness and the range of knowledge, skills and services it encompassed. Casework, it was declared, was a band-aid type of help that was no longer needed. In fact, it might well be seen as harmful to society, especially if it encouraged individuals and families to accept the status quo rather than motivate them to change their social reality. It was feared that psychotherapy might diminish interest in dealing with the real causes of society's ills by helping people to obtain superficial relief from stress, thus removing the incentive to understand and alter the cause of such suffering.

This dialogue will probably continue in social work as long as it exists, but a psychosocial approach to practice at least offers the hope that the therapist and the social activist can coexist in the social worker, since it provides a conceptual continuum that stresses the importance of both perspectives rather than seeing practice as a dichotomy.

The Hollis book played an important part in this debate. It reaffirmed for the profession the continuing importance and essential nature of the treatment of individuals and families from a social perspective. At the same time, it laid a conceptual basis that supported the role of the larger systems approach to practice. The presentation of *psychosocial* therapy as a thought system placed clinical social work in an interdisciplinary and therapeutic role. Thus, the book as a whole reaffirmed the profession's dual commitment to personal and societal change, which dual commitment contributed to the clarification of an autonomous role for the social worker.

It would be a mistake to argue that the Hollis book was published solely as a response to these challenges to casework. However, it did serve to provide answers to criticisms and to open new and expanded perspectives of the profession's mandate concerning individuals, families, and groups. It did this by clearly underscoring the twofold commitment of the profession to the social and the psychological components of the human experience, to man as a psychosocial being.

In the years since Hollis's book was first published, a marked increase in the use of this term can be observed within writing about social work, not only as it touches on clinical practice, but interestingly on the other interventive roles of the social worker, such as work with communities or in larger policy areas. Although the term did not originate in our profession, in the 1960s it was most frequently associated with social work. This has now changed. A growing use of the term by other professions can be observed as individuals and disciplines become increasingly aware that psychosocial therapy represents a distinct theoretical orientation that results in a unique approach to therapeutic endeavors.[2]

Definition

Psychosocial therapy as it is currently practiced is not presented as a dramatically new or revolutionary approach. Rather, it is seen as an evolutionary development that draws on the knowledge, experience and thinking of the past. It represents only one of many continuing efforts to provide a conceptual basis from which to develop a procedure for understanding and seeking to alter the behavior of persons, families, and small groups. Unlike some other theories or thought systems, it is not a simplifying but rather a complex and many-faceted system. Evolutionary in its origins, it remains dynamic and open. It attempts to move from the selective use of various other systems in an eclectic way to an ongoing search for interconnections between ideas, to an interlocking of conceptual frameworks. It builds on the conceptual and professional wisdom of decades of practitioners in many disciplines who have contributed to the growing understanding of the complexities of human behavior and of the many ways in which humans are influenced. It seeks to avoid the risks of a unitary perception and to exploit the advantages of a plurality of perspectives.

Therefore, as an approach to psychotherapeutic practice, we offer the following definition of psychosocial therapy:

> That form of psychotherapeutic practice in which the bio-psychosocial knowledge of human and societal behavior; skills in relating to individuals, families, groups and communities; and competence in mobilizing available resources are combined in the medium of individual, group and familial relationships to help persons to alter their personality, behavior or situation in a manner that will contribute to the attainment of satisfying, fulfilling human functioning within the framework of their own values and goals and the available resources of society.

Historical Origins

SOCIAL WORK

A thorough search of the literature covering several disciplines did not result in the discovery of a single source of origin of this term.[3] Rather than the contribution of any one person, the term appears to have emerged as the result of many efforts to build conceptual bridges between and among various disciplines interested in the understanding of man. Social work cannot claim to be the originator of the term or the idea. Indeed, it might be argued that social work emerged as an autonomous profession from the developing awareness that any psychotherapeutic intervention requires an understanding of the blending of social and psychological factors.

From the late nineteenth century, as social work first emerged as an avocation and shortly thereafter as a profession, a continuous thread of commitment to this dual perspective can be observed, a thread that has emerged in the full flowering of a distinct theory.

The term "psychosocial" seems to have been used first in social work literature in 1930 by Frank Hankins of Smith College.[4] Hankins was clearly underscoring the crucial need for the social worker to understand man in both a psychological and a sociological framework.

The idea of a duality of professional thrust goes back to the origins of our profession and its literature. Certainly over the decades, the relative importance accorded these two thrusts has varied as has the tendency to keep them separate.

In *What Is Social Case Work?* Mary Richmond insisted on the dual thrust of practice. This is reflected in her well-known twofold division of intervention, which she described as "direct action of man on man" and "indirect action through the social environment."[5] In the book she argued that the central thrust of casework is the development of personality.[6] Her dual emphasis is clear in her famous definition of social casework as "those processes which develop a personality through adjustments consciously effected, individual by individual, between men and their social environment."[7] The psychosocial orientation, although Richmond did not call it that, can also be seen in her earlier and better known work *Social Diagnosis,* written in 1917. There she described diagnosis as a process which aims to present "as exact a definition as possible of the social situation and personality of a given client."[8] Although emphasizing personality, Richmond tended to take it almost for granted; throughout her later writings she put more stress on the gathering, analyzing and reporting of the social systems in which the client functions. Her vocabulary reflects the stress on the social component of the duality in such phrases as "social evidence," "social diagnosis," and "social treatment."

Throughout her writing Richmond emphasized that her man-and-milieu approach to social work was a continuation of a tradition of planned helping that went back to the early nineteenth century. She commented on the ideas of Chalmers in Glasgow in the 1820s and of his successors, who saw the goal of their work as the "release of energy, the regeneration of character, or the multiplication of health opportunities, opportunities of training and the like." Richmond also mentioned the later work of the London Charity Organization Society, whose members stated as their goal "to release the latent possibilities within persons." Later she mentioned that Octavia Hill continued this focus and described her desire to know the "passions, hopes and histories of people and to assess what resources can be brought to bear to move, touch and teach them."[9]

Moving on from Mary Richmond, the psychosocial theme can be traced through the thirties and forties, from the early work of Hollis[10] to the work of Gordon Hamilton. In 1949, Swithun Bowers collected and analyzed thirty-four prior definitions of social casework.[11] With varying degrees of clarity, most of these definitions continue the emphasis on the twofold influence of personality and society. The definitions differ principally in the relative weight given to the psyche and the social. Thus in 1926, Taylor talked about the purpose of treatment as "understanding individuals as whole personalities and the adjustments of these individuals to socially healthy lives."[12] Here the understanding of the person as a psychological entity is given emphasis. In 1935, Bertha Reynold gave more stress to the societal function of man, defining practice as "that form of social work which assists the individual while he struggles to relate himself to his family, his natural groups, his community."[13] Bowers proceeded from this analysis of an emerging definition of practice to his own definition, in which he further developed the psychosocial concept. He defined casework as a process of "mobilizing capacities in the individual and resources in the community appropriate for better adjustment between the client and all or part of the total environment."[14]

The psychosocial theme, clearly traced in Bowers's work, was picked up and developed by Gordon Hamilton in the two editions of her major work, *The Theory and Practice of Social Casework*.[15] The preface to her Second Edition underscored the fact that throughout the 1940s the concept of "the psychosocial case" had become steadily clarified with advances in psychiatry and the social services,[16] but she included the caution that "the social worker traditionally concerned with the environment is today committed not only to understand the structure and dynamics of personality but also to rediscover the use of environmental or social therapy." In this comment we see reflected the profession's growing awareness of the temptation and tendency to overemphasize either the psyche or the social environment. Even in 1950, Dr. Hamilton was urging the rediscovery of social therapy. This tendency to imbalance will be seen to mark the next twenty-five years.

Just a year before publication of the second edition of Hamilton's book, Annette Garrett[17] commented on the identifiable swings in the evolution of social work, especially casework, from an emphasis on modifying environments to an emphasis on modifying persons. She noted that at no time was either concept excluded.

> The pendulum swings went from a scarcity of knowledge about the factual and emotional factors in a case to an excessive piling up of facts and information without focus or direction; from indiscriminate use of resources to exclusive exploration of emotional factors; from early overactivity and directiveness to excessive passivity and drifting; from over-intellectualized analysis of cause and effect relationships to unscientific wallowing in feelings and belittling of intellectual knowledge.[18]

Within social work this twofold thrust to practice has had continuous importance. What has been difficult is the integration of the perceived twofold viewpoint into a conceptual whole. This difficulty has at times played into a concomitant sociological question of professional identity and professional boundaries. An example is the aforementioned dispute about perceived similarities and differences between casework and psychotherapy and efforts to resolve the dispute along disciplinary lines. Thus attitudes and practices emerged that maintained the importance of intrapsychic man and societal man but divided responsibility for these two territories by profession. Social work was proclaimed to be expert in the "external" factors in a case and psychiatry in the "internal" ones. Those who worked through this era of the 1950s know how much time, effort, and concern was spent on this division-of-labor question.

Clearly the distinction was never made by practitioners themselves in anything but a rhetorical and fragmentary way. The social worker's need to maintain a dual focus continued in practice and was supported in the literature.

In the mid-1950s Hollis published a paper on personality diagnosis[19] focused specifically on the need to differentially understand the personality structure and functioning of the client. Even so, she acknowledged the need to understand the client's total life situation, his physical functioning as well as his personality, in order to intervene effectively in his life. The interface of these systems was identified by Hollis but their boundaries were kept quite separate. In a similar vein Helen Perlman, writing in the late 1950s, noted that although the essential goal of social casework is to facilitate the person's social functioning this must include attention to the functioning of the personality structure.[20]

By the late 1950s there was growing concern that we had once again let the pendulum swing away from using our knowledge of significant environments to an overemphasis on the psychological structure of man, especially his unconscious and preconscious functioning. There is no doubt that social casework was highly influenced by psychodynamic thinking even though this influence has been overemphasized, oversimplified, and overcriticized. It is also clear that this interest in intrapsychic man resulted in a diminshed interest in his social perspectives during this period. Never, of course, was this phase of the profession's commitment entirely abandoned, as seems to be implied at times.

The Stein and Cloward book *Social Perspectives on Behavior,* published in the late 1950s, made a significant contribution to the emergence of psychosocial therapy as a system of practice.[21] An important argument of the book is that the psychosocial dichotomy should not be allowed to become a point of controversy; rather, we should continue to seek interconnections. To this end, Gordon Hamilton, in her foreword to the Stein and Cloward book, had stressed the need for the social worker to be competent in weighing the balance between inner and outer forces. The importance of this balance was underscored by the editors in their own preface: "By blending the psychological and the social, as our knowledge in both areas increases, the uniqueness of our professional discipline will be increasingly clarified" (p. xix). The content of this work clearly reflects and emphasizes two important concepts: first, a demonstration of the rich material available to the social worker from a broad spectrum of disciplines in the social sciences; second, and more important, the fact that a more diversely selective and enriched turning to the social sciences by the social worker is a challenging and difficult activity.

In spite of the Stein and Cloward appeal to search for a balance, the social as opposed to the psychological understanding of man continued to gain ground, and during the 1960s and 1970s the trend was toward an emphasis on social therapy rather than psychotherapy. Social therapy, it was argued, is what social workers do, not psychotherapy! Thus James K. Whittaker declared that the purpose of social work was to "improve social functioning and coping with social problems."[22] Hence, as mentioned earlier in this chapter, the first edition of Hollis's *Casework: A Psychosocial Therapy* was important in again insisting that clinical practice in social work was not an either/or situation but a balance.

GROUP WORK

Up to now the development of psychosocial concepts has been examined principally from the point of view of casework. This is not to imply that casework was the only component of social work that was developing from a psychosocial foundation. Certainly, the development of group work as a component of social work reflected much the same conceptual basis. Group work evolved from somewhat different roots than casework and was focused more on the social and interpersonal functioning of man. But never was this focus social to the exclusion of the psychological. Group work, like casework, was influenced by the psychoanalytic school and also became a part of the mental health movement. And so, in a similar way, group workers also faced controversies around the question to what extent, if any, group work was a part of therapy.

An important development of the 1960s for both group workers and caseworkers was the growing acceptance of the notion that the same practitioner could be competent working both with individuals and with groups. This was a moving away from the earlier tradition which supported the idea that a person practiced in only one discipline. It would be incorrect to claim that it was psychosocial thought that fostered this change; indeed, it could be argued that in an earlier time it may have hampered it. What can be said is that with the growing understanding of a psychosocial approach as a distinct form of practice, and with increasing attention to the implications for practice deriving from the theory, the possibility of and indeed the necessity for a multiskilled psychosocial therapist became more evident.

The term psychosocial as an identifying concept does not appear to have become a part of the group work literature until the late 1960s. We find Helen Northen using the term several times in her 1971 book *Social Work with Groups*.[23] In the early pages she acknowledges that a psychosocial viewpoint underlies her understanding of the practice of social work. Later in the book she refers to Hollis to explain her perception of person–situation interaction and emphasizes the need to have knowledge of "the psychosocial development of individuals" (p. 146).

FAMILY THERAPY

It is surprising that the term psychosocial has not been used as frequently in the family therapy literature as in that concerned with the treatment of individuals and nonfamily groups. Certainly the psychosocial concept of psychological man in interaction with significant others has been and is still an essential conceptual basis of family therapy. Undoubtedly the dramatic interest in family therapy that began in the 1950s did not represent a new direction so much as a conceptual enrichment of practice stemming from a psychosocial tradition, principally in social work.[24]

Hollis certainly saw the emergence of family therapy as a logical development in the psychosocial tradition. This is reflected in the attention she gives it in the second edition of her book on psychosocial therapy, in which she invited Isobel Stamm to write a chapter on family therapy and its relevance to the book's focus. In the same year that the second edition of Hollis was published, an interesting collection of writings on various components of family life was published under the title *The Psychosocial Interior of the Family*. The book clearly takes the viewpoint that the psychosocial orientation is a discrete thought system that gives a distinct quality to understanding and altering family life.

OTHER DISCIPLINES

An examination of the last thirty-five years of the *American Journal of Orthopsychiatry* reveals that the term "psychosocial" does not appear in the earliest years. However, even as early as 1940 the idea of considering man "in his life situation" and emphasizing "social feelings" in psychology were mentioned by

Ann Shyne in an article about Adler.[26] By 1947 Jules Henry was emphasizing the importance of understanding cultural and environmental effects on the psychological functioning of an individual.[27] Later, in 1948, Bettelheim wrote about inner and outer forces and how the development of personality is affected by both environment and interpersonal relationships.[28] And again in 1948, James Cunningham quoted an article published two years earlier in a British medical journal in which the term "psychosocially" was used to attempt to link these two realities.[29]

Although the term "psychosocial" is not frequently used in this period, the underlying concepts are present by implication in several works.[30] One exception to this is a 1954 article by Maurice Friend and Otto Pollack, entitled "Psychosocial Aspects in the Preparation for Treatment of an Allergic Child,"[31] in which they referred to the influence of both Hollis and Hamilton on their thinking. Following them, a range of social science writers used either the term "psychosocial" or such variations as "psychosituational," "psycho-social,"[32] "psychocultural" and "psychopolitical" to indicate the importance of developing bridging concepts between various disciplines and various approaches to man.[33] In general those sociologists and anthropologists who viewed man as a product of the interaction between inherent dispositions and environmental factors can be thought of as belonging to a "psychosocial" school of thought even if they used different terminology.

Conceptual History in Social Work

From the data currently available, three phases in the history of psychosocial thinking can be identified. First, a general psychosocial orientation has always been a significant component of social work's tradition although it has not always been identified as such.

The second phase developed during the period of the late 1940s and early 1950s, when the well-known diagnostic–functional school debate was in the foreground.[34] It was during this debate that the ideas contained in psychosocial thinking began to take on a more specific identity. The diagnostic school's position on casework was clearly different from the functionalist's viewpoint. Although the term "diagnostic school" came to identify this form of practice, Hamilton, as we have seen, used the term "psychosocial approach" in ways that made it equivalent to what other writers meant by "diagnostic school," without perhaps appreciating that it was the beginning of a new thought system.

This controversy faded in importance as new issues began to emerge for the profession and new knowledge began to be absorbed. It was out of a desire to reflect the new knowledge and broadening base of practice that Hollis published in 1964 a book giving the term "psychosocial" a prominent position. As suggested earlier, Dr. Hollis saw her book not as a declaration of a new approach to practice but as an updating of the tradition that had emerged out of the diagnostic school.

But the book provided the basis for a new controversy. In the 1960s a tendency could be observed among some groups of social work clinicians to identify with the writings of either Helen Harris Perlman[35] or Florence Hollis as the foundation of practice. Their two books were seen by some practitioners as taking opposite positions. It would be incorrect to attribute too much importance to this perceived difference, which seemed more a declaration of loyalty by their respective followers than a formal conceptual split. Nevertheless, it did reflect the fact that for a while these two viewpoints were the only ones clearly articulated for social workers. In a very short time, however, it was clear that several thought systems rather than only two were influencing practice. This situation was identified in the significant and very timely publication of the Robert and Nees book *Theories of Social Casework* in 1970.[36] Here, for the first time since the earlier diagnostic–functional writing and the later short-lived Perlman-Hollis rivalry, an attempt was made to identify the similarities and differences in particular approaches to practice. This book more than Hollis's highlighted the growing awareness that "the psychosocial approach to practice'' was indeed distinct from other approaches and that it represented a thought system in its own right.

It is here that the third phase of the psychosocial development began: the emergence of an approach to practice that came from the earlier diagnostic school but was distinct from it as a thought system. This third phase, which had begun with the Robert and Nees book, was continued in an article by Hollis in the 1971 *Encyclopedia of Social Work*[37] and further developed in the revised edition of her book in 1972 and Turner's *Social Work Treatment*.[38]

Although the thesis of the present book is that psychosocial therapy is a distinct approach to clinical practice, I do not mean to suggest that it is a novel or original development. As Hollis mentioned, one of the distinguishing features of the psychosocial approach is that it is a theory of intervention that has been built up from practical experience. Although frequently referred to as the "traditional" school of the practice of clinical social work, in fact it is probably the most contemporary. This stems from a long-standing commitment to be open to new ideas and approaches wherever these are found to enhance practice.

Thus the psychosocial tradition has had two sources of development. The first is experiential and empirical in that there has been a constant effort to codify and generalize the accumulated wisdom of searching, committed practitioners. These efforts at conceptualizing have taken the form of practice-based articles and formal research and scholarly writing by students and practitioners. The other developmental source has been an openness to new systems of thought. In the theoretical orientation of psychosocial practitioners over the past four decades, selected components of the major theories or thought systems then influencing current practice in the various helping professions can be found.

The fact that psychosocial theory has developed from a spectrum of sources can of course be regarded as one of the strengths of the system or as a source of potential weakness.

But in its search for increased effectiveness a clear commitment of the psychosocial approach has always been to the development, enlargement and strengthening of the theoretical
base. There has never been adherence to an impressionistic approach to practice. The client is to be understood, the situation to
be studied, the process to be utilized consciously, the setting and
its limitations to be recognized, manipulated and, throughout the
process, evaluated. None of this, of course, is to be carried out at
the expense of the essential interaction of the persons involved in
the process.

To sum up, the psychosocial school in its earliest days was
heavily influenced by the sociological theories of persons such
as Ruth Benedict and R. M. MacIver of the late 1920s. These
beginning efforts to understand man in interaction with the significant environment experienced the impact of the first wave of the
psychoanalytic school. There were few major spokesmen for the
psychoanalytic school, including Freud himself, who did not
have an influence on the psychosocial school at various times.
Some of these influences, such as the work of Otto Rank and the
development of the functional school,[39] challenged previously
held positions and caused us to rethink. In addition to the better
known authors of the analytical school there were many
psychoanalysts who directly influenced practice through their
contacts with social workers in the role of teachers, therapists,
cotherapists and consultants.

Harry Stack Sullivan, Karen Horney, Erik Erikson, and Heinz
Hartman[40] all made further elaborations of psychoanalytic
thought, especially in the later emergence of ego psychology.
Their refinements on the first formulations of Freudian theory
gave a more social-interactional interpretation of man and fit
closely into the development of the psychosocial school. As mentioned earlier, in the late 1950s we had to relearn and enrich our
knowledge of the social realities by turning back to the social
sciences, with a special emphasis on cultural anthropology and
sociology. We had to rediscover the sociology of socioeconomic
classes, ethnic origins, and the family and small groups, as well

as to develop a new appreciation of the political and economic components of our clients' environments and our own. Whether as cause or effect, the rediscovery and reunderstanding of these significant influences on clients stood us in good stead during the troubled days of the 1960s and early 1970s.

As we struggled to understand these important societal developments we looked to new thought systems and their implications. Role theory and systems theory helped us to begin to interrelate the complexities of human psychosocial functioning, though we were careful not to forget that man is a biological and spiritual being as well. With the growing appreciation of intersystemic man and the myriad of influences that affect his social functioning, the psychosocial school of thought became more comfortable with a multimethod approach to intervention. Thus the use of significant environments, persons and things, individual intervention, group intervention, family intervention, neighborhood intervention and behavioral techniques have all been included in the theoretical basis and practice profile of psychosocial therapy. In the same way, communications theory, the various forms of cognitive therapy and existential theory are all helping to enrich and shape psychosocial practice.

The thesis of this book, then, is that psychosocial therapy stands as a distinct approach to practice. Even in claiming its autonomy, we recognize that it is an approach to practice that has been influenced by a wide range of theories from psychology and sociology. It is a multitheory-based system that has sought to interlock a wide range of viewpoints and techniques as these proved helpful to understand and effectively intervene in the lives of clients. And while it is still an emerging system, it has already become one that has been adopted as the basis of practice for many social workers, psychologists, and psychiatrists.

Notes

1. Florence Hollis, *Casework: A Psychosocial Therapy* (New York: Random House, 1964; 2nd ed. revised, 1972).

2. Gerald Handel, ed., *The Psychosocial Interior of the Family: A Sourcebook for the Study of Whole Families*. (London: George Allen and Unwin, 1968).

3. I am particularly grateful to Joanna Martin, a graduate Social Work student, who conducted a thorough literature search into the origins and development of this concept.

4. Frank Hankins, "The Contributions of Sociology to the Practice of Social Work," in *Proceedings of the National Conference of Social Work, 1930* (Chicago: University of Chicago Press, 1931), pp. 528–535.

5. Mary E. Richmond, *What Is Social Case Work?: An Introductory Description*. (New York: Russell Sage Foundation, 1922), p. 102.

6. Ibid., p. 90.

7. Ibid., p. 99.

8. Mary E. Richmond, *Social Diagnosis* (New York: Russell Sage Foundation, 1917), p. 51.

9. Ibid., pp. 25–37.

10. Florence Hollis, *Social Casework in Practice: Six Case Studies*. (New York: Family Welfare Association, 1939).

11. Swithun Bowers, "The Nature and Definition of Social Casework," reprinted from the *Journal of Social Casework,* October, November, December 1949, in Cora Kasius, ed., *Principles and Techniques in Social Casework* (New York: Family Service Association of America, 1950), pp. 97–127.

12. Ibid., p. 102.

13. Ibid.

14. Ibid., p. 127.

15. Gordon Hamilton, *Theory and Practice of Social Casework,* 2nd ed., revised (New York: Columbia University Press, 1951).

16. Gordon Hamilton, "Basic Concepts in Social Casework," *The Family* XVIII (July, 1937), pp. 147–156. Gordon Hamilton, "The Underlying Philosophy of Social Work," *The Family* XXIII (July, 1941), pp. 139–147. Grete Bibring, "Psychiatry and Social Work," *Journal of Social Casework* XXVIII (June, 1947), pp. 203–211. Irene M. Josselyn, *Psychosocial Development of Children* (New York: Family Service Association of America, 1948). Helen H.

Perlman, ed., *Charlotte Towle on Social Work and Social Casework* (Chicago: University of Chicago Press, 1969).

17. Annette Garrett, "Historical Survey of the Evolution of Casework," reprinted from the *Journal of Social Casework,* June 1949 in Cora Kasius ed., *Principles and Techniques in Social Casework, op.cit.,* p. 396.

18. Ibid., p. 399.

19. Florence Hollis, "Personality Diagnosis in Casework" in H. Parad, ed., *Ego Psychology and Dynamic Casework* (New York: Family Service Association of America, 1958), pp. 83–96.

20. Helen Harris Perlman, *Social Casework: A Problem Solving Process* (Chicago: University of Chicago Press, 1957).

21. Herman D. Stein and Richard Cloward, eds., *Social Perspectives on Behavior* (New York: The Free Press, 1958).

22. James K. Whittaker, *Social Treatment* (Chicago: Aldine Publishing Co., 1974), p. 49.

23. Helen Northen, *Social Work with Groups* (New York: Columbia University Press, 1969).

24. Nathan Ackerman, "Emergence of Family Psychotherapy on the Present Scene," Morris I. Stein ed., *Contemporary Psychotherapies* (New York: Free Press, 1961), pp. 228–244.

25. Handel, *op. cit.*

26. Ann W. Shyne, "The Contribution of Alfred Adler to the Development of Dynamic Psychology," *American Journal of Orthopsychiatry* 12 (April, 1942), pp. 352–359.

27. Jules Henry, "Environmental and Symptom Formation," *American Journal of Orthopsychiatry,* 17 (October, 1947), pp. 628–632.

28. Bruno Bettelheim and Emily Sylvester, "A Therapeutic Milieu," *American Journal of Orthopsychiatry* 18 (April, 1948), pp. 191–206.

29. James M. Cunningham, "Psychiatric Case Work as an Epidemiological Tool," *American Journal of Orthopsychiatry* 18 (October, 1948), pp. 659–669.

30. Norman Cameron, *The Psychology of Behavior Disorders: A Biosocial Interpretation* (Boston: Houghton Mifflin, 1947). Lawrence Frank, *Society as the Patient: Essays on Culture and Person-*

ality (New Brunswick: Rutgers University Press, 1948). In the preface the author identifies a "psychocultural approach" as a unifying variable. David F. Aberle, "The Psychosocial Analysis of a Hopi Life History," *Comparative 4 Monographs* vol. 21, no. 1, ser. 107 (Berkeley: University of California Press, 1951). C. Kluckhohn and H. Murray, *Personality in Nature, Society and Culture* (New York: Knopf, 1953). Berta Fantl, "Integrating Psychological, Social and Cultural Factors in Assertive Casework," *Social Work* 3 (October, 1958), pp. 30–37. Alfred H. Katz, "Some Psychosocial Problems in Hemophilia," *Social Casework* 40 (January, 1959), pp. 321–326. Julian Huxley, "The Evolutionary Vision," in Sol Tax and Charles Cullinder, eds., *Evolution After Darwin*, vol. *III, Issues in Evolution* (Chicago: University of Chicago Press, 1960), pp. 249–261. In this paper given in 1959 Huxley argues that man's evolution is not biological but psychosocial.

31. Maurice R. Friend and Otto Pollak, "Psychosocial Aspects in the Preparation for Treatment of an Allergic Child," *American Journal of Orthopsychiatry* 24 (January, 1956), pp. 63–72.

32. Rudolf Deikuss, "The Adlerian Approach to Psychodynamics," in Morris I. Stein, ed., *Contemporary Psychotherapies* (New York: Free Press, 1961), pp. 60–79. Erik Erikson, *Childhood and Society,* 2nd ed., revised and enlarged (New York: W. W. Norton, 1963). In this book and the earlier edition Erikson develops a psychosocial theme. The only place that he actually uses the word psychosocial is in a footnote on p. 250, Theodore Lidz, *The Person: His Development Throughout the Life Cycle* (New York: Basic Books, 1968). The author identifies that it was Harry Stack Sullivan and Erik Erikson who linked psychoanalytic theory and the behavioral sciences. He describes Erikson's eight stages as a "psychosocial orientation." B. Schoenberg *et al., Teaching Psychosocial Aspects of Patient Care* (New York: Columbia University Press, 1968). Bernard Shoenberg *et al., Psychosocial Aspects of Terminal Care* (New York: Columbia University Press, 1972). This book is a multidisciplinary approach to psychosocial factors of terminal care. Roy Grinker, *Psychiatry in Broad Perspective* (New York: Behavioral Publications, Inc., 1975). The author describes

psychiatry as a biopsychosocial system and points out the need to understand the intersystemic homeostasis that promotes growth.

33. Jules Masserman, ed., *Psychoanalysis and Social Process* (New York: Grune and Stratton, 1961). Morris I. Stein, *Contemporary Psychotherapies* (New York: Free Press, 1961).

34. Cora Kasius, ed., *A Comparison of Diagnostic and Functional Casework Concepts,* Report of the Family Service Association of America to Study Basic Concepts in Casework Practice (New York: Family Service Association of America, 1950).

35. Perlman, *op.cit.*

36. R. Roberts and R. Nee, eds., *Theories of Social Casework* (Chicago: University of Chicago Press, 1970).

37. Florence Hollis, "Social Casework: The Psychosocial Approach," *Encyclopedia of Social Work II* (New York: National Association of Social Workers, 1971), pp. 1217–1226.

38. Francis J. Turner, "Psychosocial Therapy," *Social Work Treatment: Interlocking Theoretical Approaches,* ed. F. J. Turner (New York: Free Press, 1974), pp. 84–111.

39. Shankar A. Yelaja, "Functional Theory for Social Work Practice," in F. J. Turner, ed., *Social Work Treatment* (New York: Free Press, 1974), pp. 147–180.

40. Harry Stack Sullivan, *The Interpersonal Theory of Psychiatry* (New York: Norton, 1953). Karen Horney, *New Ways in Psychoanalysis* (New York: Norton, 1939). Erik Erikson, *Childhood and Society,* 2nd ed., revised and enlarged (New York: Norton, 1963). Heinz Hartmann, *Ego Psychology and the Problem of Adaptation,* translated by D. Rapaport (New York: International Universities Press, 1958).

Chapter 2

The Target of Intervention: A Psychosocial Perspective of Personality and Problems

The Nature of the Person

The primary object of interest for social workers is the individual person, as he is in himself, as he interacts with others and as he functions in society. The primary goal of the psychosocially oriented social worker is change; change that may take place in persons, groups, families or situations. The nature of the change that is sought is related to the potential of the person, the goals and attitudes for which he is striving, his values and aspirations, and the resources available to him. Such a professional objective presupposes that the helping person has an understanding of man in general and in particular as well as an understanding of situations in general and in particular.

In the psychosocial perspective people are viewed within an optimistic framework. Human nature is considered to be essentially good. Man is seen as committed to his own development and the satisfaction of his goals and objectives within a social context in which the interests, goals and aspirations of others are acknowledged and accommodated.

Human nature is also considered to be free; free not in an absolute way but free in a nondeterministic way. This perception of freedom does not deny that man is greatly shaped by his genetic endowment, marked by his early history, influenced by his developmental course, and conditioned by his significant environments. But within all these influences there is a part of the human being that is free to choose among alternatives, that is able to rise up above and beyond his history and his endowment, a part of him that is unique and unpredictable.

Each human being is also seen as transcending the world, as being a distinct and special part of the life process. Both as an individual and as a member of the human family, each person is thus worthy of special respect and honor from the instant he exists until his death, regardless of his stage of development or deterioration.[1]

This belief in the nobility of man can be manifested in a variety of perspectives. It can be reflected in a wonderment at the evolutionary process that has resulted in the human genius. It can come from a philosophical appreciation of cause and effect that argues to a first cause uncaused. It can also derive from the conclusion developed from a theological orientation that acknowledges man's spiritual origin. Regardless of our individual perspective, the human being as the object of our professional activities is a creature of respect and wonderment for us.

The human being is believed to be free because he possesses reasoning powers. Because of this, he is seen as having a right to self-determination. Thus, he is to be treated as an individual capable of responsibility for his life. He is therefore to be permitted to experience the outcome of his choices and actions. Clearly, this question of autonomy is not absolute. Social workers are well aware of the extent to which man's capabilities as a unique human being can be and are limited by a wide variety of experiences and situations. But it is the awareness of the potential of individuals that underlies the social worker's optimism and assurance in helping, encouraging, and at times leading the client to goals beyond his present situation.

Further, the human being is seen as growth-oriented, highly flexible, and endowed with curiosity. It is these essential qualities that provide the potential for change and the ability to seek and achieve one's goals, to learn from others, from one's own experiences, and from access to new opportunities and resources. Most of what makes up a person has been learned. It follows that such learning is capable of modification and conditioning.

People are also understood to be dependent and interdependent. This is another way of saying that human beings are social in nature. The completely isolated person is seen as a variant case. Only in the most extreme and unusual cases is it possible to function without some direct or indirect dependence on the skills, knowledge, and resources of others.

The attribute of dependency is an important concept underlying the therapeutic endeavors of the social worker. It can be a powerful adjunct to such endeavors as well as a potential detriment. As a social being, man becomes aware of his need for and his dependency on others. This becomes the source of both anxiety and uncertainty. Anxiety about the dependability of others and the adequacy of resources to meet one's needs and the needs of others, and uncertainty of one's destiny haunt man throughout his entire life. And again, like his dependency, anxiety and uncertainty are a source of both problems and strengths in the therapeutic encounter.

These comments, of course, are not original or exclusive to the psychosocial therapist. They are rather a cluster of assumptions and conclusions that have been debated by philosophers and theologians for centuries. They are basic conceptual tenets underlying psychosocial therapy and thus must be understood to fully appreciate this approach to the therapeutic process.

Within this general understanding of man, the social worker is particularly interested in the personality of each individual. Personality, like many terms that we commonly use, is not easy to define. In attempting to define personality it is easy to get into a circular process where one ends up using the terms with which one began. In the psychologically oriented literature there are many definitions of personality, some referring to the person's predominant effect on other people, others highlighting a particular aspect of readily perceived qualities in a person. Each effort to describe personality, however, seeks to include a concept of uniqueness, complexity and humanness.[2]

Personality in the context of this discussion is defined as that dynamic organization of biological, psychological, and social systems that comprises an individual's unique adjustment to society.[3] The important characteristics of this definition include the concept of dynamic—that is, a perception that the personality is changing and interdependent. It also highlights the concept of organization. Further, it stresses a concept of intersystemic influence, balanced by a concept of uniqueness. Finally, it points to the importance of interpersonal influence. It is this dynamic organization, or personality, that is the primary sphere of activity of the social worker.

This perception of personality leads the social worker to ask himself the following questions about each client:

1. How is this client like every other person I have known?
2. How is this client like some other persons I have known?
3. How is he/she like no other persons I have known?

Our definition of personality includes the concept of intersystemic interaction, especially between the biological, psychological, and social systems. That is, the personality develops its unique profile of characteristics and behaviors in relation to the intersystemic experiences that occur. The way in which each of these systems is perceived, understood and weighted in turn affects the nature of activities intended to influence the action of the personality—that is, the therapeutic process.

Although social workers have never proposed or attempted to be physicians, from the earliest days of our professional practice there has been a clear awareness that the biological endowment and functions of individuals are of great importance in understanding their behavior. It follows that the therapeutic endeavor must pay attention to this component of our clients for a proper understanding of them and their functions.

With the great advances made in recent years in the field of genetics, we are now much more aware of the very beginning of the biological process. We know that from the very instant that two sets of chromosomes meet and interact, some immovable boundaries are set for the individual. Much about the individual is fixed at this point relating to his or her appearance, potential size and shape, intellectual abilities, propensity to some diseases, motor skills and even to some extent length of life. The complexity and uniqueness of the hereditary process have important implications for many of our clients. Indeed, of such importance are these matters that with the expanding knowledge in the field of genetics, a field of specialized social work has emerged that focuses on assisting persons to resolve such questions as the choice of marriage partner, the bearing or not bearing of children, the continuing or terminating of some pregnancies, and the terrible value dilemma that these types of decision create.[4]

Immutable as is our genetic endowment, at least at the present level of human knowledge, as social workers we know all too well the impact of a person's physical endowment on psychosocial functioning. Consider the case of a very pretty, bright fifteen-year-old in a correctional institution for girls. She was five feet eleven inches in height with the appearance of a woman years older than her chronological age. Her unusual height and the fact that she was perceived as a much older person than she was were at the root of many of her difficulties. She was sought after by older men, whom she in turn threatened because of her height. This resulted in serious problems of self-image and role identification. At only fifteen she had gained access to an adult world and become involved in a wide range of socially unacceptable activities, which eventually resulted in her being placed in a training school.

In the folklore of our society we talk of redheaded personalities and jolly fat men; we wonder if blondes indeed have more fun. We know that dangerous as stereotypes are, society does respond in a patterned way to a person's appearance and that reciprocally a person's self-concept develops from the messages and cues received from the response of others as well as from the person's own perception of his or her physical appearance.

Indeed, in an earlier day, a psychology of personality was developed around physical types. The shape of one's head or one's body build was seen as an indicator and predictor of one's behavior. Although this is no longer a popular approach, we know that attention must be paid to how a person views himself, how he is seen by others and how others react to him. This is an important variable, one that is not always sufficiently addressed by therapists.

Along with physical appearance as a variable that affects a person's interaction with the world, a further component of the genetic and hereditary endowment is a person's intellectual capacities. Clearly, the possession of normal intelligence and the range and diversity of intellectual, perceptual and motor skills that usually accompany it dramatically affect the development of personality; thus, intelligence is of considerable interest to the therapist. This component of personality greatly influences the opportunities that are available for some kinds of behavioral change.

In addition to the way persons appear and the intellectual and psychobiological skills they possess, their physical feelings of well-being or lack thereof are dramatic determinants of personality functioning with both short- and long-range implications. From a short-range viewpoint we all know how self-conscious we feel when we have a temporary facial blemish or an accidentally acquired black eye. We know that this self-consciousness greatly affects the way we fulfill many of our daily roles. We also know how drastically altered are our feelings and attitudes if we are suffering from even so mild an illness as a cold. Our understanding of the effect on us of such small things helps us to develop an appreciation of the importance of a person's general state of health as a determinant of personality, greatly affecting his or her self-image, dependency patterns, problem-solving activities, mobility, social-interactional patterns, access to alternatives and attitude toward life and the future. The nature of an individual's reaction to their health will of course vary according to the seriousness of the health situation and its extent over time. But it is an important determinant of a person's psychosocial functioning that must be accurately appraised in the helping process.

In addition to the genetic endowment a person brings to the world, the type of care he has received and the patterns of response to him in his very early interactions with society are important determinants of his personality. From the very start of life—indeed, even while still in the womb—the child begins to interact with the world. The prospective mother frequently has had an anticipatory perception of the child that is shaped by many experiences, including the difficulty or ease of the pregnancy. From the child's earliest hours in the world, through the first months of life, the type of behavior that is reinforced, the patterns of response to expressions of feeling that are experienced, begin to shape his or her sense of autonomy, the experience of trust, and the nature and extent of anxiety and trust which will continue to mark the adult personality.

In recent decades much work has been done in charting the stages of normal personality development and how it takes place.[5] This detailed and tested understanding of the developmental process has been of dramatic assistance to the helping professions. A psychosocial perspective requires that development be understood from the viewpoint of the interaction of many earlier significant influences. These various determinants and the extent of their influence must be taken into account in developing an understanding of a person. We all know well that even though it is possible to chart averages, identify patterns and predict stages of development, the life history of each person is different. Thus from birth onward the peculiar interaction of each person, with his unique genetic endowment, with significant persons and events will differ. Even though we all pass through certain stages, as described by Erikson and others, each of us does this in a unique way, and we both mark and are marked by the world in a distinctive way. Thus the range of specific determinants is understandable only in a general sense. All that we can do at present is to begin to identify and categorize the major components of these influences without being able to fully evaluate the exact effect of each factor on us or on others whom we are seeking to understand.

Although an important concept of psychosocial thinking is the understanding that the young child in his early developmental stages influences his significant environment, obviously this influence is slight compared to the extent that he is influenced.

Thus, many or indeed, in some senses, all patterns of behavior that we have developed are learned from the world around us. In particular, the patterns of personality and behavior learned in our earliest years are critical to the person we become. We know that they can be modified and changed. But we know that this can be done only with difficulty and only over a long period of time. Learning and unlearning, of course, presuppose a cognitive process, but people are more than cerebral entities.

The difficulty of determining fully the importance of some factors in the functioning of the individual is further complicated by the multiple components of personality. Thus, in addition to being rational, man is also irrational or nonrational and nonconscious. This is, of course, related to an important component of the psychosocial approach to the nature of personality, the unconscious.

Although the psychosocial school of thought has in many ways moved far beyond Freudian and other psychoanalytic theories of behavior, the concept of the unconscious is still an important one. The debate about the legitimacy of utilizing the unconscious as a component of therapy has subsided in the past decade.[6] By now there are few persons in the helping professions, if any, who do not hold to the viewpoint that there is a significant component of the personality that is not available to the conscious mind except in rare circumstances, that along with the parts of the personality that can be readily known and understood there is a further component or layer that is not apparent. But the unconscious cannot be overlooked as a partial determinant of personality even though we may not always be in a position to deal with its structure and content but only with the results. As will be elaborated in subsequent chapters, social workers often begin to appreciate the power of unconscious reactions in terms of the client's relationship with the therapist.

The fact that we cannot fully quantify the impact of early life experiences on the development of personality does not mean that we know nothing about their relative importance. We do know something of the importance of nurture and love and care in the early months; we do know how important parenting is in the early years; we are growing in our knowledge of the importance of the father and mother, even though we have underplayed the father's role for a long time.[7] We know much more now about the effects of some specific kinds of early life adventures such as illness, moves, death, or separation.[8] But although we take these elements of early child care for granted, it is well to remember that it is only in the past thirty or forty years that we have come to realize how important they are. Indeed, it was this understanding that early deprivation of parental care over and above basic physical needs could cause the condition known as marasmus, a situation that can eventually result in death through lack of attention.[9]

A factor of early parenting that is vital to the prescription of the well-known T-L-C is the need for consistency. Hence the impact of a child's separation from a parent can be most serious. Dramatic progress has been made toward understanding and lessening the traumatic impact of the inevitable hospitalization of some children and the role parents can play during this period. Awareness of the need for consistent parenting has resulted in marked changes, especially after World War II, in our perception of the risks involved in the institutionalization of young children and in a renewed interest in foster care of children.

Thus illnesses in parents, serious illnesses of other family members that put heavy demands on parents, deaths and separations are all dramatic events in the personality development of children. We probably do not fully appreciate the tremendous personality strain put on many children in current society by the increase in new forms of marriage and the high frequency of remarriage, with various recombinations of sets of siblings.[10]

Obviously an important determinant of personality in a psychosocial framework is the family into which a child is born. Without attempting to do more than touch lightly on the nature and intensity of this factor in personality, we shall list only the key factors.

In the first decade of life the family is the essential influence on the emerging personality. We begin with the fact that the first language the child will speak will come from the family. In addition to language such things as ethnic and racial identity, socioeconomic status, access to material goods, attitudes, values, role perception, self-identity including self-worth, trust, anxiety and adequacy, and likes and dislikes of a wide range of stimuli all come from the family in which the child is raised. Even though many of these components of the person may be changed, we know that he or she keeps many of them, be it a dislike for a particular food or a preference for some activities over others.

Sibling position is a determinant of personality related to family to which clinicians used to give considerable attention. Whether a person is first-born, last-born, an only child, a second child, a twin or a middle child may still be an important aspect of personality development deserving further study. We know that when parents compare notes about their children they have some clear ideas about differences related to birth order and are prepared to make generalizations from these perceptions. Some sociological research strongly supports the importance of birth order. There are findings, for example, which indicate that first-born children can be expected to be found in top levels of industry or other leadership positions and professions, especially if the first-born is male. Other studies have looked at similarities and differences in the behavior of twins.[11]

There are two additional, interconnected factors that are important determinants in the developing structure of personality. The first can be subsumed under the general idea of a person's history. As the developing child moves beyond the family of origin and finds that not everyone sees the world as he does, that people react to him differently, that he in turn reacts differently to them, his personality is in turn altered and expanded. He is taught many things, his perceptions are widened, he learns new ways of responding and functioning, he learns new skills, he develops new priorities. His uniqueness remains, he is still himself, but the structure and attributes of this unique personality are altered.

This dynamic historical component is ongoing and includes the whole interface of a person-in-situation that is increasingly complex for much of our society. The exciting aspect of this expanding spectrum of cognitive, affective, and interpersonal stimuli, with which we are bombarded is that the human person seems to be capable of limitless flexibility in dealing with a vast range of new responses, ideas and situations. It is fashionable to predict that we are now approaching the saturation point in dealing with complexity, but this is only speculative.[12] I think there is at least as much evidence that man has only begun to appreciate his potential for change, development and learning.[13]

A further component related to the impact of our individualized histories on our odyssey through life is the values and attitudes we develop. An important individualizing factor in personality structure is the set of values with which we view ourselves, others, and the world around us. This component of personality, once relegated to the philosopher and the theologican, is now regarded as of great importance to the sociologist, psychologist, educator, and social worker.[14] It is increasingly evident that each individual has to come to terms with a variety of basic situations that in turn will affect how he sees the world and how he relates to it. Thus how he views man's basic nature, how he comes to terms with individuality versus membership in groups, how he perceives the nature of his activities are some of the basic value orientations that are essential to persons and in turn differentiate personalities. This applies, of course, to families and groups as well. Kluckhohn, Rokeach, and others have examined this field and are continuing to make considerable progress in identifying the range and clusters of values between and among people as well as how values are learned and changed.[15]

In a psychosocial theory of practice, the development of that unique quality we call the individual personality is seen as a multifaceted process in which the biological, psychological, and social components all have critical roles. The extent to which these are to be ordered in a hierarchical way is still a topic of debate. Presuming some adequate biological endowment, we seem to have moved in this school of practice from a position which made the early psychosocial history the key factor in understanding a person to the more optimistic position that sees learning as continuing all through life, facilitating changes and ongoing development. This ability to change and modify who we are is obviously of great importance in instances where the therapist hopes to bring about change in psychosocial functioning.

Although it may be seen as a profession of faith instead of a demonstration of scientific fact, there appears to be one final determinant of personality of such strength and importance that it cannot be ignored. This is the basic life force in each person that makes him or her much more than the sum total of a genetic endowment and the events of a history. It is that special, spiritual, individualistic, nondetermined component of human nature that permits the individual to choose not to be influenced or not to be conditioned. It is the quality that seeks growth and change, that permits one to shake off his past and move beyond it. Important as it is to try to assess the determinants of an individual's personality, we must also try to include in our assessment and to respect his own special piece of life that leads him to say "I am" rather than "I have been made to be."

The Normal and the Abnormal

Within this broad concept of personality and its significant components, the helping person must develop a set of working concepts related to normal and healthy functioning and its opposite, abnormal and unhealthy functioning. Although the concepts of the normal and the pathological have been criticized as having a judgmental or medical-model basis, there is no way of avoiding some form of continuum. Even when these terms in themselves are rejected, some related terminology must be developed to replace them. Regardless of one's conceptual stance, responsible therapeutic practice demands that each client be assessed from the viewpoint of what about him and his potential is contributing to his ability to function in a satisfying way and what about him and his resources is preventing this kind of functioning. That is, we must constantly ask what there is about the client and his situation that is normal and growth-enhancing and what there is about his functioning that is not normal. If we do not have working concepts related to this dichotomy, we lack conceptual guidelines that will tell us to be worried about some clients, to be pleased about others, to perceive when a client has progressed in his psychosocial functioning and when he has regressed.

It is understandable that there has been strong resistance in the helping professions to the use of categories or classifying concepts. This issue will be discussed again when the topic of diagnosis is addressed in the next chapter. The fears expressed relate to two things: (1) a perceived risk of making judgments about people that are unfounded or value-laden, and (2) a perception that practice will be viewed as dealing only with pathology or abnormalities. Both of these fears relate to a misuse of concepts rather than to invalid concepts.

Always we must respect the limits of our knowledge and the awesome responsibility we take in making judgments about people. But to fail to assess people and categorize people vitiates any claim to practice-based knowledge. The fact that we make judgments about the adequacy or inadequacy of a client's personality does not mean that this is the essence of our practice. We know that among many caseloads we will be dealing with situations where our assessment tells us we have a normal person who is experiencing problems, just as we will be dealing with nonnormal persons with problems. On the other hand, we will be dealing with normal persons without problems, as well as with nonnormal persons without problems. To know this requires that a judgment be made and hence an assignment to a classification.

NORMALITY

In the psychosocial tradition, a person is considered normal who possesses an adequate biopsychosocial endowment, a strong sense of self, an ability to exert himself within the range of his capabilities, an ability to function within the acceptable demands of society's systems and subsystems, and finally a reasonable access to the persons, goods, and services of the society in which he lives in a manner acceptable to his values.

As here described, normality is a complex concept including both normative and relative elements.[16] It is not a concept that lends itself to precise definition. Contained in the above description are six elements: First, "normal personality functioning" does not mean the same thing as ideal functioning. That is, the concept does not require that an individual possess all human qualities in a state of perfection but only to that degree which is considered adequate. An analogy to our physical condition helps clarify this. We all know that even when someone is considered to be in a state of physical well-being allowance is made for a wide range of small physical defects, lacks and imperfect functioning; thus there is a wide variation between persons. A careful physical examination of the healthiest of persons would turn up a range of conditions concerning weight, teeth, eyes, posture, and digestion that would not be ideal but certainly well within the range of normal and healthy functioning. This same concept of adequacy is carried over to a perception of personality functioning.

The second element in the concept of normality is that it is different from the concept of average. This is an important point. It helps the practitioner to avoid viewing situations as unchangeable or not needing change because they are the common condition of many people. It is important to know the potential of the human endowment and the human condition so as to adequately assess the situations which are not normal even though they are shared by a wide number of people.

The third element of normality relates to the biological endowment a person possesses. This contains two concepts: his physical endowment and his intellectual endowment. Both factors involve two further concepts: one, that there are no serious lacks or abnormalities in the organisms themselves, and secondly, that they are functioning well. For example, a person may have a fully intact body which is not functioning well because of disease. On the other hand, a person may be seriously handicapped because of the absence or malfunction of a limb or an organ.

The fourth element of normality concerns a person's sense of self, more commonly designated as his identity. That is, a normal person is one who knows who he is and likes himself as he is. This includes several elements, such as being free from acute internal suffering, anxiety, fears, compulsions, anger or psychosomatic complaints. It also includes having a sense of usefulness, of knowing that he belongs somewhere, that he is a part of something that is significant and important in his eyes. Related to this is the possession of a sense of fulfillment, the feeling that one is doing something that is worthwhile, that is leading to an objective that is desirable and acceptable to him.

A further factor in self-identity concerns having a sense of self-control, control of one's inner as well as one's outer life. Clearly, "control" is not meant in an absolute sense but in a more general, managerial sense. That is, I am in control of me and the things around me in most areas of my life.

The fifth element of normality from the psychosocial viewpoint is related to the ability to function within significant societal expectations and demands. The idea of *ability* is stressed here to avoid the normative concept that normal functioning includes functioning in a socially useful fashion or in a way that requires a person to make full use of his or her potential in an achieving, growing way. Clearly, this moves us into the realm of cultural norms and values. For the therapist, the important component is whether the person is capable of functioning within society's expectations if he so chooses, not whether he indeed is so functioning. Certainly, if a person chooses to exercise his autonomy in a manner that knowingly and willingly brings him into conflict with society, we cannot call this abnormal even though it is potentially painful to the person involved, harmful to others and strongly rejected by significant others in his life.

The sixth and final element of normality relates to an individual's access to persons and things outside himself. Inherent in the psychosocial system is the idea that man is a socially oriented being who finds his identity and fulfillment in relationship with others and in the enjoyment of material and cultural resources. What is adequate in this area is heavily culturally defined but the concept is clear. For an individual's functioning to be considered normal he must have access to other individuals with whom to relate, have an adequate share in the material goods and services that are appropriate to the culture and times and be able to participate comfortably in the resources of the society in which he lives. The importance of access to other persons and resources as a necessary determinant of normal psychosocial functioning is reflected in the attention that is given in psychosocial therapy to changes in a client's external environment.

ABNORMAL FUNCTIONING

The concept of normality includes the possibility of nonnormality or abnormality. In assessing a situation, the characteristics of normality are applied to that situation. Hence in our practice we find persons who are deficient in their ability to function because of lacks in their physical or intellectual endowment. Just as a minor temporary illness can effect our own moods, attitudes, and abilities to solve problems, relate to others, and discharge expected roles, these effects are magnified when a person is afflicted either temporarily or permanently with a physical or mental disorder. In more pathological situations, we see the depths of suffering in such symptoms as depression, depersonalization, or paranoia.

In addition, families and groups may be under stress from the standpoint of their perception of themselves. People may be confused and anxious about who they are; they may be overwhelmed with anxiety, inhibited because of a sense of uselessness, immobilized by feelings of being unloved, rejected, unfulfilled, or unwanted. These feelings can range from very minor and transitory reactions that are a part of all our lives to the stage where they clearly are beyond the realm of normal functioning and can cause pain, suffering, and loss of potential that can be properly designated as abnormal.

Persons may also be under stress because of their inability to get along with others, to function in their chosen roles in society, or to operate within institutions and structures of that society.

As with all problem areas, rarely is the situation caused by a single factor. Certainly, a person may be unable to function in some segment of society because of a physical limitation or a personality deficit. But it may also be that his inability to function results from society's perception of him and the transactions that take place between the individual and other individuals and groups in society. That is, the behavior of persons can be considered variant for any one of the numerous reasons that have been and continue to be the source of value-laden perceptions of people.

Assaults on normal personality functioning can also result from a lack of the materials and services required to function. Clearly, there is a strong relativistic component to what is adequate, what is essential, what is desirable, and what is inappropriate. In our society the difference between essential needs can vary considerably in places within a few miles of each other. For example, elevators in an urban high-rise apartment must be seen as essential, but snowmobiles would be a great luxury in such a setting. However, only a few miles away, for a rural family in an area subject to heavy snowfalls a snowmobile would be essential and an elevator a useless luxury. Thus in no way can these needs be considered interchangeable. Absence of these resources for the two families involved would be critical from the viewpoint of survival in times of crisis. It is this relativity of need that makes planning so difficult in general programs of public assistance in North America. An example of the relativity of programs was seen in a recent trip to the Arctic. One of the settings visited was a detention center for sentenced male adults. A part of the program of this center was to issue the prisoners hunting equipment, including rifles, to go out on the land and hunt caribou, which in turn was used to supply meat for the old people in the settlement who were no longer able to hunt. This obviously is a program that would hardly be followed in an urban correctional center.

Psychosocial therapy has as its primary goal the facilitation of satisfying, growth-oriented psychosocial functioning. It is evident that within the factors included in the concept of normal personality functioning a wide range of situations can develop or may exist that will inhibit or restrict optimal functioning.

I am not suggesting that the psychosocial therapist is seeking to develop a utopian world; rather, he is committed to dealing with the situations that can be changed and where there is an appropriate desire to change. In this approach to psychotherapeutic practice, a problem is seen as a stress-producing situation which inhibits satisfying functioning and with which an individual or group does not have immediate resources to cope.

These situations, the proper target of intervention, can be classified in four main categories. Two of these categories are within the person; deficiency of an endowment or the inability to make use of one's potential. The remaining two are external to the person; lack of adequate resources that restrict the person's achievement of potential and a lack of access to existing resources.

The psychosocial therapist is committed to understanding the personality and its determinants as well as those things within both the person and the society that contribute to enhanced growth and development as well as those that contribute to problems of functioning and suffering.

Notes

1. Felix Biestek, *The Casework Relationship* (Chicago: Loyola University Press, 1957).
2. C. Kluckhohn and H. Murray, *Personality in Nature, Society and*

Culture, 2nd ed. revised and enlarged (New York: Knopf, 1953), pp. 53–67.

3. Calvin S. Hall and Gardner Lindzey, *Theories of Personality,* 2nd edition (New York: John Wiley and Sons, 1970), pp. 1–28.

4. William B. Neser and Grace Sudderth, "Genetics and Casework," *Social Casework* 46 (January, 1965), pp. 22–25. Sylvia Schild, "The Challenging Opportunity for Social Workers in Genetics," *Social Work* 2 (April, 1966), pp. 22–28. Amelia Schultz, "The Impact of Genetic Disorders," *Social Work* 2 (April, 1966), pp. 29–34. Amelia Schultz and Arno Motulsky, "Medical Genetics and Adoption," *Child Welfare* 50 (January, 1971), pp. 4–17.

5. Gordon R. Lowe, *The Growth of Personality: From Infancy to Old Age* (London: Penguin Books, 1972). Erik H. Erikson, *Childhood and Society,* 2nd ed. revised and enlarged (New York: Norton, 1963). Jean Piaget, *The Origins of Intelligence in Children* (translated by M. Cook) (New York: International University Press, 1952). Arnold Gesell, *The First Five Years of Life: A Guide to the Study of the Preschool Child,* 9th edition (New York: Harper and Row, 1940).

6. Florence Hollis, *Casework: A Psychosocial Therapy,* 2nd ed. (New York: Random House, 1972), pp. 185–202.

7. John Bowlby, *Maternal Care and Mental Health,* 2nd ed., World Health Organization Monograph Series no. 2 (Geneva: World Health Organization, 1952).

8. Nes Littner, *Some Traumatic Effects of Separation and Placement* (New York: Child Welfare League of America, 1956).

9. O. Spurgeon English and Gerald H. J. Pearson, *Emotional Problems of Living* (New York: Norton, 1945), p. 38.

10. Irene Fast and Albert Cain, "The Stepparent Role: Potential for Disturbances in Family Functioning," *American Journal of Orthopsychiatry* 36 (April, 1966), pp. 485–491. F. Turner, ed. *Differential Diagnosis and Treatment in Social Work,* 2nd ed. (New York: Free Press, 1976), pp. 676–682.

11. Gerry E. Hendershot, "Familial Satisfaction, Birth Order and Fertility Values," *Journal of Marriage and the Family* 31 (February, 1969), pp. 27–33. Kenneth Kammeyer, "Sibling Position and the Feminine Role," *Journal of Marriage and the Family* 29 (1967), pp. 494–499. Theodore D. Kemper, "Mate Selection and

Marital Satisfaction According to Sibling Type of Husband and Wife," *Journal of Marriage and the Family* 28 (1966), pp. 346–349. Atlee L. Stromp and Katherine J. Hunter, "Sibling Position in the Family and the Personality of Offspring," *Journal of Marriage and the Family* 27 (1965), pp. 65–68. Elsa G. Welins, "Some Effects of Premature Parental Responsibility on the Older Sibling," *Smith College Studies in Social Work* 35 (1964), pp. 26–40.

12. Alvin Toffler, *Future Shock* (New York: Bantam Books, 1971).

13. Russell Ackoff, *Redesigning the Future: A Systems Approach to Societal Programs* (New York: John Wiley, 1974).

14. Francis J. Turner, "Values and the Social Worker," in J. R. Meyer, ed., *Reflections on Values Education* (Waterloo: Wilfrid Laurier University Press, 1976), pp. 201–210.

15. Florence R. Kluckhohn and Fred L. Strotbeck, *Variations in Value Orientations* (Evanston: Row Peterson and Co., 1961). Milton Rokeach, *The Nature of Human Values* (New York: Free Press, 1973).

16. Norman Cameron, *Personality Development and Psychopathology: A Dynamic Approach* (Boston: Houghton Mifflin, 1963), pp. 8–13.

Chapter 3

The Nature and Scope of Psychosocial Treatment

A Question of Terminology

In the first chapter we referred to the debate in the 1950s as to whether social work intervention was to be considered a form of psychotherapy or some other form of help. Athough the debate was in fact more concerned with the nature of the profession than the nature of therapy, its resolution on the side of therapy had important implications for the psychosocial school. For in asserting a commitment to therapy, this system was also accepting the responsibility inherent in the concept. It was acknowledging that the intervention process was based on a body of testable and communicable knowledge and skills utilized in a respectful, understanding, and supportive way for the benefit of the client. It was also recognizing that the therapist would be held responsible for his actions.

There are persons who challenge the use of the word "therapy" because of its derivation from the medical tradition and the mistaken belief that it therefore assumes that disease or pathology is basic to all aspects of the human predicament. Thus such terms as the "helping process," "counseling," "intervention," and "client-worker interaction" have been proposed as preferable. Clearly, there is nothing wrong with these other terms, but neither is there anything wrong with the term "therapy." The added advantage of using "therapy," in its correct context, is the implication it carries for accountability and responsibility and for an intense commitment to the never-ending process of expanding and strengthening the empirically verified basis of practice. Nevertheless, any of the other descriptions of the process is valid as long as it contains this commitment to the concept of responsible, knowledge-based practice.[1]

In a parallel way the concept of the social worker as therapist is important in the psychosocial tradition. As with "therapy," the term "therapist" includes the dimensions of personal responsibility, training, social accountability, and social authentication. It also includes the idea of knowledge and authority. It includes, finally, the concept of an acceptance of and a commitment to the client in a noncondemning, authentic way.

Again, for some, "therapist" is an unacceptable word. It seems to convey the idea of disregard for the client's autonomy, an unchallenged use of authority, a sociological distancing from the client, a negatively tainted, establishment-based membership in a closed association. But as with other terms, these critical comments represent misuses of the term rather than inherent deficiencies. Any other term, be it "helper," "enabler," "facilitator," "counselor" or "helping person," is again acceptable as long as it includes a commitment to the responsible, accountable use of knowledge for the client's good.[2]

Who Is the Client?

For the psychosocial therapist, the definition of a client is more complex than it might appear to be. Certainly it is easy to perceive who and what a client is in situations where an individual, family or group has asked for the services of the social worker for a specific reason related to a psychosocial situation. In these instances, a client can be defined as a person or a group of persons who have sought the services of a social worker and to whom the social worker has made a professional commitment to offer his knowledge and skills.[3]

However, including a contractual concept in the definition of a client does not hold in situations where the client is an involuntary one because of age, situation, or setting. Thus, a person who is ordered by the court to see a social worker for a specific period of time is far from being in a position of seeking to contract for professional services. A further situation that obfuscates the clarity of the client concept relates to intermediary services. It frequently happens in practice that the primary area of concern is a particular child, even though the recipient of the social worker's services might be, for example, the child's teacher, who is being helped to find different ways of coping with the child in a manner that is helpful to the child.

The definition of client becomes even more diffuse in community work, where the effects of the social worker's activity might influence persons and groups with whom the worker has no direct contact or even knowledge.

Although difficult, the question of who the client is must be addressed in any discussion of a specific approach to practice. To the psychosocial therapist, a client is an individual or a group of individuals about whom the worker has professional knowledge, for whom he has taken responsibility, on whom some professional influences will be brought to bear, for which society will hold the professional accountable.

The Scope of Therapy

In clarifying the essential components of the therapeutic process the goal of the process must be kept paramount. For the psychosocial therapist, the goal is the achievement of optimal psychosocial functioning within the client's potential and in a manner that recognizes and respects his value systems.

This goal is sought within three broad contexts: the medium of human relationships, the material and service resources available, and the human resources of the client's significant environments. Within these parameters, five types of change can be identified that can result from a therapeutic experience with a psychosocial therapist: cognitive, emotive, behavioral, material, and relief from suffering. It is to be understood that this classification is intended to convey not discrete categories but, rather, useful clustering to permit a clearer understanding of the process. Rarely does change that takes place in a case occur in only one category. More commonly it touches on several areas. More importantly, it is to be understood that these various forms of change do not reflect a hierarchy; no one type of change is of greater merit than another. The client's needs must be kept paramount, rather than the therapist's preference or the profession's ranking of types of change.

One further point needs to be made. This fivefold classification describes the range of possible changes. It does not of course suggest that any one psychosocial therapist has or should have an existing range of skills, knowledge and resources to help all clients in all situations. Rather, the kinds of change that can be sought are being laid out; whether these changes occur or not in a specific case will depend on the skills of the therapist, the potentials of the client and the intensity of the problems that are being addressed.

COGNITIVE CHANGE

Of all the many changes, both subtle and dramatic, that can take place during the helping process, the importance of cognitive change is most frequently underestimated by therapists. It seems that our perception of ourselves as therapists more often focuses on the emotional life of the client than on his or her intellectual sphere. Yet, we have experienced in our own lives how important it is to know and understand what is happening to us and to those around us. In addition, we are aware that knowledge or information can expand our perspectives, open up new opportunities, and enhance our potential for increased autonomy over our destiny. On the other hand, we have all experienced anxiety, confusion and frustration when we did not have full information and understanding about choices, resources, or procedures.

Thus in psychosocial practice, a significant part of any change that occurs in a client's psychosocial functioning will result from cognitive changes. Clients will acquire new knowledge about themselves, their motives, feelings, reactions and attitudes. They will expand their knowledge about their behavior and its impact on others. They will learn more about significant others in their lives, about societal subsystems with which they are involved and most importantly about resources of goods, services, opportunities and people that can help them achieve the goals to which they have committed themselves. Knowledge in itself is a form of growth, whether it be the growth that takes place in a woman who finds that she can continue to work because of the new information about daycare services she has obtained or the more basic growth that takes place when a man learns that his long-standing pattern of aggression has been creating problems for him and that this pattern can change.

EMOTIVE CHANGE

An essential component of psychosocial therapy, indeed of any form of psychotherapy, is modification of the emotional life of the client. The complex range of feelings that comprise the person's functioning, can be rich and satisfying, but we also know that these feelings can be restricting, painful, and confusing. The uncovering, redirecting, freeing and refocusing of feelings have of course been among the distinguishing objectives of psychotherapy.

Rational as man is, and enabling as his rationality is, we know that his emotional life, both conscious and unconscious, is also a basis for much of his motivation and personal growth just as this same emotional life can be restricting and inhibiting. Without attempting to describe the total myriad of emotional complexities that can inhibit functioning and growth, there are several major situations that can be emphasized.

All therapists, regardless of their orientation, realize the extent to which many clients we meet in practice are greatly inhibited because of a distorted, damaged or scarred self-image. This self-directed negativism, which can take many forms, leads to an underestimation of one's potential, an inability to make use of available resources and a distortion of aspects of one's significant environments.

In addition to an individual's image of himself, his ability to utilize his potential may also be curtailed because of debilitating feelings of anger, fear, anxiety, uncertainty and hurt. Each person develops an idiosyncratic pattern of mental mechanisms, both conscious and unconscious, to deal with his emotional life. It is essential for the therapist to understand both this pattern and the pattern of compromises, limitations, and restrictions that a pattern of behavior brings to an individual's search for development. Much of the change of feeling that takes place concerning a client's sense of himself begins in the experience of being accepted, understood, supported, and encouraged in the client–therapist relationship. Often, this type of change then frees the client to experience similar changes in himself and others both in his present and also from his past.

BEHAVIORAL CHANGE

It appears that in earlier decades behavioral changes were not seen as a direct goal of treatment but rather as an outcome of treatment. As a client came to understand himself and his responses more clearly, he could alter his behavior. With the growing appreciation of intersystemic influences that has resulted from our ongoing contact with systems theory, there has been an enriched appreciation that just as changed feelings can result in changed behavior, so changed behavior can bring about changed attitudes and changed understanding of oneself. We have always know this in regard to our children. Frequently, we encourage them to risk engaging in some new behavior and observe their increased pleasure in themselves and their own autonomy. What we have not done is to make sufficient use of this same knowledge in therapy for the benefit of our clients.

There are two principal ways in which therapy aims at bringing about this type of change. First, there is the change that takes place indirectly, within the medium of the relationship. Here the client can learn new patterns of response, new skills in communication, and new approaches to problem solving through the process of interacting with the therapist. This type of behavioral influence on clients is frequently underestimated by therapists, often because we do not see the changed behavior clients have learned from us and hence do not include it in our assessment of our interventions. Indeed, clients themselves may not be aware that they have changed but may be aware only that some formerly stress-producing situations have been altered.

Changes are also directly and planfully sought in psychosocial therapy. Clearly, interest in and detailed attention to this component of therapy has been greatly expanded with the dramatic development of behavioral therapy in the past decade. Many therapists in the psychosocial tradition have expanded their repertoire of techniques by making use of these carefully studied and researched methods to bring about specific behavioral changes.[4] Others have drawn on the learning-theory basis of these techniques to understand better how behavior is learned and modified in a less structured way.[5] Whether in the tradition of the behavior modifier or in the more conventional role of the therapist as teacher and advisor, much current psychosocial practice consciously aims at modifying client behavior. This can be as simple as teaching a mother new ways of coping with a highly active child or as diffuse as helping a couple learn new patterns in dealing with their disagreements through some carefully designed program of reciprocal reinforcement. It can be as basic as teaching a young adult how to groom himself better in searching for a job or as advanced as helping a mother to recognize and alter emerging symptoms of depression that have formerly incapacitated her.

ENVIRONMENTAL CHANGE

A principal tenet of psychosocial therapy is to stress the essential influencing power of an individual's significant environments on the development and modification of personality. It follows, therefore, that in treatment planned change will also be sought in these milieu aspects of the client's life. As mentioned earlier in the discussion of behavioral change, the theoretical basis of milieu change is the belief that alterations in a client's outer world can bring about changes in behavior, emotional responses and understanding, just as changes in emotional responses can help the client modify his or her external world.[6]

There are two principal areas in which this type of change takes place. The first encompasses those activities intended to increase the client's access to material resources. These activities, long the hallmark of the social worker, involve the ever widening and increasingly complex range of resources to which a social worker must turn in a busy practice. None of us has to go beyond our own life experience to be aware of the limitations on functioning, the drains on our emotions and the assault on our identities that can result from even a minor and transitory limitation of resources. We also know reciprocally how helpful it can be to acquire resources or access to them in a particular situation.

Along with the direct provision of material assistance, changes in the client's environment are also brought about by the provision of services. The list of services that have been developed is myriad. We know that in a society such as ours it is not sufficient to be willing to achieve our goals and to have the personal ability to do so. In addition, we all require an intricate network of services to assist us. Day-care for children, substitute care for the aged, educational, and recreational resources are just a few of the services essential to the adequate functioning of persons, families and groups. The psychosocial therapist uses his skills both to ensure that such services exist and to understand their potential in a manner that permits him to draw upon them for the good of the client as he knows and understands him.

The manner in which we bring about changes in the client's significant mileu is of course a complex and involved topic. It requires vast knowledge of the client and of the persons, resources, and services in the community. No less, it requires an array of skills necessary to bring client, person, service, and resource together in a manner than can most assuredly result in the sought-after change. Of such importance is this component of practice in this system that it will be the topic of a subsequent chapter.[7]

RELIEF FROM SUFFERING

Before leaving this classification of the types of change that are sought in psychosocial therapy, one additional topic needs to be mentioned. There is some question as to whether it stands as a topic in its own right or whether indeed it underlies all the other changes. Many of the clients with whom we come in contact professionally are hurting in a myriad of ways. It may be a primitive hurt stemming from earlier deprivation or the existential anxiety of searching for meaning. It may be the pain of frustration, the weight of depression, the drain of anxiety, the terror of hallucination or the confusion of a deteriorating personality structure. It may also be the emptiness of hunger or the suffering of want. It is this human hurting and the resultant loss of fulfillment and drain on potential that is our motivating force. Thus in our practice some of the change we will seek is the alleviation of pain and suffering. But this we do more as a means than as an end. Perhaps we take it so much for granted that we do not want people to suffer unnecessarily that we forget to find out where our clients are hurting. Some of the obvious hurts we can relieve rather quickly either through our own efforts or with the aid of colleagues and other disciplines. Some of the hurt that we over-look and thus fail to seek to change is of a less obvious nature such as that of persons struggling to know who they are, where they are going, and how they are going to get there. Our existentialist colleagues have aided us in this topic and remind us of the need to be more aware of this sphere of our clients' reality.

The Resources of Treatment

The foregoing summarizes the kinds of change the psychosocial therapist seeks to bring about in the lives of clients. Just as the possible outcomes are varied, so are the resources and the means available to the practitioner.

RELATIONSHIP

The first and certainly the most critical resource in psychosocial treatment is the relationship between the therapist and client. From its earliest roots in the writings of Mary Richmond, psychosocial therapy has emphasized the power of person-on-person, the ability of one human being to change the ideas, perceptions, feelings, actions, and life-styles of another. The helping relationship has been seen as so powerful that at times it seems almost to have been given a mystical identity in itself and viewed as a magical, mysterious force.[8] Happily, we are now moving away from this perception, and in the past decade there has been growing interest in trying to understand and describe how people influence each other, in what circumstances and with what duration. This trend implies no lessening of respect for the power of this essential component of human resources.[9]

We know that we influence each other; we know that at times this human-on-human influence is of critical significance; we know also that this influence is not necessarily a positive one. We know all too well how the spell-binding charm and charisma of a leader can cause masses of people to take action that can be in no way considered as beneficial to them; we also know that on a one-to-one basis people can espouse a life style that directly contradicts a previously strong commitment to its opposite.

This component of treatment will be addressed again in Chapter 4; at this point we want only to identify it as a most powerful resource in the treatment process in the psychosocial tradition. As mentioned earlier, the influence of person-on-person has long been understood as one of the most powerful agents in human development, healthy and unhealthy, and in human growth, warped or fulfilled. Awareness of the power of the relationship and how to manipulate it for the benefit of the client is, and long has been, an essential component of the psychotherapeutic tradition.

Critical as the therapeutic relationship is, in the psychosocial tradition it is not seen as the only variable in treatment. Therapists can easily move into a situation where the helping relationship becomes the predominant component or indeed the sole component of treatment when we see how powerful and influential it can be. Many of the persons we meet in contemporary practice have been so deprived of significant, caring relationships that their response to a professional use of the relationship is dramatic. So often in our practice we forget that there are many individuals in society who have not had the experience of receiving an uninterrupted, concerned, respectful, accepting hearing, and we marvel at how freeing and enabling this can be. We frequently underestimate the extent of our influence in enhancing growth in clients as a result of brief contact with them. Of equal importance is the awareness of how harmful such an encounter can be when badly handled.

THE THERAPIST

Important as the relationship is and as the knowledge and skills of therapy acquired through professional training are, the uniqueness of the therapist as a person is no less important as a component of the therapeutic process. Who the therapist is will partly affect how he is seen by the client, what kinds of persons he can help, in what kinds of settings he can most effectively practice, and with what kinds of problems he can deal efficiently.

Clearly, the commitment and goal of professional training is to reduce the idiosyncratic nature of practice in so far as possible, but it can never eliminate it entirely. There will always be individuals for whom the unique person of the therapist will be the key factor that fosters positive or negative development in a way that is essential to the particular case. This uniqueness should keep us humble as practitioners.

Because of the importance of the person in the therapeutic process, the question of societal accountability is of grave importance. In North American society there has been an interesting dyad of phenomena related to the professions that for a while tended to neutralize each other. In the late 1960s and early 1970s there was a strong individualistic, antiprofessional bias that put emphasis on the individual practicing in his own manner. Professions were seen as self-protective, restrictive, self-serving bodies; hence questions of licensing, control and professional accountability were minimized. This viewpoint was reinforced by the antitherapeutic viewpoint that emphasized a peer style of practice based on a model of relationship with friendshiplike qualities. In this style first reactions, impressions and immediate responses were the basis of helping.

At the same time, there was another shift of value that supported the appropriateness of seeking help and a turning outward for professional help. The numbers of persons seeking help increased, but for a time this increasing demand was almost invisible because of the influence of the antiprofessional trend. This has now changed, and with the interest in formal helping services, unprecedented societal demands are being made upon professional groups for accountability. There is a concomitant societal disillusionment about persons who do not identify themselves with a recognized and sanctioned professional group which can hold them accountable for their knowledge and skills.

With the increased demands for help and accountability there was a growing appreciation of the potential dangers of unethical or unacceptable help and of the need for standards, controls, and sanctions to protect clients against these hazards. This in turn has put heavy pressure on professional bodies to find the essential line between the necessary autonomy and individuality of each practitioner and the need for standardized levels of practice and accountable codes of behavior.

It is this recognition of the need for both autonomy and accountability that accounts for the strong insistence within the psychosocial tradition that the therapist, especially in his first years of practice, receive some form of professional supervision or consultation. As will be mentioned later, the nature and form of supervision have varied over the years and among practitioners, but not the insistence that responsible practice, at least in the early stages, requires that the therapist be involved in a process of supervision.

THE SERVICE NETWORK

By setting, in this context, is meant both the structure in which help is given, such as the agency or clinic, and the actual physical environment in which the process takes place, such as a home, a ward, or an office.

Although a more detailed discussion will follow in Chapter 8, it is important to make brief mention of these factors in this discussion of the components of professional intervention. One of the important features of the psychosocial viewpoint is the commitment to use all the factors that might bring about desired change.

Before addressing the setting as a unit it is useful to comment on setting from a network perspective. It appears that we have greatly underestimated the extent to which the very existence of a helping system is in itself a form of indirect help-producing activity. Although it would be incorrect to overstress the efficacy of this indirect form of help, neither can it be ignored. When an individual, family, or group in need is aware that persons and places exist to which they can turn, this in itself is a component of a helping process. The expectation that help is available and that it will be efficacious creates a climate of involvement that in many cases can be productive. At times, this expectation and optimism can carry some clients through some inadequate and unhelping intervention.[10] Although the importance of the agency as a sociological component of society has long been understood,[11] less attention has been focused on the physical attributes of agencies and their influence on the helping process. This dearth of data is remarkable, especially from the social work viewpoint, in view of the fact that as a profession, social work has championed the importance of adequate physical resources for psychosocial development. We have not been able to translate this concern into knowledge and practice. Our own clinical experience as well as the accumulated data of the social psychologists and the human engineers have underscored the extent to which we are all influenced by the physical environments in which we carry out our various social transactions. We know how our comfort, security, and sense of importance are all greatly affected by the physical surroundings in which we find ourselves. We know also that there are emotions which are affected by our physical environments. Reciprocally, we are well aware of how our perception of others is influenced by the physical situations in which they function, be it a dentist's office or a car salesman's showroom. A comfortable private office, tastefully decorated and furnished, can contribute greatly to a client's sense of worth and respect just as the same lack of privacy and comfort can detract from the trust and security required to make use of available help. These factors are all considered to be influencing variables in the helping process, to be assessed and utilized according to a plan.

LOCALE

A related variable to which attention must be paid in the helping process is the locale of the therapist-client contact. By locale, we mean the place where the interaction takes place, be it an office, a home, a job setting or some informal place. For decades members of the helping professions have worked with clients in a wide range of settings. Often, the choice as to which setting was to be utilized was a pragmatic one based on the exigencies of available time and convenience. Little detailed data are available on the impact of different locales on the therapeutic process.

In the late 1950s, with the rediscovery of the sociocultural influences and the wave of enthusiasm about family therapy, the home visit assumed prime importance.[12] But unfortunately, this aspect of treatment, long a part of child welfare, public assistance, and the practice of the rural social worker, became a cause rather than a reasoned, examined, and tested variable in practice. Again, more data are needed to clarify the effects of different locales on practice. Without turning far from our own psychosocial lives, we know that we do react differently to situations and to people depending on where we see them or interact with them. We know, for example, that our perception and confidence in a lawyer, physician, or clergyman is greatly affected by their flexibility to be available in particular situations of need.

Time

Like setting and locale, the factor of time has not been addressed properly as an empirical component of the helping process. Certainly one of the traditional values linking time and treatment, and reflecting the strong influence of the psychoanalytical school, was the often unstated conviction that the helping process is more effective if extended over a long period. This is reflected in the view of many that long-term treatment is more valuable than short-term treatment in effecting fundamental changes in personality, while short-term treatment is temporary and has something in common with the administration of first aid in cases of physical injury. This viewpoint is changing. There is a growing awareness based on research and experience that short-term treatment can be as effective and at times of more benefit than long-term treatment. Related to the new interest in short-term treatment is a concomitant interest in crisis intervention and an awareness that the right amount of appropriate help given at the right time can be of fundamental importance.[13]

Although much more work is required to fully understand time as a variable, we already know some of the ways in which it is related to effective intervention.[14] Thus, how soon a client gets seen once he has made an initial request for service is an important variable. We have moved from the point where being able to tolerate a waiting period was seen as a test of motivation to the point where we emphasize the need for instant service in some situations. We know that some people are able to work out very appropriate solutions to situations when left on their own, just as others must be seen at once. What kinds of persons and what kinds of situations respond best to immediate service and which respond best to a waiting period before service is given are not matters of established fact but remain in the realm of speculation.

We know also that the duration of the helping process is an important variable. Some clients seem to reach a point where continued contact, rather than being helpful, is detrimental.[15] Thus one of the most critical decisions in the therapeutic process is knowing when to terminate.[16] Again, we have moved through fads in this issue without sufficient data. The continuance of clients in therapy at one time was seen as an indicator of effective helping and unplanned terminations as a sign of failure. As we began to appreciate the risks of inappropriate dependency we moved away from overvaluing long-term treatment. In fact, we seem now to have reached a position that holds that the shorter the contact, the more valuable the process. Clearly, this cannot be a question of fads but must be based on tested experience and the needs of clients.[17]

A further factor related to time as a treatment variable is the question of length and spacing of interviews. Again, much practice is based on a tradition that has found it convenient and manageable to establish a once-a-week, one-hour contact as the norm of therapy. Every experienced worker has experimented from both choice and necessity with variations in the spacing of interviews as well as in their duration, but for the most part this has been done on an impressionistic basis rather than as planned experimentation.

Not every client can tolerate a one-hour interview, while some persons can function effectively in a two-or three-hour interview. Some people need a week between interviews to make maximal use of the interview process; other get more benefit out of a more frequent type of interview. Clearly, some of the variables that affect these differences are related to level of internal stress, frustration tolerance, intellectual ability, physical condition, and the type and nature of service and problem.[18]

Time can also be seen as a variable in another way. Frequently, the kind of development or change that is required or desired by a client will take place as a part of a healthy maturational process that cannot be hurried. In these instances our task is one of sustaining the client in a situation until nature and nurture can fulfill their predictable functions.[19] Thus a young adult, overwhelmed by the realities of autonomous functioning, may need only the experience of living for several months and demonstrating to himself his potential to function on his own to achieve a strong, healthy self-identity. The therapeutic responsibility in this instance is to ensure that the process is structured in such a way that the client has time to fulfill his own potential. To push too hard, to get overinvolved, to terminate too soon could have such negative impact as to interfere with and indeed undo the maturational process. The application of time as a resource of treatment, then, can vary between spending only a few minutes on the phone with a client in an accepting, supporting way to keeping active with a client over a period of years so that sufficient support is available to facilitate the growth potential of the person and his significant social system.

ENVIRONMENTAL RESOURCES

As mentioned earlier, psychosocial practice is based on the strong conviction that many factors influence growth and enhance development and that the purpose of therapy is to understand these factors and bring their influence to bear appropriately to achieve a stipulated therapeutic goal. Thus, the armamentarium of the sensitive and imaginative psychosocial therapist contains a broad range of external resources that he can call upon. One of the most important is that spectrum of other individuals and groups who are generally described as the significant others in a client's life. In earlier pages, we have emphasized the critically significant role that the interaction of person-on-person plays in growth and development. This factor, when properly understood and used, is a most powerful resource beyond the specific utilization of the therapist-client relationship.

There are many ways in which the therapist will involve himself with the significant others in a client's life. Some examples may help. The skill of a therapist in working with the husband of an anxious wife, the friend of a depressed student, the teacher of a disturbed child, the boss of an addicted man, the family of a schizophrenic youth, or the child of an aged person can be the key to successful intervention. In working in this sphere of significant others the same skills of assessment, diagnosis, and intervention are needed as in working with the primary client. Indeed, from a psychosocial perspective it is frequently difficult to determine who is the client.

Over and above the planned building of relationships with others there are three major components of the environmental resources available to the therapist. These are: information, services and material resources.

INFORMATION

First, the therapist is aware of the potential for help that the providing of information to a client can be. Frequently we forget how overwhelming and debilitating the complexity of life may seem to many persons in the urban environment in the 1970s. The sense of being overwhelmed can lead to great anxiety, even to the point of immobility. To a great extent this immobility can come from not knowing how to find needed services and resources or not understanding procedures, alternatives, requirements, expectations and limitations. We have all experienced how tense we can be in new situations—for example, when we move to another city. We also know how quickly this tension and anxiety can be lifted as we accumulate the required information about the resources we need and want. Most of us underestimate the skill this requires and how adept we have become at acquiring the requisite information about many components of our lives. But there are many persons we meet in our practice who lack both information and skills in acquiring it.[20] I am increasingly convinced that one of the most critical functions of the professional in today's world is to be a provider of information. Over and over again, we have observed in our practice the liberating effect on our clients when they become aware of the helping services that exist even when they do not need to make use of them.[21]

SERVICES

The psychosocial therapist also considers the function of helping a client gain access to available resources an important variable in treatment. This function is included partly in the process of making information available but is more complex than that. It is one thing for a mother to know that there are day-care facilities for her physically handicapped child, but it is another thing for her to gain access to that resource. When the process is facilitated in a helpful manner, we know that the outcome can have a dramatic and positive effect on the client's self-image and ability to function. We forget how much knowledge we ourselves take for granted about the availability of resources in a community and how to gain access to them. We underestimate how restricted some clients' lives are because of lack of access to such resources. This was clearly demonstrated to me in the excitement and pride evident in a group of working-class mothers in a large Canadian city when a volunteer arranged to take them on a tour of Government House and their increased pleasure when they learned that they in turn could take their children on a similar tour. Each of these women was in active contact with a social worker about some of the problems of self-identity related to being a single parent. In many ways, finding the resources that were available to them in the city was of more help than the relationship with the therapist had been. This is only a minor use of resources, but it emphasizes how important the gaining of access can be for enhanced living.

It is so easy to overlook such situations. I remember well a client who had been talking about his concern for his mother, who had moved to a distant nursing home. I raised the question of his writing to her but found considerable resistance to this suggestion. I spent some time trying to find out the source of resistance until by chance I stumbled on the fact that the man could not write and was ashamed to admit it to me. It took some time to help him work out his feelings of inadequacy about this, but as a result of our efforts he was able to get special help through the educational system and eventually to return to school. At the same time he was also able to reestablish contact with his family, the original focus of the case.

MATERIAL RESOURCES

A final component of resources as a facet of therapy is the provision of material assistance. This is a sensitive subject in the helping professions. The stereotype of Lady Bountiful bringing a basket of food to the poor family does not fit our current image of ourselves as relationship therapists helping to reconstruct personalities through our professional skills. Yet, if growth is our goal, whatever facilitates growth must be considered appropriate and not denigrated. If one is hungry, food is what is needed, not relationship. I think we are over this dilemma now and are more comfortable in seeing ourselves as variously utilizing different resources. But because of our heritage, I think we are still less knowledgeable about how to make use of material assistance as a facilitator of growth in our clients. Social norms of course make this difficult for us.

It is still easier to get a client very expensive professional services than to get him ten dollars in cash. As a young social worker in a psychiatric setting, I was first puzzled and then angered to learn that with one phone call, I could arrange for a client to receive prescriptions for highly expensive drugs but could not get him twenty-five cents for a busfare downtown to look for a job. Similarly, I could get the most expensive legal counsel available in the city for a teenager in trouble but was not able to get him money to buy a guitar or lessons to learn to play it. There is still a very important place in the psychotherapeutic approach for the provision of material resources to clients as part of a process of finding and mobilizing their potential for growth. This is so whether it be the provision of a small gift to celebrate a significant event or long-term financial maintenance of a family to enable it to function. We need to see this as a growth-enabling process, to be studied and used systematically, rather than as an issue about professional behavior, self-image or political entanglement. It is just as wrong to provide financial aid to a client who needs intensive crisis intervention as it is to provide relationship therapy when what the client needs is a new place to live.

Technology

The final component in the spectrum of therapeutic resources is the use of technology. This is a relatively new aspect of therapy, but one that has resulted in some interesting literature. Included in this topic is the therapeutic use of audiotapes, videotapes and a variety of other technical appliances and resources available in our society. In keeping with the commitment to diversity in the psychosocial approach to practice, such resources should be seen in a neutral way. That is, they are neither good nor bad in themselves but only as they are used to facilitate or hinder growth. It is interesting that already we probably know more about the utility of these resources, which have come into their own in the past decade, than we do about the impact of material resources, mentioned in the previous section.[22]

We know something about the beneficial results to some clients who are able to hear themselves in interpersonal arguments through the medium of an audiotape. Many families have been helped by watching themselves function through videotapes. Other individuals have learned about reducing stress through the use of various instruments to monitor physiological changes. Groups have learned to make excellent use of films as a basis for discussion and later group interaction. Just as we have not yet fully realized the importance of the physical setting for clients, neither have we begun to appreciate the extent to which many components of technology can be of help to us. No doubt, as in other developments in practice, there will be sins of excess when in our overenthusiasm some of our offices will look like space-center control booths. But up to the present our practice has tended to move in the other direction, underusing what is currently known and available to us and failing to examine what is available in other fields that we might adapt to our own practice and research.

This, then, is the range of major resources from which the psychosocial therapist draws in working with clients. Most of these have been commented on only in summary fashion but are dealt with at greater length in subsequent chapters.

Therapeutic Skills

A principal theme of this chapter is that the process of therapy rests on a profile of skills acquired through training in the application of relevant knowledge. It is difficult to categorize precisely the range of skills required of the competent therapist yet it is important to address this question. There are the inevitable two extremes to be avoided. On the one hand, there is the identification of a range of skills that is so generalized that little of use is conveyed. Hence, to describe the psychosocial therapist as one skilled in establishing and maintaining relationships and in utilizing environmental resources is of little help. On the other hand, a listing of skills that attempts to identify each component of the assessment, diagnostic, and interventive stages of the process would be tedious and confusing. In such a list one would have to mention that a therapist should be able to specify clearly, to ask questions, to focus discussion, to deal with silence and on and on through the myriad of activities that make up any planned human encounter.

In attempting to identify the range of clinical skills required by a therapist, four major headings can be identified:

1. *Involvement skills.* Under this heading are included that range of complex activities required to involve individuals, families, and groups into a process resulting in the giving and receiving of information, services, or resources. Included in this process of involvement are those activities related to interviewing, such as listening, sustaining, communicating empathy, competence and trust, the facilitating of verbalization and reflective thinking.

2. *Organization and management skills.* The psychosocial therapist must be capable of dealing with large quantities of information, impressions, viewpoints, and attitudes coming from many sources, and order and manage these in a way that is useful to the process. In current society this skill is needed by all persons at a certain level. But it is of particular necessity that therapists possess this skill at a high level as developed through training and practice. A lack of this skill results in a treatment process that becomes fragmented, disorganized, and directionless.

3. *Synthesizing and abstracting skills.* Not only must material be elicited, managed, and organized, it must also be synthesized and rank-ordered in a manner that permits it to be examined from a theoretical perspective to give focus and direction to the interventive process. It is proficiency in this area that

permits accurate and useful diagnostic formulations in specific cases.

4. *Implementation skills.* The psychosocial therapist must be capable of planning and implementing a strategy of therapy specific to each case. This requires a broad range of interpersonal techniques, thorough knowledge of societal resources, access to these resources, and a high degree of flexibility necessary to establish, maintain, and orchestrate a multifaceted program of intervention.

The Risks of Practice

Before concluding this discussion of the essential characteristics of psychosocial therapy some brief attention must be given to a topic not frequently addressed, namely, the risks involved in this endeavor.

A frequent criticism of social work treatment is that we often create undesirable dependency in clients that inhibits growth rather than promotes it. Indeed, so sensitive is this matter that at times we treat all dependency as undesirable. This, of course, is wrong. Dependency is a healthy and productive component both of normal growth and development and of the therapeutic process. But like other aspects of normality, it can be detrimental. Individuals can be too dependent on significant others. This phenomenon is a risk of the therapeutic experience. The therapist can take on an importance in a client's life that is detrimental. He can be seen as all-powerful, all-wise and all-giving to the extent that the client relinquishes his autonomy to retain the support of the therapist. I think, though, that we are now sufficiently aware of this possibility that it is no longer a general problem. In fact, perhaps we have overreacted to the point that we inhibit ourselves from fostering or facilitating dependency in clients, thus neutralizing a most effective component of therapy.

Nevertheless, there are real risks involved. Because the essential thrust of any therapeutic process is healing and helping, we tend to view it principally in a positive framework and to avoid the real danger that it may be a hurting and damaging process to the clients involved, to society and to the therapist himself.

THE CLIENT

In a general way, all clients who involve themselves in a therapeutic relationship risk themselves in embarking on an uncertain venture. There is the risk that they will not get competent help, that they will not be understood, or indeed that they will be harmed. Anyone who has been in practice is well aware of the reality of such risks. There are clients on the verge of suicide whose call for help is unheard by the therapist. There are persons on the verge of a serious depression or a psychotic break or persons facing critical life decisions who are not assessed correctly and thus, rather than get the help they need, end up in a much worse situation than when they first asked for assistance. It would be inappropriate to assume all responsibility for clients and the outcome of treatment, but neither can we always avoid the charge that we have failed clients and brought harm to them.

SOCIETY

The risk of incompetent therapy is borne not only by individual clients and families but also by society at large. Only a few of the potential societal harms need be noted. For years social workers in the child welfare field have been involved in planning and frequently enforcing various break-ups and rearrangements of families. Each child who is removed from a home and placed either temporarily or permanently in a foster home has had his life and environment essentially changed. Much of this work has been successful yet no one who has been involved is unaware of the harm that has been caused through incompetence. The awful question of accurate diagnosis in child welfare cases has been brought to mind dramatically in recent years in cases of child abuse. Here the social worker and members of related disciplines must frequently face the choice of leaving at home a child who is in risk of abuse or even death or removing him, with the attendant problems of separation and permanent trauma.

Another type of societal risk related to diagnostic competence is involved in decisions about clients who are potentially dangerous to society. There are persons so angry, so disturbed, and so distressed that they are capable of harming or even killing others. Again, we should not always take full responsibility when such things occur; the state of our knowledge is not precise enough to predict such outcomes. But terrible is our responsibility if we have not made use of the knowledge, skill, and resources that are available to us.

THE THERAPIST

The third area of risk pertains to the therapist. Aside from the risks mentioned above stemming from assaultive, homicidal, or paranoid clients, there will be people who are angry at us, such as a marital partner whose spouse has left the marriage with our support or parents angry because we have fostered independence in their children. Some of these risks are only emotional, the loss of affection or respect; others are more serious in terms of the possibility of revenge and assault.

The rapid growing demand from society for competent professionals is a new phenomenon in social work practice, one that brings on further type of risk. In a way it is a status achievement for social work that we too are now open to litigation from clients who believe that they have been abused. Such risks have the effect of making us more precise, specific, careful, and humble, all desirable attributes in any professional person.

Notes

1. Florence Hollis, *Casework: A Psychosocial Therapy*, 2nd ed. (New York: Random House, 1972), pp. 197ff.

2. Annette Garrett, "Historical Survey of the Evolution of Casework," reprinted from *The Journal of Social Casework* (June, 1949) in Cora Kasius, ed., *Principles and Techniques in Social Casework* (New York: Family Service Association of America, 1950), pp. 393–411.

3. Helen H. Perlman, *Social Casework: A Problem-Solving Process* (Chicago: University of Chicago Press, 1957), pp. 6–26.

4. Richard B. Stuart, "Behavior Modification: A Technology of Social Change," in F. J. Turner, ed., *Social Work Treatment,* (New York: Free Press, 1974), pp. 400–419.

5. Edwin J. Thomas, ed., *Behavioral Science for Social Workers* (New York: The Free Press, 1967), Derek Jehu, *Learning Theory and Social Work* (London: Routledge, 1967).

6. Richard M. Grinnell, Jr., "Environmental Modification: Casework's Concern or Casework's Neglect," *Social Service Review* 47 (June, 1973), pp. 208–220.

7. See Chapter 7, p. 148.

8. Felix Biestek, *The Casework Relationship* (Chicago: Loyola University, 1957).

9. G. T. Barrett-Lennard, "Significant Aspects of a Helping Relationship," *Mental Hygiene* 47 (April, 1963), pp. 223–227. Also in *Canada's Mental Health* 13 (July–August, 1965), supplement no. 47.

10. Perlman, *op. cit.*, pp. 40–52.

11. Gordon Hamilton, *Theory and Practice of Social Casework* (New York: Columbia University Press, 1951), pp. 115–144; Yeheskel Hasenfeld and Richard A. English, eds., *Human Service Organizations* (Ann Arbor: University of Michigan Press, 1974), pp. 1–23.

12. Mary Larkin Bloom, "Usefulness of the Home Visit for Diagnosis and Treatment," *Social Casework* LIV (February, 1973), pp. 67–75.

13. Lydia Rapaport, "Crisis Intervention as a Mode of Brief Treatment," in Robert W. Roberts and Robert H. Nee, eds., *Theories of*

Social Casework, (Chicago: University of Chicago Press, 1970), pp. 267–311.

14. Ruth E. Smalley, *Theory for Social Work Practice* (New York; Columbia University Press, 1967).

15. William J. Reid and Ann W. Shyne, *Brief and Extended Casework* (New York: Columbia University Press, 1969).

16. Edna Oberman, "The Use of Time-Limited Relationship Therapy with Borderline Patients," *Smith College Studies in Social Work* 37 (1967), pp. 127–141.

17. Selma Brown, "Time, Content and Worker as Factors in Discontinuity," *Smith College Studies in Social Work* 36 (1966), pp. 210–233.

18. R. Baker, "Client Appointment Preferences in a Child Guidance Centre: An Exploratory Study," *British Journal of Social Work* 2 (1972), pp. 47–56.

19. Carel B. Germain, "Time: An Ecological Variable in Social Work Practice," *Social Casework* 57 (1976), pp. 419–426.

20. Charles Zastrow, "The Current Status of Community-Wide Social Data Banks," *Social Worker* 40 (1972), pp. 107–112.

21. Phyllis Willmoth, *Consumers Guide to the British Social Services* (Harmondsworth: Penguin Books). This is an excellent example of a useful guide written for the general public about social services, the type of thing that would be useful in other countries and regions.

22. Ian Alger and Peter Hogan, "Enduring Effects of Videotape Playback Experience on Family and Marital Relationships," *American Journal of Orthopsychiatry* 39 (1969), pp. 88–94. Bonnie C. Rhim, "The Use of Videotapes in Social Work Agencies," *Social Casework* 57 (1976), pp. 644–650.

Chapter 4

The Process of Psychosocial Treatment

Anyone who tries to conceptualize a process as complex as psychotherapy faces the challenge of steering a difficult course between two extremes. Like the mythological navigator one has to avoid the Scylla of the position that regards the therapeutic process as so individualized from the viewpoint of therapist and client that one cannot talk about rules, regularities and proper procedures. The Charybdis, the other viewpoint, holds that the therapeutic process is a technical one that can be examined and translated into precise rules and directions to be taught and evaluated.

Although the psychosocial tradition has always tried to avoid being pushed into either of these extremes, it does tend more strongly in the direction of a formal process rather than an impressionistic, nonrationalized one. Certainly, the importance of the uniqueness of persons and situations is fully acknowledged. But this viewpoint does not negate the essential though difficult task of studying the process in an empirical manner to identify regularities and effective and noneffective procedures and thus to advance understanding.

One of the difficulties in discussing the process descriptively and analytically is the danger of giving its various facets an identity that is more discrete than exists in reality. For example, the process of intervention has traditionally been described as a tripartite structure made up of information-gathering, assessment and diagnosis, and finally treatment. At the same time, it has been emphasized that these components should not be seen as separate and time-bound phases of treatment but rather as three activities that go on simultaneously throughout the entire process even though each may be emphasized differently at different times in treatment. Clearly, mistakes have been made in both directions. On occasion new practitioners indicate that they have not yet formulated their assessment because they are still in the data-gathering process, or that they plan to start treatment only after they have completed diagnosis. This attitude has been reinforced in practice in agencies where there are distinct admissions or intake procedures in which a variety of data are gathered, followed by diagnostic or assessment meetings or committees, followed in turn by assignment to a therapist to begin the interventive process. Frequently, each stage of the process is the responsibility of a different person or group of therapists.

The other extreme is to insist that the processes are so interconnected that they cannot be considered separately. Some would go further, questioning whether they exist at all. If they do not exist they can be ignored. The outcome of this attitude is avoidance of establishing any clear point at which decisions are made about the adequacy of the data, the clarity and certainty of the assessment, and the goal and procedures of treatment.

In a psychosocial therapy, these two extremes are avoided by underscoring the importance of seeing the components of treatment as both processes and facts. That is, the activity of gathering data can be therapeutic, as can the assessment process. Yet it is still essential that clear decisions be made about the sufficiency of available information and possibility of precise assessment in the formulation of appropriate kinds of intervention.

The above discussion clearly underscores the commitment of the psychosocial system to a rationalized process based on a full and clear understanding of the client and his motivations, the situation, the available resources, the joint establishment of appropriate goals, the reassessment of such goals as appropriate, and the carrying out of a planned, evaluated process of intervention. This commitment of course is not the sole prerogative of the psychosocial system. Most approaches to practice identify with the triadic structure except, perhaps, those schools of thought that stress dynamic and spontaneous interaction between client and therapist and the nonnecessity of formalizing the process.

Data Gathering

Because of the commitment to understand the person in a specific situation, the gathering and assessment of information are essential parts of the psychosocial therapeutic process.[1] But also because of the spectrum of subsystems that are considered significant for the full understanding of a person-in-situation, an essential skill in the gathering of data is selectivity. As mentioned above, mistakes have frequently been made in the direction of excess; that is, the inexperienced therapist has a tendency to gather masses of data about all components of a client's life before beginning a formal therapeutic process. I well recall my first days in child welfare, where we spent much time collecting and putting together extensive amounts of information about a client. This information was gathered from a large number of persons other than the client. The goal of this activity was to find out everything we could about the client before we considered ourselves to be in a position to act. Although this was allegedly done out of concern for getting the full picture, in retrospect I suspect that it was frequently done because we did not know what to do and wanted to feel necessary.

Thankfully we have now moved to a point where we are much more selective in our fact-gathering activities. In this regard, one of the interesting phenomena in current psychotherapeutic practice in our communication-oriented society is that our problem is not in obtaining information but in being selective about the masses of information available from both the client and his milieu. Responsible practice suggests that the nature and amount of information that is required or needed should be dictated by the client, the setting and the service required. Thus, if it is clear that a client is asking only about the range of available resources in a particular area, we need to know little about him except what we have observed in his interaction with us. This is in contrast to what would be appropriate for a person under intense stress who is trying to sort out complex problems about himself and his place in the world. In such instances it may be necessary to have information from a wide range of sources and persons.[2]

The first and certainly the most desirable source of data about a client is the client himself. The approach involves both encouraging respect for the person and a commitment to involving him in his own processes and destinies. How a client sees himself, his history, his world, his aims, concerns, and future aspirations tells us much about who he is, what he wants, what he can do and how he can do it.

The way the client perceives himself and his significant environments and whether his perceptions fit our own perception of him is also an essential point of information-gathering. When these two sets of observations differ it is important for the therapist to consider the reasons for the discrepancy and to ask if further information is necessary. Often the very task of clarifying and reviewing with the client areas of understanding and perception is part of the therapeutic process and indeed may well become the content of the process itself.

It may also be necessary for the therapist to seek information beyond the client himself.[3] Frequently the first system addressed is that of significant others in the client's life. Close persons such as family or friends often can give us information and perceptions about a client that can expand our understanding in an appropriate way. For example, a wife sharing with the therapist the fact that her husband's mother died a few months before the beginning of his difficulties with his job helps the therapist better understand the nature of the stress the client was experiencing.

Included in the concept of significant others is the range of persons who may influence the client's life or be influenced by the client—bosses, teachers, other professionals, friends neighbors or associates. All of these may be able to contribute some understanding of the client in a manner that is helpful to the therapeutic endeavor. In turning to others, the practitioner must be ready to understand the extent to which a client is helped as well as hindered by various significant others. Such persons may be sources of information but also sources of strain. A potential pitfall for the unwary therapist is to accord a higher level of validity to persons who are not clients and to tend not to give the client a hearing.

Along with significant others in a client's life there are professional others who may be sources of information about strengths and limitations in the client's psychosocial existence. Thus the psychologist, other social workers, the physician, the public health nurse, the clergyman, the teacher may be able to provide information about the client emerging from prior contacts, or we may wish to make use of their skills and experience to bring us further information. The use of such persons will be discussed further in Chapter 7; here we are only identifying them as sources of information about clients.

An interesting sociological phenomenon stemming from the social worker's interest in significant others and in significant subsystems beyond the client has been a tendency to see these areas as the principal responsibility of social workers on the multidisciplinary team. Because of this social workers have come to be viewed by some as mainly information gatherers. Thus in the earlier phases of the mental health team the social worker was frequently seen as the history taker, a function that was not considered part of the direct helping process. Important as this role is, it became a problem when assigned only to the social worker thus excluding him from a role perceived as being more therapeutic.

Records left by other professionals can also be an important source of information about the client. We are just emerging from a period in the early 1970s where some colleagues spoke against the use of prior records in working with clients. It was argued that the therapist who read such records would be biased about the clients and locked into a perception of them before the first interview. Those who argued this position failed to see that such an argument marked them as highly impressionable persons unable to think for themselves or to sort out a range of perceptions.

In addition to other professionals and their reports as sources of information, existing agency records or professional records can occasionally serve the same purpose.[4] In spite of a current viewpoint that tends to disparage ongoing records as sources of accurate data about clients, intelligent and responsible use of such records can be of great assistance.[5] The use of appropriate records can save the client from having to repeat data that may be sensitive and it can help the therapist to understand prior history and to communicate this understanding to the client in a way that can be useful.[6] Such interest can manifest concern and responsibility on the part of the therapist that in themselves can facilitate the therapeutic process.

Records and their use can sometimes indeed be detrimental to an effective helping process, but the same can be said of any component of the process that is not understood fully or utilized responsibly. Since individuals' strengths and limitations are significantly related to their past histories, it can be useful to know some aspects of the history gathered for some previous professional purpose.[7]

A further source of data frequently misunderstood or underestimated is the information we have about the client based on our own observation of the client in interaction with us or others in his environment. This is a very strong source of information and one that we should use as part of our overall assessment.

In addition to other sources of information, the therapist's knowledge of significant aspects of the client's life can contribute to the requisite data. Thus knowledge of a neighborhood and its values and traditions or the demands of a particular occupation, an acquaintance with the mores of a school or of an ethnic or cultural group can all enrich and expand a therapist's perception of a client and the reciprocal interaction of the significant components of his psychosocial reality.

The psychosocial therapist looks in many directions and to many sources to understand the client. This tradition of a broad-based perception and assessment has sometimes resulted in the earlier mentioned perception of the social worker on the mental health team as being the gatherer of data and the formulator of histories. As a reaction to this, and in the desire to seek a more secure position as a provider of therapy, there has been a tendency to play down this role and to negate the usefulness of broadly based data about clients.

A necessary skill for the psychosocial therapist is the ability to select and use broadly based sources of data. The decision to seek data beyond what the client can provide should be based on professional judgment rather than on status seeking for the profession. Certainly most therapists function from the law of parsimony in the question of client involvement. That is, in so far as possible, we settle for less rather than more detail about the nature of the problem and try to see the client as the provider of the necessary information. When the decision is made to go further, with the client's permission, then our activities should be selective and purposeful rather than a haphazard gathering of material in the hope that something will turn up. Thus the client should not be subjected to a series of tests, interviews and assessment procedures on the chance that we may discover something we do not know. However, once a decision has been made to seek further data in a carefully planned way, the sensitive professional who turns to other components of a client's life can be performing a most important part of the information-gathering process. Indeed, this type of activity can also be a part of the helping process, showing the clients our interest and concern for them.

A further advantage of moving out into the client's world is that it necessitates leaving our offices and agencies. Time-consuming as this process is, it can be a most important opportunity for us to come into direct contact with the client's world in a manner that can be growth-enhancing for us. A particular aspect of this outward movement by the therapist is found in the home visit. Social workers have long known the advantages of the home visit as a major source of understanding clients. This long-practiced activity was given new legitimization with the re-vitalized interest in family therapy that emerged in the early 1960s, when the home visit became almost a status symbol for the family-oriented therapist.[8] In addition, viewing the client's place of work, the neighborhood in which he lives, the schools he attends, and the kind of places where he spends his leisure time is an important aspect of the pyschosocial tradition, an essential part of the first component of the interventive process, the gathering of information.

Assessment

As has been suggested above, it is the use to which available data are put that is the mark of the responsible therapist. The range of professional judgments that we make about the data are essential in shaping the direction in which the client and therapist will move together.

The goal of the data-gathering component is to understand the client, his potential and limitations, the sources of strengths and stress, the resources for change and the barriers to desired change. Thus accompanying the information-gathering process is a cotemporal process of assessment. By assessment is meant the formulation of a professional judgment about the data obtained from the viewpoint of the nature and objective of the interven-tion. This is an important concept, one frequently overlooked by professionals. The assessment component separates the profes-sional activity of information gathering from a mere reporting, or gathering role and ensures that it is a responsible, selective, de-velopmental, and professionally accountable activity.

The assessment process contains two elements. The first is the decision concerning what additional data are required at any given time in the life of a case and where such data are to be obtained. The second element is the judgments made about the data. For example, it is not sufficent to be able to describe only the physical living conditions of a client; the psychosocial therapist must in addition decide to what extend this environment is contributing to the client's ability to function. Similarly, it is not sufficient to know and describe the family situation of a client, it is also necessary to evaluate to what extent the family's interaction contributes to or interferes with the client's search for psychosocial growth and development.

And so in every case, each of the significant persons, systems and components of a client's life that are considered must be assessed from the viewpoint of their potential strengths, from the viewpoint of the client's needs and aspirations and also from the viewpoint of their role in the problematic situation being considered in the therapeutic process.

The sensitivity and accuracy with which the psychosocial therapist makes this wide and diverse range of assessments will, as always, depend on his knowledge and sensitivity to the significant components of a client's personality and milieu and the objectives of the intervention.

Diagnosis

The assessment process lies midway between the data-gathering stage and the diagnosis.[9] The concept of diagnosis has long been a part of the psychosocial framework so much so that at one period the psychosocial approach to practice in social work was known as the diagnostic school. Like concepts or terms mentioned in earlier chapters, the word "diagnosis," in itself a clear and useful one, has become an emotion-laden term that frequently precludes dispassionate discussion. The term as it has been used in the psychosocial tradition has the same meaning given to it in other professions; that is, it is the process of distinguishing, or the art of knowing, the sources of a phenomenon. Diagnosis has been more closely attached to such helping professions as medicine, where it has tended to be interpreted as the process of understanding a disease process from its observable manifestations.

The disease-related connotation of the word is of course far from its original meaning, viz. to distinguish. The skill of the diagnostician lies not only in recognizing what is wrong and why, but also in recognizing what is right and healthy and, even more important, being able to assess that there is nothing wrong.

In the psychosocial tradition, diagnosis has been used in this broader sense. Thus it is a process in which the therapist consciously attempts to bring together the sum total of his information, impressions and experiences so as to come to a conclusion, albeit tentative, as to the nature of the person, situation and request. It is out of this process of synthesizing, restructuring, refocusing and organizing that goals are established and patterns of intervention are developed. It is the skill, thoroughness and precision of the diagnostic process that render the psychotherapeutic activity responsible, accountable, sensitive, flexible and effective.[10]

The diagnostic process implies a looking inward by the therapist and a commitment to organize thoroughly the range of data, the intermeshing of fact and impression, the recognition of knowledge gaps, the elimination of what is irrelevant, and the struggle to reach conclusions. The nature, content, and intensity of diagnosis will be related to the nature of the client, the setting and the point in the life of the case.

Diagnosis has a twofold nature, as both a process and a fact. As a process, it relates to an ongoing activity that is almost intuitive to any therapist. It is an activity in which the therapist is always ordering, classifying, rejecting and reformulating the constant streams of stimuli that are a part of the professional activity. But the diagnostic process must also be a fact. A part of any responsible, accountable, professional activity that seeks societal sanction requires that our perception of the situation and the objectives we set in any instance be visible to those who are mandated and competent to assess our activities.[11]

As mentioned earlier, several criticisms have been brought

against the use of the term "diagnosis," and these make discussion of the concept difficult. First, it is said by some that diagnosis is the prerogative of the medical profession, where it has its own precise meaning, and that its use by other professions, regardless of the rationale for doing so, is improper and thus to be seen only as some form of status seeking.

Second, as used in the medical profession, the term "diagnosis" refers to the exploration of a disease process and thus implies the existence of a pathology. The diagnosis is considered to be complete once a label has been assigned to describe the presenting difficulty. It is then argued that since psychosocial therapy is oriented to health and growth, it does not always presume the existence of a pathological process and that use of the term diagnosis is therefore inappropriate.

A third criticism of the use of the term "diagnosis" comes from those who see the concept as a search for a label or classification of a situation. That is, diagnosis is seen as a process of searching through a preset list of existing problems of pathology or disease entities and from this list selecting the one presumed closest to the presenting situation. The selection and application of such a label is said to be the diagnosis.

If these premises are accepted, then the term diagnosis is indeed inappropriate for use by the psychosocial therapist. We are far from a point where we have a closed classification system of problems or persons which would describe each and every situation we meet in our practice. As will be mentioned below, this is not to discount the need for such systems in our practice, it is only to remind ourselves that at this point they do not exist.[12]

A fourth criticism of the diagnostic concept again relates to the perception that diagnosis consists only in a judgment on the part of the professional involved for which he must be accountable and in which the client or patient has no say. That is, the diagnosis is seen as assigning to a client a label based on the judgment of the professional. It is argued that no psychotherapeutic process is unilateral to this extent. Always the client is to be involved in setting objectives for intervention and in clarifying situations.

Indeed, the very process of helping a client frequently consists in focusing on the gradual clarification of a stress-producing situation and the search for ways of coping with it more effectively. In this process the client is seen as having an important role. Thus the process is a bilateral one. Hence it is argued that the use of the word "diagnosis" is inappropriate.[13]

Finally, it is argued that even if it is desirable to use the term "diagnosis" in the limited sense described above, the state of current knowledge is such that we are not yet able to make such precise judgments. It follows, therefore, that we should not aspire to the term.

Clearly, none of these areas of criticism can be dismissed lightly. For the most part they represent the concerned thinking of responsible colleagues. There is no doubt that some psychotherapists have misappropriated the concept of diagnosis. For some, indeed, it has consisted in a search for pathology. For others it has represented only a commitment to categorize. It also has served some as a model for emulating others, and finally it has been carried out as a unilateral process. Thus it is understandable that the term has been challenged.[14]

Nevertheless, all of the criticisms of the use of the word "diagnosis" are really criticisms of a misuse of the term or a translation of the term from a narrow and incorrect perception of its correct meaning. Unless an equally precise word can be found, it is our contention that "diagnosis" is the preferred term to describe that synthesizing intellectual process, the hallmark of the responsible professional, in which an effort is made to formalize and order perceptions of the client's psychosocial situation from the viewpoint of the presenting situation. If we do not diagnose, then we cannot call ourselves responsible professionals. Our work becomes, of necessity, impressionistic and takes on the characteristics of benevolent meandering. Regardless of theoretical orientation, each of us does formulate a synthesizing decision about the relevance or irrelevance of various components of a client's life. We do decide and order the significant interconnections between systems. We do attempt to identify the checks and balances to various areas of stress and strength and to identify what needs to be changed and what can change.

Clearly a commitment to an accurate conception of the diagnostic process helps us to respect the responsibility we bear and fosters a sense of humility as we grow in awareness of the imprecisions with which we must work.

Earlier it was emphasized that the diagnostic component of treatment must be both process and fact. The emphasis on factual components helps us to stress a search for precision in the ordering of our perceptions, assessments and conclusions about the client.

In performing a diagnosis, it is important to describe the client's current psychosocial situation as we see and understand it, to identify those aspects of the client's history which we consider to be significantly influencing the presenting situation, and to assess the client's current psychological functioning, identifying both the stresses and the strengths under which he is operating.[15] In addition, a particular aspect of this part of the diagnosis is assessment of the client's attitudes about the therapeutic process, including his motivation or lack thereof and his perceptions of the helping process and his place in it. Further, we must identify the significant others in the client's situation as well as the significant environments in which the client is living. In conjunction with this we must attempt to assess the interaction that is taking place between these systems and identify those areas that we consider to be of greatest importance for the therapeutic task. In all of this we must attempt to state whether we see the client as falling into a recognized classification of problem or personality. At the same time we must individualize the client in a way that helps us and others to focus on the specific differences that set this case apart from other, similar cases. It is the constant attempt to organize our perceptions in a visibly objective manner that helps to bring discipline to our own work and to provide an opportunity for others to observe it, learn from it, and assess it. Such objectivity will also enable us to know when indeed we have achieved the goals to which we have committed ourselves with the client.

Contract or the Setting of Goals

Diagnosis, whether as a process or a fact, is not an end in itself but leads to the process of goal setting. It aims at the clarification of goals and the establishment of the realistic objectives related to goals. The establishment of clear objectives is a component of the helping process that can be and frequently is avoided in therapy, especially if there is a concomitant perception that treatment consists of an impressionistic, spontaneous, experiential exchange between client and therapist. But even when there is a commitment to an objective process there is a further factor that contributes to the avoidance of goal setting. This is the complexity that usually characterizes the presenting and ongoing situations of the clients one meets in practice. Often the life situations of our clients are made up of a wide spectrum of deficiencies, many unexpected problems and a critical lack of resources; thus it is extremely difficult to establish fixed goals except in an impressionistic way. But difficult as it is, it is essential that we constantly attempt to formulate and work toward goals even if they have to be frequently redefined during the life of a case.[16]

A commitment to goals includes the important concept of flexibility that allows for the necessary realigning and rethinking as situations change, as new data emerge and as new priorities develop.

As suggested earlier, it has always been considered important that objectives not be imposed upon a client but that the client be included in setting them. This practice is not always followed. Clients are often not fully aware of the goals toward which the therapist is working. In recent years, as a way of correcting this deficiency, there has been growing interest in a more explicit and shared formalization of treatment goals through the medium of a therapeutic contract. In such a contract the goals of the process and the mutual expectations of both client and therapist are set out, sometimes informally and sometimes in the form of a signed and co-signed written contract.

The advantages of such a formal setting of goals are several. In the first instance, it necessitates the therapist's formulation of a clear diagnosis so that realistic goals can be set with the client. It also requires that the therapist discuss and share with the client his diagnosis and the goals he proposes. This, in turn, ensures that the client is involved in the process of goal setting and presumably is in agreement with the content of the contract or some modification of it.

One of the most important, but often overlooked, factors in this renewed stress on a formal contract setting is its importance in facilitating evaluative research. Frequently, it has been difficult to assess the efficacy of intervention because the objectives of the process have not been spelled out.[17]

Although there is currently high enthusiasm about the importance of the therapeutic contract as a way of establishing and sharing the goals of therapy, the experienced therapist is aware that the extent to which he is able to share his perceptions and goals with the client will vary from case to case depending upon the ability of the client to understand and accept some objectives. Presumptuous as this sounds, the therapist does at times know better than the client and may have goals that should not be shared with the client. This is a part of responsible assessment practice. For example, it might be obvious to the therapist that a particular relationship in which the client is involved is detrimental to the client's functioning and is heading for termination even though the client's objective in treatment is to examine it and assess how it can be changed to make it less stressful. Such instances are rare, for the majority of situations the client should be actively and fully involved in the process of goal setting.

The Therapeutic Relationship

The next component of the therapeutic process is the establishment and maintenance of the therapeutic relationship. As described in Chapter 3, psychosocial therapy is built on the premise that one of the most powerful agents in bringing about change is the influence of person-on-person within the discipline and knowledge of the therapeutic relationship. For some time this relationship was seen as so unique and so sacred that it was rarely studied in an empirical way. As a result much writing about this relationship was in a prescriptive or exhortative style. Hence much of what went into an effective therapeutic relationship was unknown. This fortunately is now changing, and there is growing empirical evidence that the qualities that make up an effective relationship can be understood, taught, acquired and improved. Thus it is known that the client has to feel he is accepted, respected, understood and heard before he can invest in the process. In addition, the process has to be seen as a safe one for the client, and the therapist must be perceived as interested, competent, open and congruent—that is, as a person whose words and actions give similar messages.[18]

An important part of a therapeutic relationship to which the psychosocial therapist gives particular attention is the phenomenon of transference.[19] Transference, a concept originating in earlier psychodynamic thought, refers to the process in interpersonal relationships whereby we respond as if the person with whom we are relating is a significant individual from our past, usually a parent or a parent substitute. All of us can see examples of this in our close relationships if we devote some time to examining our emotional responses to people. We find ourselves looking for parental approval from some persons or expecting parental disapproval from others in a manner that is inappropriate to the reality of the relationship. We find emotions stirred up in our interactions with people that on examination clearly belong to earlier, often forgotten, experiences. Frequently it is not possible for us to understand the origin of some of these feelings readily as they lie repressed in our unconscious. Nevertheless we do know that if we can let ourselves be sensitive to such responses in our relationships, we can see that some emotions we experience and the intensity of these emotions are inappropriate to the context.

Transference is not given as much attention in psychosocial thought today as it was twenty years ago. Nevertheless it is still an important concept. When properly understood, assessed and put into perspective it provides us with a basis for understanding many of the surprising and inappropriate responses we note in clients during the process of treatment. Because so much of our contact with clients is related to their feelings, experiences and perceptions of others, and because of the intensity of the emotional investment that is made by clients in us, the phenomenon of transference takes place much more frequently than is currently appreciated. This process, when sensitively recognized and skillfully managed can be a tremendous asset to the outcome of a relationship, just as a misunderstanding of it can result in an ineffective or indeed a hurt-producing process between client and worker.[20]

So accustomed do we become in meeting an ongoing succession of new persons, each of whom brings to us his own experiences, aspirations, hurts and, frustrations, that we often forget how unusual it is for him to find someone truly interested who hears, understands, and reaches out to him. Thus, we both underestimate the long-term effectiveness of our contact with people and fail to understand the extent to which we can bring about negative responses in a relationship, especially through the effects of transference reactions.

Frequently in practice we behave as if all transference reactions are in the client and none in ourselves. A full understanding and utilization of the transference reactions that take place in relationships requires attention to the co-relative term "countertransference." By this is meant, of course, that therapists can have responses to clients that are inappropriate to the situation and that indeed are carried over from earlier experiences, both positive and negative. There are clients who will anger us, who will frighten us, who will entice and arouse us in a manner that on examination will prove to be a reaction that belongs to earlier experiences from our developmental histories.[21]

Certainly not all of our emotional reactions to clients are components of transference, but some of them may well be. It is this kind of situation that reinforces the commitment in the psychosocial tradition to the self-discipline of being constantly intraobservant, to the need for skilled supervision as a part of the educational process, to the requirement of supervision and consultation throughout our practice and to support for the desirability of one's own therapy when required.

The Temporal Phases of Treatment

In looking at the therapeutic process and its component parts, it is helpful to examine three temporal stages of the process, namely beginnings, middles, and endings. In an earlier period of professional literature the functional school paid particular attention to these temporal components of practice. They pointed out that, as in normal living, there are phenomena specific to each of these periods that, when properly understood, can facilitate the helping process and conversely, when not understood, can be detrimental to the smooth client-therapist interaction. Although not as much attention is currently paid to some of this earlier material, these concepts are still of importance and deserve further considereration.[22]

BEGINNINGS

The beginning of a therapeutic process is a difficult period for the therapist as well as for the client because of the range of tasks that must be accomplished with a minimum of data.[23] The client must be quickly involved in the process in a manner that will be beneficial to him. He must early find that it is a safe and useful process that respects his right to be there, the dignity of his person, the extent of his autonomy and ability to manage his own life. It must also recognize the feelings that he brings to the process, ambivalent and complex as they may be. In this regard it is important that the place where the process begins is taken into account. It can greatly assist the client to experience the trustworthiness and integrity of the process. Along with involving the client the worker must also hear him, understand him and help him grasp some of what he can expect and what will be expected from him.[24]

There are several factors that are of assistance to the therapist in the initial stage. Usually the client is in a situation where at least part of him wants help and where the enthusiasm and curiosity that most persons have about new situations can be productive.[25] As has been suggested before, therapists frequently underestimate how helpful and facilitating they can be even in a one-contact situation with a client. In some situations just being available to the client and communicating interest, concern and respect for him can enable a client to look at himself, others and the alternatives open to him and find solutions to problems within himself. Further, the client may find release from anxiety and concern in a first contact so that the growth process can be restarted. There are many persons in our society who have rarely if ever had the experience of being listened to by a sympathetic, understanding, knowledgeable, skilled person and such an experience can be a freeing, enabling experience.[26]

These comments are meant to further underscore the utility and importance of short-term contacts. (Within this therapeutic tradition there are still traces of a viewpoint that the effectiveness of therapy is directly related to its length.) Thus both the novelty of the beginning and the allaying of anxieties regarding the risks involved are important components of the beginning of therapy that can be built upon.

MIDDLES

The middle or ongoing component of therapy has received the least attention in the psychosocial literature. This is surprising because it is this phase of the process that is the most demanding and requires the greatest level of skills. The challenge to the therapist and client comes from the increased risks of routine and disillusionment during this period. The initial enthusiasm is over, the first impact of the professional charisma has passed. The first gains and relief that were experienced have already been forgotten. The client realizes that change in person and situation is not easy; there is much hard work ahead. The pain of self-examination and possible behavior change is acute. The goals seem less desirable. Doubts begin to emerge about the competence of the therapist, the usefulness of the resources and the ability or desire to sustain the effort.

On the worker's side a similar reaction takes place; the initial curiosity and enthusiasm about a new situation have passed. The similarity to many other cases is apparent. There are few surprises to be expected. The difficulty of making additional progress is clear. The client's discouragement, dependency and doubt can be draining. It is easy to become both bored and irritated by the client who is struggling with expanded perceptions of self and significant others and alternative choices that are clear to the therapist. The case can easily become bogged down, objectives forgotten, material repeated again and again, and unprofitable and diverting areas pursued. Patterns of avoidance become reinforced and reciprocal denial supported. Some of the intense feelings related to transference and countertransference that may take place can become troublesome, whether recognized or unrecognized.

The skilled therapist must be aware of the risks in the process and capitalize on the less visible but nevertheless critical developmental factors that arise. The objectives first set out must be reviewed with the client, the autonomy of the client must be recognized and encouraged, the importance of the process must be reinforced, the pain and ambivalence of the client must be empathically responded to and a constant search must be conducted to help the client recognize and experience the satisfactions of change and growth.[27]

Clearly the process of the middle phase varies from case to case, and it would be wrong to convey the idea that all cases are the same. This is true especially in the psychosocial thought system where heavy emphasis is laid on the involvement of significant others and resources, and where many components of the client's life may be in change, turmoil or even conflict. The middle phase of the helping process may be anything but a settled routine. In fact, many cases appear never to reach the middle stage. They consist instead of a series of beginnings or a series of very short beginnings and endings so that there is no chance of becoming bored or bogged down. In such cases, rather than the possibility of ennui, the challenge is to avoid becoming so irritated and frustrated by the endless series of new demands, problems, and failures that it is difficult to maintain a focus and retain objectives as well as to contain the disappointment and frustration of the client. But even in such active and turmoil-laden cases it is easy to fall into patterns of a middle phase where long-term objectives are forgotten, small gains go unrecognized, the client's ability to keep trying goes unsupported, and his needs become overlooked. The heavy drain on the therapist that this phase of a case creates is often not appreciated and thus the concomitant self-protective activities of the worker are hidden by denial or projection. This further removes the client from the recognition of his own abilities to alter himself or his life style. Most therapists, even in the earliest days of their professional practice, have little difficulty in involving the vast majority of clients in the helping process in the beginning stages of treatment. The difficulties stem from not being able to sustain the process by building on the strengths of the beginning phase. This results in the all too common phenomenon of unplanned terminations.

TERMINATIONS

Most writing on terminations has been quite negative, probably because many of the terminations that take place in our field are unplanned[28] from the therapist's viewpoint. The client is often the one who decides when the process is over.[29] This is clearly of concern to the helping professions because it contradicts the image of the therapist as a person in control of the therapeutic situation.

From the positive side, the ending is the most critical component of treatment. If planned, it marks the culmination of the whole process, the point toward which the entire process has been working. The client and therapist have decided that the process has reached its culmination in that the goals toward which the process has been aimed have been reached or a decision has been made that they cannot be reached and it is not desirable to continue.[30]

Just as beginnings when properly utilized can be growth-producing in themselves, so too with endings. The ending can convey the confidence of the worker that the client is now able to function without his assistance. It can thus represent an achievement for a client which is in itself ego-enhancing. The ending also gives client and worker a chance to review, to examine what has taken place and even more important to understand why. It provides an opportunity for the client to reflect on why this relationship has been helpful, to see what roles he has played in it, to recognize the progress that has taken place. These phenomena are further components of a growth-enhancing process.[31]

Another facet of the ending stage is to examine those components of the process that have not gone as expected. The sensitive worker will be aware of this possibility and respond to it. Being able to share limitations, disappointments, and frustrations about the worker–client interaction can be an additional form of progress for the client, helping him to learn how to deal with this kind of material as well as to experience the satisfaction of success in meeting a new challenge.[32]

Of course it may well be that the outcome has not been successful for a variety of reasons. Again, reviewing this with the client can be helpful in being able to think about why, to look at what else may have happened and to avoid experiencing this lack of success as another failure that further defeats his desire to try again.

In the ending process there is also an eagerness to tie up any loose ends. Therapists frequently find that material is introduced in a last interview that has not been mentioned before but can be dealt with in a helpful manner.

But just as the ending process can be helpful to a client it can also be detrimental. The therapist may fail to appreciate some of the concerns of the client. He may not recognize the resistance to separate and may fail to respond to some of the client's hurt, anger and disappointment about termination. Further, the worker may not recognize that some new material can be dealt with as a part of the ending process but rather may see it as the client's wish to go on or his uncertainty about ending. Thus, the worker who encourages the client to prolong the relationship because of the introduction of new material in the final stages may be reinforcing feelings of dependency and fears of autonomy.[33]

Certainly it is possible for the process to terminate too soon. This is especially so today when short-term treatment has achieved new status. If in an earlier day we kept cases open too long, surely we have now moved in the opposite direction, closing many cases too soon.[34]

There are insufficient data available on how individual workers deal with the termination phase. It is suspected that frequently the review process is omitted and the case is closed on the achievement of some goal. A sensitive looking back with the client, if only for a few minutes, can both reinforce and expand the gains that have been made and differentiates a merely acceptable termination process from a highly skilled and sensitive one.[35]

A final aspect of the termination process is for the therapist's benefit. When it is done in a disciplined manner, the worker can also review with himself whether the original objectives were achieved and whether they had changed from the beginning. And of equal importance is the consideration of why the goals were achieved or not achieved. Such review can help the therapist to expand and improve his skills by becoming aware of what has helped and why and, equally important, by identifying what improvements can be made in technique and procedure.

In considering the timing of the case ending one possibility must not be forgotten, that of the worker not wanting to terminate. All of us have had cases that we have enjoyed or clients to whom we have particularly become attached and have put off the termination phase. Obviously, our professional commitment to accountability must guard against this.

Differential Diagnosis and Treatment

One of the most difficult questions facing the aspiring clinical social worker is how to tie up the two topics discussed in the last two chapters, the resources of treatment and the process of treatment. Once I understand what is wrong and right about a client, once I know the things I can do for him, how do I decide which ones to do? This the heart of the challenge facing the therapist, especially the psychosocial therapist. There are inevitably two extreme viewpoints. The first suggests that the idiosyncratic nature of clients and their life structures makes it impossible for any generalizations to be made. Each case is different, each therapist's style individualized, each setting unique; therefore, the management of each case will be different. The other position holds that psychosocial behavior is understandable and predictable and hence so is the desired therapeutic process. All that is needed is a more precise classification of persons, problems, and situations and further analysis of the impact of different components of therapy. It will then be possible for us to accurately describe how to achieve a particular goal with a particular client.[36]

The psychosocial viewpoint leans toward the latter position but recognizes that it is simplistic. It is true that each case is different, that the variations in person and situation are innumerable. But it is also true that there are patterns of behavior, similarities of problems, and predictable effects of the components of therapy. Still, given the vastness of the spheres of interest of psychosocial therapy and the current state of knowledge, we can only aspire to some generalizations about the management of various attributes of clients and problems; the therapist must still adapt these generalizations to fit the combination of persons, situations, and resources with which he is confronted.[37]

All therapists from time to time have fantasized about the situation of being able to consult a book, chart, or computer about the optimal plan of therapy, given a particular set of circumstances. We are far from this point. Nevertheless, it is still important that we use much more precision in our practice.[38] Much has been learned about dealing with various kinds of cases and clients. For the most part this knowledge is still scattered throughout the rich periodical literature of our own and related fields. To an increasing extent, efforts are being made to draw this material together in ways that will help therapists to draw more easily on the tested and accumulated wisdom of colleagues.[39] It is not the purpose of this book to attempt to generalize from these accumulated data; this is a task that must be faced in a future work.[40]

It has long been my conviction that we know much more about precise intervention for specific presenting problems than we give ourselves credit for. Several analyses of the literature have attested to this.[41] What appears to be a useful next step is an analysis of the profiles of diagnosis and intervention of many hundreds of cases from a wide range of experienced therapists and to begin to identify, by means of computers, patterns of intervention and their different effects on case outcome. Today we have the resources for such an undertaking, and there is sufficient tested commonality of terminology within segments of the field to permit the gathering of large amounts of related data from practice.[42]

At the same time, the process of examining the literature and abstracting therapeutic principles from it that can be organized into classification systems must be continued. This is the principal challenge in the psychosocial field and the area in which great progress will be made in the next decade.[43]

Notes

1. Florence Hollis, "The Psychosocial Study," *Casework: A Psychosocial Therapy,* 2nd ed. (New York: Random House, 1972), pp. 247–259.

2. Mary Mason, "The Contribution of the Social History in the Diagnosis of Child Disturbances," *British Journal of Psychiatric Social Work* 9 (1968), pp. 180–187.

3. Mary Ellen Richmond, *Social Diagnosis* (New York: Russell Sage Foundation, 1917), pp. 38–80.

4. Rosalie A. Kane, "Look to the Record," *Social Work* 19 (August, 1974), pp. 412–419.

5. James R. Seaberg, "Case Recording by Code," *Social Work* 10 (October, 1965), pp. 92–98.

6. Maureen McKane, "Case-Record Writing with Reader Empathy," *Child Welfare* 54 (1975), pp. 593–597.

7. Mary Wong Chea, "Research on Recording," *Social Casework* 53 (March, 1972), pp. 170–180.

8. Florence Hollis, *op.cit.*, pp. 260–268, M. Dorsey Tobin, "Diagnostic Use of the Home Visit in Child Guidance," *Smith College Studies in Social Work* 38 (June, 1968), pp. 202–213. Marjorie Behrens and Nathan Ackerman, "The Home Visit as an Aid in Family Diagnosis and Therapy," *Social Casework* 37 (January, 1956), pp. 11–19. Nathan Ackerman, *The Psychodynamics of Family Life* (New York: Basic Books, 1958), pp. 129–138. Constance C. Hansen, "An Extended Home Visit with Conjoint Family Therapy," *Family Process* 7 (March, 1968), pp. 67–87.

9. Hollis, *op.cit.*, pp. 268–280.

10. Werner A. Lutz, *Concepts and Principles Underlying Social Casework Practice,* Monograph III, Social Work Practice in Medical Care and Rehabilitation Settings (Washington D.C.: National Association of Social Workers, 1956).

11. Doris Campbell Phillips, "Of Plums and Thistles: The Search for Diagnosis," *Social Work* 5 (January, 1960), pp. 84–90.

12. Alfred Kadushin, "Testing Diagnostic Competence: A Problem for Social Work Research," *Social Casework* 44 (July, 1963), pp. 397–405.

13. Bertha Reynolds, "Is Diagnosis an Imposition?" in *Social Work and Social Living* (New York: Citadel Press, 1951), p. 97.

14. Helen H. Perlman, "Diagnosis Anyone," *Psychiatry and Social Sciences Review* 3 (8:1969–1970), pp. 12–17.

15. Florence Hollis, "Personality Diagnosis in Casework," in H.

Parad, ed., *Ego Psychology and Dynamic Casework* (New York: Family Service Association of America, 1958), pp. 83–96.

16. Hollis, *op.cit.,* pp. 283–300.

17. Werner Gottlieb and Joe H. Stanley, "Mutual Goals and Goal Setting in Casework," *Social Casework* 48 (October, 1967), pp. 471–481.

18. Carl R. Rogers, "Characteristics of a Helping Relationship," *Canada's Mental Health,* Supplement 27 (Ottawa: Department of National Health and Welfare, March, 1962).

19. See Chapter 5, pp. 103–104.

20. Annette Garrett, "Transference in Casework," in Cora Kasius, ed., *Principles and Techniques in Social Casework* (New York: Family Service Association of America, 1950), pp. 277–285 (reprinted from *The Family,* April, 1941).

21. Hollis, *op.cit.,* pp. 232–242.

22. Ruth Smalley, *Theory for Social Work Practice* (New York: Columbia University Press, 1967).

23. Gale Goldberg, "Breaking the Communication Barrier: The Initial Interview With an Abusing Parent," *Child Welfare* 54 (1975), pp. 274–282.

24. Elvira Hughes Brigg, "The Application Problem: A Study of Why People Fail to Keep First Appointments," *Social Work* 10 (April, 1965), pp. 71–78.

25. Phyliss R. Silverman, "A Re-examination of the Intake Procedure," *Social Casework* 51 (1970), pp. 625–634.

26. Frances B. Sark, "Barriers to Client-Worker Communication at Intake," *Social Casework* 40 (1959), pp. 177–183.

27. Aaron Rosenblatt, "The Application of Role Concepts to the Intake Process," *Social Casework* 43 (1962), pp. 8–14.

28. Jacob Kounin, Norman Polansky, *et al.,* "Experimental Studies of Clients' Reactions to Initial Interviews," *Human Relations* 9 (1956), pp. 265–293.

29. Helen H. Perlman, "Intake and Some Role Considerations," *Social Casework* 41 (December, 1960), pp. 171–177, reprinted in H. H. Perlman, ed., *Persona: Social Role and Personality.* (Chicago: University of Chicago Press, 1968), pp. 162–176.

30. Lillian Ripple, Ernestina Alexander, and Bernice W. Polemis, *Motivation, Capacity and Opportunity,* Social Service Monographs (Chicago: University of Chicago Press, 1964).

31. F. G. Clarke, "Termination: The Forgotten Phase?" *The Social Worker* 35 (1967), pp. 265–272.

32. Rose Green, "Terminating the Relationship in Social Casework: A Working Paper," *Annual Institute on Corrections,* University of Southern California, (April), 1962.

33. Jane K. Bolen, "Easing the Pain of Termination for Adolescents," *Social Casework* 53 (1971), pp. 519–527.

34. Gerard Hogarty, "Discharge Readiness: The Components of Casework Judgement," *Social Casework* 47 (March, 1966), pp. 165–171.

35. Sheldon K. Shiff, "Termination of Therapy: Problems in a Community Psychiatric Outpatient Clinic," *Archives of General Psychiatry* 6 (1962), pp. 93–98.

36. Rodney J. Shapiro and Simon H. Budman, "Defection, Termination and Continuation in Family and Individual Therapy," *Family Process* 12 (1973), pp. 55–67.

37. Dorothy McGriff, "A Co-ordinated Approach to Discharge Planning," *Social Work* 10 (January, 1965), pp. 45–50.

38. Diane Husband and Henry R. Scheunemann, "The Use of Group Process in Teaching Termination," *Child Welfare* 51 (October 1972), pp. 505–513.

39. Francis J. Turner, "The Search for Diagnostic Categories in Social Work Treatment," unpublished paper given at *Learned Societies of Canada,* University of York, Toronto, 1969.

40. Samuel Finestone, "Issues Involved in Developing Diagnostic Classifications for Casework," *Casework Papers* (New York: Family Service Association of America, 1960), pp. 139–154.

41. Werner W. Boehm, "Diagnostic Categories in Social Casework," *Social Work Practice, 1962* (New York: Columbia University Press, 1962), pp. 3–26.

42. Anita K. Bahn, "A Multi-Disciplinary Psycho-Social Classification Scheme," *American Journal of Orthopsychiatry* 41 (October 1971), pp. 830–845. Bruce P. Dohrenwend, "Notes on Psychoso-

cial Diagnosis,'' *American Journal of Orthopsychiatry* 41 (October, 1971), p. 846. John A. Clausen, ''Psychosocial Diagnosis: What and Why,'' *American Journal of Orthopsychiatry* 41 (October, 1971), pp. 847–848.

43. Francis J. Turner, *Differential Diagnosis and Treatment in Social Work* (New York: Free Press, 1968, 2nd ed. 1976). Beatrice Simcox Reiner and Irving Kaufman, *Character Disorders in Parents of Delinquents* (New York: Family Service Association of America, 1959).

Chapter 5

Individual and Joint Therapy

From the preceding chapters a reader could easily conclude that psychosocial therapy is a process that takes place principally between a single therapist and a single client. Indeed, this conclusion is one that could just as well be drawn from much of the psychotherapeutic literature. Fortunately this is not true in current practice. Since man is understood as being variously influenced in his search for and achievement of normality, a perception of therapy built on these premises must include the concept of a multifaceted approach.

In current psychosocial practice the significant divisions of therapy consist, of course, in direct work with clients and indirect practice, or work with the significant environments in a client's life.[1] Each of these two major divisions is in turn divided into several subdivisions. The components of environmental work will be addressed in the next chapter. Here we will address the subdivisions related to direct work. At this time in the development of practice there are six forms of direct work with clients. These include therapeutic activities with individuals, dyads, groups, families, multiple therapists, and the entire community.

It is of interest to note that this commitment to multimodalities has not always been a part of the psychosocial approach. In the historical development of psychotherapeutic systems, especially in the previous four decades, one-to-one treatment was the model for practice. Other modalities were acknowledged as being occasionally useful, if acknowledged at all. It is interesting that even in the psychosocial tradition the idea of a multimodality approach was resisted conceptually. This is reflected in the long-time practice of defining social work treatment as casework. The term carried a strong but not entirely exclusive implication that practice referred to one-to-one intervention. Even when a groundswell began in the helping professions in support of a plurality of methods to be practiced by the therapist, the casework terminology remained. Thus, there was an era in which the professional vocabulary contained such terms as "casework with groups," "family casework," "family group casework," "casework in the community."[2]

This usage was shortlived, and support quickly developed for the idea that a person need not be restricted to a single modality of practice. This concept of a one-person, one-modality viewpoint had been reinforced by our tradition of personalizing methods. Thus in our tradition we referred to colleagues as caseworkers, group workers or community workers, indicating a personalized style of practice rather than a discrete set of skills that various persons could practice.

But this has now changed, and it has become acceptable to differentiate among modalities. We have also accepted the possibility that of a person may be skilled in several modalities. Indeed, the psychosocial tradition takes the viewpoint even further, demanding that the responsible therapist be multiskilled and use different types of practice selectively according to the diagnosed needs of a particular case.

This viewpoint does not rule out the possibility and even the desirability of some persons becoming specialists in one or another of these modalities. But it is essential that such specialization be developed from a multifunctional base rather than from a position where one claims specialization in a particular method because he or she cannot do anything else.

One of the risks inherent to practicing from or espousing a multifaceted base is that one may develop the viewpoint that all of the various modalities of treatment are essentially the same process and that once a person has mastered any one of these he is capable of practicing all of them.[3] This viewpoint is just as dangerous and unproductive as the earlier practice that assigned different modalities to different individual specializations. In fact, it is a more dangerous position because it tends to reduce different modalities to the lowest common denominator.

Certainly, there are features common to all the methods of intervention.[4] It is because of this that it is useful to discuss the therapeutic process in general, as we have done in the earlier chapters. But it is just as important that each method be examined separately to highlight its individual identity and different utility. In the subsequent discussion of the modalities of direct psychosocial therapy the ideas and contents of the earlier chapters will be presumed as a basis.[5]

One-to-One Therapy

As mentioned above, the greatest attention by far in the psychosocial tradition has been given to the process of one-to-one treatment. This can be understood from a historical viewpoint, since the first forms of psychotherapy were of a one-to-one nature. But it is important to speculate about why therapy developed initially on a one-to-one basis. It could be argued with some conviction, that psychotherapy developed in a society that had an individualistic first-order value orientation and thus put major emphasis on the one-to-one approach. But this still begs the question. It could also be argued that if the culture had reflected a collateral orientation it would not necessarily have followed that the first approach to therapy would have been a group approach.[6]

Since the basic unit in any society is the person, it may well be that as important and useful as the other forms of practice are, help is given most effectively directly to the individual. Certainly groups, families and communities are essential to human growth and development but even these systems are always based on the individuals comprising them.

Whatever the historical reasons, therapy was first developed as an individual intervention. Even with the expanded interest in and conceptual development of other modalities, the most commonly practiced form of treatment is still one-to-one. Thus in the late 1960s, when family treatment was predominant both in the literature and in professional interest, and later, when groups attained the same place of importance in clinical practice, the actual provision of therapy was and remains today predominantly individual. Whether this will continue to be so is an interesting question for speculation.

The very fact of privacy is partially responsible for the importance and prevalence of one-to-one therapy. One of the unique strengths of therapy is respect for the individual. As was mentioned briefly in the discussion on relationship, many persons in our society have rarely if ever had the opportunity of having another human being available to respond to them in a private, safe, confidential, and helping manner. To have such an opportunity in a professional setting can in itself enhance self-worth and foster a sense of security, both major components of the growth process. It is the tremendous positive potential of the relationship of one-to-one treatment that makes it possible for the inexperienced worker to be effective in many situations when he himself is feeling uncertain and frightened in his new role.

A one-to-one approach is the format of treatment that best permits the client to find the privacy, acceptance, safety, and security that are so conducive to freeing people to look at themselves in a new way. Once a trusting relationship has been established, most clients are able to risk expressing feelings, fears, anxieties, ideas and opinions that are not the content of ordinary human interaction. Frequently the very ability to show such emotions and thoughts not only brings a sense of relief but is a source of growth. This is especially so when the client finds that the content he produces is understood and accepted by the worker. In the privacy of the relationship with the worker the client is able to look at himself from different perspectives and to find out how he is perceived by others. He can thus consider other patterns of behavior, enriched perceptions of the world, and expanded knowledge of his significant environments and his place in them. He also receives the opportunity to have his ideas tested and challenged in a nonhurting, nondestructive way that can again provide the opportunity for growth.[7]

In the psychosocial perspective it is important that one-to-one treatment not be seen as inward-looking only. It is equally important for the client to be led to think about his significant environments, including people, resources, and systems. Further, the client can be helped to understand others with whom he relates and to become aware of his impact on them. He can thus be helped to discover resources available to him and when necessary to work out some of his attitudes or misperceptions about such resources. The therapist, aware of the interaction between the client's inner life and his outer reality, remains sensitive to how important it is for the client to experiment with new behavior, to have an opportunity to fumble, falter or even fail and still feel able to come back to the relationship to review these experiences and be encouraged to try again.

Obviously there is much in common between the therapeutic relationship and the healthy, growth-enhancing parent-child relationship. There are differences as well; especially the time-bound character of the therapeutic relationship, the emphasis on client growth, and the de-emphasis on the therapist's gratification. Because of the similarities to the parent-child relationship there is frequent recurrence in the one-to-one relationship of emotions, ideas and reactions that are remnants from earlier experiences. Situations in which the client begins to act and react as if the therapist were a parent or parent figure are examples of such emotional reactions.

This phenomenon of transference is, of course, well-known. An interesting facet of the history of the psychosocial school is the varying emphasis that has been put on the importance of transference to treatment.[8] During those times when psychoanalytic thinking was the principal basis of clinical practice, the nature, extent and influence of transference were key concepts. Rather than being seen as unusual, it was taken as given that there were some elements of transference in all worker-client relationships. This phenomenon therefore had to be taken into account throughout the life of the case and carefully watched, nurtured or diffused depending on its extent and influence in relation to the goals of treatment.[9]

Transference was greatly stressed because of its great potential for enhancing functioning, since the client could be easily influenced within the aura of a transference situation. Also, as frequently experienced within a transference situation, some earlier unresolved developmental problems from the past could be worked out.

But unfortunately transference reactions are not necessarily positive; indeed they frequently are negative. When negative they hold great potential for further hurt, rejection, and suffering. Unless this is understood and managed properly the treatment process can become stalemated or more frequently abandoned by the client who is confused about himself, hurt, threatened, and disappointed. The worker also is only human and thus is capable of having transference feelings toward the client and of experiencing unrecognized reactions to the client's transferred feelings. These understandable reactions by a client or to a client are frequently misunderstood, misperceived, or even totally overlooked by the worker. What begins as a planned, objectively based problem-solving process can become instead a hurtful and confusing process of rejection that not only is not helpful, but may indeed be harmful.[10] It is because of the high possibility that such charged emotions stem from the client's and therapist's past that continued emphasis is put on the therapist's need for supervision or, when necessary, on therapy for himself. In the psychosocial tradition the worker's responsibility for self-awareness has always been strongly emphasized. Over the years, therapists have discharged this responsibility through a formal experience of psychotherapy, a thorough, regular, practice-oriented supervision, or some form of consultation.[11]

In the early seventies the need for such a backup process for therapists was challenged; rather, stress was put on present-oriented work with clients and worker autonomy. Both of these distinct trends, the desire for autonomy and the rejection of supervision, came together in the therapeutic process. One of the results of these attitudes was a growing discontent and antagonism toward the concept of supervision and even more toward the therapist's possible need for therapy. Happily, this negativism has diminished, and there is renewed emphasis on the need for a formalized process of interaction with a colleague to bring some balance to our perspectives and to ensure that we do not react improperly to clients and their frequently heavy emotional demands on us. It also helps to ensure that our own problems and blind spots do not limit our availability and usefulness to clients.[12]

There are many other purposes of supervision or consultation, including an ongoing responsibility to strengthen our therapeutic skills by drawing on the accumulated skills of others.[13] The essential point is that in the psychosocial tradition there is strong support for the necessity for some professional backup to our practice.[14]

This discussion brings us to another component of psychosocial history, the place of the unconscious in this approach to practice. This topic has been discussed frequently in the literature. Like other questions mentioned earlier, the use of the unconscious as a component of treatment has been a sociopolitical battleground. This was related to the struggle over whether social workers provided psychotherapy or whether this was done only by other professions. Since for many the term "psychotherapy" was related to if not identified with the concept of the unconscious, the use of unconscious material became a status symbol and a hallmark of the psychotherapist.

It appears safe to say that, once the helping professions became confortable with the Freudian idea that much of man's psychic life was outside ordinary consciousness, the psychosocially oriented practitioner adopted this as an important framework within which to understand the interactions and behaviors of clients.[15] Understanding the impact of the client's unconscious life on his behavior was seen to be essential to an understanding of unrecognized transferred feelings that took place in treatment as well as of his resistances, anxieties, and projections. This is as important a concept in today's practice as it ever was. Dr. Hollis's summary of the use of the unconscious is a useful and still relevant summary of this topic.[16]

It is unfortunate that both the unconscious material itself and the techniques designed to elicit the material took on such value and status implications for some therapists. For them the extent to which unconscious material is used was and still is held to be the distinguishing mark between "intensive treatment" and "superficial work." The struggle around this issue seems to be a semantic one for the most part, reflecting therapeutic ideologies rather than what takes place in practice.

At present few data are available that indicate that psychosocial therapists from a quantitative perspective use much unconscious material directly in their work with clients. Indeed, it is doubtful that there are many therapists apart from traditional analysts who deal with unconscious material to any great extent. But this in no way negates the importance of unconscious material in current therapy. Indeed, the understanding of this component of man's personality remains an essential component in the understanding of psychosocial man.

In recent years excellent audio- and videotapes of a wide range of interviews have become available. One observation that can be made from the tapes is that most of what therapists and clients discuss relates to the events of day-to-day living and the anxieties, hurts, concerns, problems, and decisions surrounding them. It is also clear that the sensitive and perceptive therapist strives to assess and understand the unconscious components of this material simultaneously in order to respond to the client in an effective manner. Undoubtedly there are occasions in the treatment process when a therapist leads a client to look directly at the unconscious sources of some of his feelings, personality patterns, or behaviors. When this does occur it usually is brief and done in a manner that permits the client to understand how particular material or behavior is related to past experiences. Frequently this is sufficient to free the client from these bonds and their restricting influence on current behavior. Since all clients bring all of themselves into the therapeutic experience, it is essential to be sensitive to and aware of the unconscious components of their lives. It is not essential that all of the therapist's observations and sensitivities to these materials be shared or looked at as a part of treatment. Usually it is our understanding of the transference elements of the relationship that helps us to free the client in a general way. from problem-producing past experiences.

This is usually done when the specific focus of the process is a maturationally freeing one. Recently I saw a client who was talking with great intensity about her conflicting feelings about her daughter. After a few minutes, she began to get her pronouns mixed and soon was talking about herself and her own mother. It was helpful to this woman to spend a few minutes talking about some of her unresolved feelings about her own mother and their relationship, which came to the fore with some beginning awareness of hitherto unrecognized patterns from the past. The beneficial component of this material was the way it could be used to help the client understand her current feelings rather than to attempt to resolve the complexities of this earlier relationship. As she began to gain confidence in her own maternal role, she later came back briefly to her relationship with her mother, who was still alive and a part of her life, but only to report that the relationship was now much more manageable even though still not fully understood.

I am not suggesting that it is inappropriate ever to focus directly on the client's unconscious life. There is no doubt that there are some clients, and they seem to be on the increase, who come into a therapeutic process quite sophisticated psychologically and who want and can benefit from a close and intense examination of their feelings, motivations, and behavior, conscious and unconscious, current and past.[17] Even though we know that our therapy for the most part deals with current material, it need not be exclusively so. A client who wanted, needed, and could benefit from an intensely introspective, past-oriented therapeutic relationship would be seriously underserved by a therapist who refused to deal with anything but current issues. This type of case is indeed demanding and frequently is the type of case for which supervision is most appropriate and helpful for the therapist. Because cases of this sort are not the typical situation in practice, therapists must be particularly careful in their management. They are clearly within the competence of the well-trained social worker and should not necessarily be referred to another professional only because the client wishes to work at a more intense level.

Over the years a range of efforts has been made to describe with more precision what takes place within the one-to-one interviewing process. One of the difficulties in approaching such a task is to find a level of measurement that is neither too gross nor too refined to be useful.

Dr. Hollis's work in this area has been beneficial and represents a major contribution to the field.[18] Her research indicates that in the interaction between client and worker there are six general types of activity that the worker engages in with the client, and in four of these the client has a correlative activity. These will be described briefly in the following pages. For further detail in using this outline as a research tool the primary writings should be consulted.

In this paradigm the first activity of the therapist is that of *support,* an activity undoubtedly essential to all helping processes. This category includes the whole range of verbal and nonverbal activities and actions that convey to the client the therapist's interest, support, appreciation, concern, and encouragement.

Secondly, therapists also make use of their *authority* in the interview situation. The use of authority, once thought as being contraindicated in the helping process, is now recognized as a highly effective component of therapy when used selectively and sparingly. Such authority can range from the subtle suggestion that a particular form of behavior might be preferable to another to the therapist's taking an overt stand about some course of action considered important for the client.

Therapists also engage in *eliciting information and feelings* from clients ranging over everything, from the day-to-day events of the clients' lives, including behavior, to the client's most intimate feelings. The process of helping clients talk about themselves, their significant environments, their feelings, attitudes, concerns, and aspirations is the heart of much of the client–therapist activity. As has been suggested earlier, the very fact of having the opportunity to share this material in a safe, understanding, supportive setting can be a relief-giving and growth-enhancing cathartic process.

In addition to helping clients talk about themselves and their interests and concerns, the skillful therapist moves the client to think reflectively about this material. The process of *inducing a reflective attitude* on the part of the client about selected components of his psychosocial reality is a distinguishing feature of the psychosocial approach. It is during the activity of reflection that the essence of therapeutic work can take place. When reflective thinking is used appropriately, the client begins to take responsibility for himself, his decisions, and his behavior and to think of alternatives that will help solve specific problems or achieve designated goals and objectives.[19]

These reflective activities of thought are carried out in three major areas of the client's reality. First, the worker leads the client to consider his or her own current reality and immediate past. Such thinking can be about persons in the client's life, his behaviors, feelings, and attitudes, including his attitudes toward the helping process itself. This thinking about the current reality of a client's life is the principal medium of the change that is sought in the therapy.

Second, the therapist fosters, or the client initiates, reflections on patterns of behavior as components of his personality. Such reflections help the client understand how various aspects of his behavior or responses fall into categories which are interconnected and patterned. This type of reflection can be an important basis for altered self-perceptions and subsequent modified behavior.

At a third level, the therapist engages the client in reflective thinking about early influences in the client's significant past that appear to be affecting current reality. This use of past material, be it events, feelings, attitudes, or memories, was once thought to be the essence of good therapy and thus the hallmark of the successful therapist. Research over the past decades has indicated that important as such considerations of the past are, reflective thinking about it is much less prevalent than some literature would seem to indicate and some therapists would wish.

The six activities of a therapist described above comprise the entire gamut of the therapeutic intervention within the worker–client relationship. These summaries run the risk of oversimplification in that they tend to underplay the many subcategories and subtleties in each major area. Of these there are two that are particularly significant and need to be identified in their own right.

The first relates to the activities of the therapist which lead a client to talk about or reflect upon the interaction between worker and client—that is, upon the very process of treatment. Earlier chapters have described the importance of the client–therapist interaction and how it can be a source of comfort in which the client finds strength to risk new behaviors or to consider new perceptions and alternatives. In addition a client can learn much about himself, his feelings, attitudes, and patterns of relating by looking at and reflecting upon the relationship itself. This focusing on the relationship is a rich source of learning for the client and is a component of therapy and growth. Too often, however this type of reflective thinking is used only in situations where there are difficulties in the client–therapist relationship, such as those which involve questions of transference. Certainly when this type of difficulty is present, it must be dealt with and can thus be turned to the client's benefit. What is suggested here is that a less problem-focused orientation to the relationship can be a source of experience and learning for the client as well and is a potentially rich activity in the therapeutic encounter.

A further component of the worker's activity, which will be discussed in more detail in a subsequent chapter, is the use of information as a resource in the one-to-one relationship. The role of the therapist as a source and provider of information is appropriate as well to other modalities of intervention.[20] Not enough attention has been given to the positive therapeutic impact of information. So often in a busy psychotherapeutic practice, where much of our focus is on understanding the client's personality structure and its interaction with persons and systems, we tend to underestimate how reassuring, expanding, and enabling new information can be to a client. Information about how others behave, about the many resources of a community, about possibilities and alternative courses of action can be of tremendous help to a client.

In summary, one-to-one therapy is still the most frequently utilized of the various modalities in psychosocial therapy. It is a process that respects and builds upon the autonomy and individuality of each person. It draws heavily upon the growth-enhancing qualities of the therapeutic relationship in which a client can safely and securely look at himself, at others, and at resources and their importance for him. It is a modality of treatment that continues to be important in our culture where lack of privacy, intimacy, and autonomy are of increasing concern, and the one-to-one situation is welcomed by the client searching for improved psychosocial functioning.

Joint Interviewing

Although much of the literature of therapy presumes that it is provided to individuals, groups, or families, there is an additional form of therapy that requires more attention than has been given to it up to now. It is the process of joint interviewing, in which two clients and one therapist are present.[21] Most frequently this type of interviewing has been discussed from the standpoint of a husband and wife in therapy and on occasion from a parent–child perspective.[22] No doubt these are the instances where it is used most frequently. Nevertheless, it would be incorrect to restrict this modality to these situations. Rather it should be viewed as a modality that can be used for any two persons involved in some type of common reality who can make use of the particular advantages of the joint interview.

Much of what has been said of the interventive process at the one-to-one level applies to this modality as well. In addition, there are some differences that need to be considered. First, the presence of a third person in the interview destroys the potential for the intimacy of one-to-one situations. This can be a source of resentment in the client as well as a source of reassurance. The resentment can come from having to share the worker with someone else. But on the other hand, the presence of another person can provide the security that the client will not be overwhelmed and will have help available from someone else if the therapist gets too close or too probing.

In deciding to make use of the modality of the joint interview, the worker must assess the potential and perspectives of the client. From the therapist's viewpoint, having two interacting clients before him brings a different kind of reality to the situation. Rather than describing what he says and does in relation to another, the client can enact it before the worker's eyes. The worker, too, can get involved in this process for he does not and cannot remain a neutral observer but becomes a participant in a different kind of process than that which takes place in a one-to-one setting.

The existence of the triangle creates potential relationship stresses that can result in intense rivalry between the two clients for the interest and support of the worker. The therapist can easily be drawn into this type of struggle and indeed may become allied to one of the clients against the other. This was clearly brought home to me in a case in which the husband was a fellow professional and the wife was not. At one time early in the relationship, I found myself having been drawn into what amounted to a case conference with my fellow professional about the wife, but in her presence. She made it clear that this was not her perception of a helping situation and after some effort the roles were sorted out and the therapeutic process reinstituted.

But when the process of the joint interview is working in a more positive way, great progress can be made in helping people to look at their behavior, to reflect on their actions and reactions, to learn to see each other in a different light and to test out with the therapist's help new viewpoints or behavioral patterns.

A further advantage of the joint interview is that the client can also be an observer and can learn from that role. Thus he may learn new behavioral styles in observing the worker in interaction with the other client. For example, a husband may see that there are other ways of dealing with his wife's attacks; a mother may learn other ways of dealing with her child's angry outbursts; two friends may learn about each other by listening to the other person describe himself or his actions.[23]

It would be a mistake to overemphasize the potential risks of the joint interview such as the problem of rivalry referred to earlier. This style of practice can also be seen as a safe, secure situation that permits the parties involved to say things to each other and the worker knowing that the worker will protect them from themselves and from each other. Probably the statement that therapists most often hear in the joint interview is "I never heard him say that before." Over and over again people are able to share things or reveal things that bring great relief and help to the other and subsequently to their relationship.

From the viewpoint of content, joint interviewing tends to be more present-centered and participant-centered than one-to-one therapy. By "present centered" I mean a tendency to look at the immediate interaction taking place in the therapeutic process and then to build from that.[24] In the same way it tends to be "participant-centered," with only occasional focusing on significant others outside the process. Thus the decision to use modalities of joint interviewing should originate partly from the diagnosis and the objectives that are being sought.

But there is a component of joint interviewing in which some effort is made to have one or both of the participants look backwards to their developmental history in order to better understand themselves, to help the other understand them better and thus to alter mutual expectations or to consider alternative behaviors. Thus a client may find that what is happening in a relationship is strongly influenced by the background of the other. Recognizing such a pattern frequently permits adjustments in behavior.

A further risk of the joint interview is that one or both of the clients may find that they are not able or prepared to share some aspect of themselves or their behavior in the presence of the other. This need to hold back can of course be detrimental to the process and thus be seriously counterproductive. It is because of this possibility that some therapists will schedule one or two separate interviews with each client if there is a perception that something of this nature is taking place and then decide whether to proceed with joint interviews.[25]

An additional component of the decision to use a joint interview is the question of value orientation. There are clients who have a clear perception that therapy should be one-to-one or that therapy should be joint or even that therapy should be of some other modality. In these cases, barring other contraindications, the clients' preferences should be respected. Frequently in practice we forget to take sufficient account of a client's feelings about how help should be given. To an increasing extent the general population does have some perception of what therapy is like and some preference for a particular format. I think this is especially true in marital cases, where some clients clearly prefer to be seen alone and others wish that their partners be seen with them. This is not to forget that just as clients may have preferences, we too will have our practice preferences based on experience and interests; we may well attempt to get the client to follow our suggestions. But this at times may be uncomfortable or indeed unacceptable to the client, and his discomfort may be of sufficient concern to lead us to select another modality more appropriate to the client's emotional state. We must be careful to select modalities of intervention based on our clients' needs or wishes rather than our own preference.

In summary, joint interviews have a distinctive quality. They permit close scrutiny of current behavior and attitudes; they can diffuse transference and dependency problems; they can provide security to clients and, when acceptable to a client, permit shorter periods of intervention. This is especially so when the problem is directly related to some components of the interaction between the two persons involved. On the other hand, joint interviewing restricts the intimacy of the client-worker relationship, including its privacy and confidentiality; it requires the sharing of the therapist; it inhibits detailed self-examination from a historical and developmental viewpoint and can result in destructive rivalry situations or unnecessary use of therapeutic time to negotiate difficulties related to the triadic structure rather than addressing the developmental goals of the persons involved.

Notes

1. Florence Hollis, *Casework: A Psychosocial Therapy,* 2nd ed. (New York: Random House, 1972), pp. 26–32.

2. John E. Bell, *Family Group Therapy,* Public Health Monograph no. 64, (Washington, D.C.: Government Printing Office, 1961), Sidney Berkowitz, "Some Specific Techniques of Psychosocial Diagnosis and Treatment in Family Casework," *Social Casework* 36 (November, 1955), pp. 399–406, Donald R. Bardill and Francis J. Ryan, *Family Group Casework: A Casework Approach to Family Therapy,* (Washington, D.C.: Catholic University of America Press, 1964).

3. Sara E. Muloney and Margaret H. Mudgett, "Group Work–Group Casework: Are They The Same," *Social Work* 4 (2) (1959), pp. 29–36.

4. Harriett M. Bartlett, *The Common Base of Social Work Practice* (New York: National Association of Social Workers, 1970).

5. Mary E. Burns and Paul H. Glasser, "Similarities and Differences in Casework and Group Work Practice," *Social Service Review* 37 (1963), pp. 416–428.

6. Rubin Blanck, "The Case for Individual Treatment," *Social Casework* 47 (February, 1965), pp. 70–74.

7. Frances H. Scherz, "Casework—A Psychosocial Therapy: An Essay Review," *Social Service Review* 38 (1964), pp. 206–211.

8. See Chapter 4, pp. 85–86.

9. Gerald Appel, "Some Aspects of Transference and Counter-Transference in Marital Counseling," *Social Casework* 47 (May, 1966), pp. 307–312.

10. Andrew Watson, "Reality Testing and Transference in Psychotherapy," *Smith College Studies in Social Work* 36 (June, 1966), pp. 191–209.

11. Lucille N. Austin, "Supervision of the Experienced Caseworker" in Cora Kasius, ed., *Principles and Techniques in Social Casework* (New York: Family Service Association of America, 1950), pp. 155–166, reprinted from *The Family* (January, 1942).

12. Barbara Cowan, Rose Dastyk and Edcil R. Wickham, "Group Supervision as a Teaching Learning Modality in Social Work," *The Social Worker* 40 (December, 1972), pp. 256–261.

13. Kenneth W. Watson, "Differential Supervision," *Social Work* 18 (November, 1973), pp. 80–88.

14. Laura Epstein, "Is Autonomous Practice Possible?" *Social Work* 18 (1973), pp. 5–12.

15. Sigmund Freud, "The Unconscious," in *Collected Papers,* vol. 4 (London: Hogarth Press, 1949), pp. 98–136.

16. Hollis, *op.cit.,* chap. 2, pp. 185–202.

17. Ner Littner, "The Impact of the Client's Unconscious on the Caseworker's Reactions," in Howard J. Parad, ed., *Ego Psychology and Dynamic Casework,* (New York: Family Service Association of America, 1958), pp. 73–82.

18. This material constitutes the major part of the Hollis book, *Casework: A Psychosocial Therapy,* and should be carefully read to get a full description of this typology. Note in particular Part 3, pp. 89–246.

19. Phyllida Parsloe, "Presenting Reality—The Choice of a Casework Method," *British Journal of Psychiatric Social Work* 8 (1965–1966), pp. 6–10.

20. Nicholas Long, "Information and Referral Services: A Short History and Some Recommendations," *Social Service Review* 47 (1973), pp. 49–62.

21. Some authors use the term joint interviewing to describe situations where there are several clients present as in family therapy. In our viewpoint it is more accurate to restrict it to interviews where one therapist and two clients are present.

22. Joanne Geist and Norman M. Gerber, "Joint Interviewing: A Treatment Technique with Marital Partners," *Social Casework* 41 (February, 1960), pp. 76–83.

23. Shirley M. Ehrenkranz, "A Study of Joint Interviewing in the Treatment of Marital Problems," *Social Casework* 48 (October and November, 1967), pp. 498–502 and 570–574.

24. Sanford N. Sherman, "Joint Interviews in Casework Practice," *Social Work* 4 (April, 1959), pp. 20–28, Elizabeth H. Couch, *Joint and Family Interviews in the Treatment of Marital Partners,* (New York: Family Service Association of America, 1969).

25. Bernard Hall and Winifred Wheeler, "The Patient and His Relatives: Initial Joint Interview," *Social Work* 2 (January, 1957), pp. 75–80.

Chapter 6

Co-Therapy, Group Therapy, Family Therapy, and Community Intervention

In the previous chapter individual and joint treatments were discussed. In addition to these two there are other modalities of treatment used in psychosocial therapy.

Co-Therapy

Co-therapy is the planned use of two therapists in a single case. This is a modality of treatment that only in recent years has been understood as a distinct form of treatment. It is difficult to identify in the literature a time or place of origin of this style of practice. This is probably because, like many developments in therapy, it is not attributable to any one person but rather has emerged in the practice of many people.

To date there appear to be three distinct ways in which this type of intervention is used. The first includes cases in which there are two clients in a single case each of whom is seen by a separate therapist. These therapists plan and implement their intervention in a coordinated way. During the life of the case there will be occasional combined interviews but these would be the exception rather than the rule. An example of this type of approach occurred in a case in which a couple was having difficulties with a very hostile adolescent son. By the time the case came into therapy the situation had deteriorated to the point that there was no hope for any kind of family therapy or even the possibility of the same therapist working with the parents and the son. Thus, one worker took responsibility for the son and the other one worked with the parents. The two therapists worked closely together throughout. Only after several weeks was it possible to attempt an interview with parents, son, and both therapists present. This proved helpful, although the case continued in the same divided way with an occasional additional group interview.

A second form of this type of practice consists of cases in which there are two or more clients, such as a couple or a family, and two therapists who are present together during the formal interaction with the family.[1] This modality is used frequently in family therapy and less often in marital cases.[2]

The third form of co-therapy is not nearly so common as the first two. This consists of situations where there is only one identified client but two therapists, each of whom takes responsibility for some aspect of the client's situation. Each therapist is perceived to be able to help the client find some type of desirable change in certain specific spheres of his life. For example, a young male adult might be seen by one therapist to deal with a specific behavioral difficulty such as a speech problem. At the same time, he may be involved with another therapist about difficulties in relating to members of the opposite sex. Although these two areas of functioning may be closely related, more progress may be possible when they are dealt with separately. Obviously in these situations close contact between the two therapists is necessary.

There is a further modification of the latter format that has at times been called impact therapy or multiple therapists therapy.[3] Here, several therapists are involved in a variety of combinations with the same client. This approach is used infrequently, and as yet there has been little published material on it.[4]

In looking at the various forms of this modality of treatment some general observations can be made. The principal underlying concept is that all of us are influenced differently by the persons with whom we relate. These different influences can be positive, reciprocal, mutual, and growth-enhancing when these relationships are purposefully fostered and directed. Co-therapy makes use of this reality by formally setting up a situation where the client or clients have the opportunity to experience more than one helping relationship at a time.

A further aspect of co-therapy relates to the reinforcing that can take place for clients as they receive similar feedback, support or challenge from the different therapists. This reinforcing aspect of therapy can be useful in helping to keep distortions in perspective. The distortions referred to are those that sometimes arise if the client begins to lose confidence in the interventions or interpretations of a single therapist and does not have an opportunity to test them out in other situations.

From another viewpoint, a co-therapist approach can bring clients into contact with diversity, thus making the therapeutic situation more like the reality in which they live. The very structure of the therapeutic relationship has a built-in diversity that can facilitate. It was suggested above that a similarity of approach by the two therapists can be helpful. But rarely will two therapists be exactly the same. Each may act and react in different ways to the same client. Thus the client may be faced with differing interpretations, responses, and viewpoints. Certainly, this could be confusing and anxiety-producing for the client if it is not handled properly. But it can also be a source of learning and growth that can prepare the client to deal more adequately with a complex and uncertain world.

The presence of the co-therapist can also be a source of security and perceived protection for the client in that it can prevent or neutralize feelings of being overwhelmed and taken over by the other worker. This is especially applicable in situations in which two clients are involved and the possibility exists that one client may sense or perceive an alliance forming between worker and client against him, as can happen in triadic situations.

The use of co-therapists, especially when only one client is involved, can help the client partialize the components in his life that are being looked at in therapy. Partialization in this manner is desirable when a client's difficulties are caused by multiple problems and these problems are interrelated in a manner that prohibits their being dealt with serially. At times a single therapist can deal with this type of complexity. More often parallel but interconnected intervention can greatly facilitate the process.

The foregoing comments suggest that co-therapy is not a typical form of treatment but is used only in atypical circumstances, when a single-therapist approach is seen as potentially problematic. There are three clusters of situations in which the use of a single therapist seems to be counterproductive and co-therapy is to be preferred. The first and most common is the situation where the therapeutic assessment indicates that the personality structure of one or both of two interrelated clients is so fragile that the client or clients could not deal with the added strain of having to share a therapist. Secondly, situations are found in practice where it is considered essential to separate some components of a single client's psychosocial reality to bring about desired change in these areas. For example, a client may have both serious marital problems and problems related to his perception of self. Clearly these two areas are interconnected but it may also happen that progress in both areas cannot be achieved unless the two components of the client's reality are separately addressed. Such a client may be able to begin to get a better perception of himself and his ability to function by working alone with one therapist and as a result of these self-gains may be able to take a look at the marriage with another therapist.

There is a third type of situation in practice where co-therapy appears to be the treatment of choice. It occurs when we have two clients who need to have the opportunity to observe two other interacting human beings in a therapeutic situation, who can serve as models or as a basis of reality against which the clients can test and measure their own behavior and perceptions. This is a very complicated type of therapeutic situation where at times the two therapists serve almost as spokesmen for the client with whom each is working directly. Once again, the literature has not been rich in discussing this type of situation. It has been one where therapists have experimented out of necessity and are only beginning to formulate experiences out of which further conceptualization will take place.

In addition to the situations described above in which the decision to use co-therapy is made from the viewpoint of the client's need, there is a fourth use of this approach from the viewpoint of the therapist. In a very particular way, co-therapy can serve as a check or control of reality for the therapist. Having a colleague simultaneously exposed to the interactive process with the client can provide a basis for comparing perceptions and correcting distortions as well as serving as providing a source of enriched understanding of the client. At times, this type of therapy has been utilized in supervisory teaching.[5] That is, someone is asked to sit in on a therapeutic session and later share his perceptions and observations with a view to clarifying problems that may be occurring. It is suggested here that important as this teaching role is, there is a more therapeutically directed use of this method. In it a co-therapist is present not in a supervisory role but rather in an enriching, observing and at times participating role that when properly utilized can operate to the benefit of the client or clients involved.

But this very advantage of the therapeutic process also points to some of the risks and difficulties involved. First and most importantly, successful co-therapy requires a high level of mutual trust, respect, and ability between the therapists. Unlike in most other modalities, in co-therapy therapists are exposing their professional identities to each other. Without a profound mutual respect, serious relationship problems can result.[6] Sometimes these are subtle and unrecognized and can quickly complicate the therapeutic endeavor. To an extent this can be indirectly painful, harmful, and anxiety-producing to the client. It can happen that co-therapists will differ about the assessment and management of a case and then find themselves unable or unwilling to consider the different perceptions of their colleague.

In addition, co-therapy can be directly hurtful to the clients. Some clients may not be able to handle the complexities of dealing with two therapists, whether this relationship is experienced with both therapists present simultaneously or serially. It is this latter point that frequently is overlooked by practitioners. Under the influence of professional enthusiasm, they may move into a co-therapist situation without fully perceiving and discussing the possible complexities and resistances to this approach by the client. The co-therapy approach can be quite surprising to some clients, who may require a considerable period of time to sort out the relationship and their own feelings about it.[7]

Another problematic situation may occur when therapists move into a co-therapy-like situation without fully realizing its nature. This occurs when a client is being seen in another setting for some other purpose. Quite frequently clients are put into conflict about the management of two relationships. There are a few cases where there are more than two relationships existing simultaneously, and hence the client's problem of managing relationships becomes compounded. The occurrence of on-going parallel relationships, the importance of which is not fully recognized, can come about from our tendency toward professional insularity, which can easily lead us to overlook some of the client's concerns and difficulties in dealing with this type of therapeutic reality. In the beginning of any relationship it is useful and important to attempt to ascertain whether there are other ongoing therapeutic relationships involved. Such information can thus put the therapist on notice that co-therapy problems could emerge.

On the positive side, other helping processes could and should be seen as additional resources. It is assumed that when a client is involved in a plurality of helping relationships the therapists involved will have a common perception of the client. But this may not always be so. It is in such a situation that the different perceptions of two therapists can be turned to the advantage of a client. That is, the very existence of different perceptions can serve as the content of some reflective thinking by the client that will permit him to understand his different effects on people and the possible reasons for it.

Apart from its use in marital situations and in family work, it is clear that co-therapy as a treatment of choice rather than as an accidental occurrence is still in a preliminary stage of development. Further accumulation and analysis of a wide range of data on co-therapy situations and outcomes are now needed so that we can better understand when it is effective and, of equal importance, when it is not. It is also important that we know for what kinds of problems, persons and settings this therapeutic stance appears to be most useful. At this point in practice, it seems to be most commonly used in the following situations:

1. when the primary treatment objective has a major interactive component and the client's personality structure is sufficiently intact to enable him to sustain the additional demands of a multiple therapeutic relationship.
2. when the client's personality is so fragile that a "best friend" or colleague is required to ensure his protection in a joint interview situation or
3. in some family situations, where it is considered desirable to move in more than one therapeutic direction simultaneously.

Group Treatment

As mentioned earlier, the psychosocial approach to therapy developed principally in a one-to-one tradition and with a more clinical orientation than existed in the group work tradition.[8] Group practice emerged from the traditions of the settlement house and the recreational fields. Thus for a long time these two modalities of practice remained quite separate. Yet, a basic psychosocial concept was integral to both the individual and the group field.[9] Nevertheless it was only in the late 1950s and early 1960s that the concept of a single therapist who is competent and comfortable with a multiplicity of modalities began to emerge. Practitioners began to be much more committed to the idea of being able to practice in several therapies. By now we have reached a point where the majority of therapists are comfortable working with groups, individuals, and families.

In psychosocial terms, the use of groups as a modality of treatment strives to build a therapeutic process based on an understanding of the role of groups in normal growth and development. It is hardly necessary to document the importance of group experiences to all normal growth and development.[10]

Groups play a different role in the development process at different periods in a person's life. For example, in the period of early latency, the individual finds in a group the satisfaction of new experiences and the pleasures of shared activities. Later, in adolescence, the group serves in a more dynamic way to help the adolescent test out differing values and mores and to find security and support for the emerging individual personality structure.

Regardless of the developmental period, groups serve some similar functions for all individuals. Thus we know that groups are able to help individuals find security, identity, acceptance by peers, opportunities to test out viewpoints, to learn new perceptions of reality and new modes of behavior, to have one's values and opinions challenged in a nondestructive way, and to find sympathy and understanding in times of pain and suffering. Obviously, the group process being referred to here is a healthy one that takes place in natural and spontaneous groups.[11]

The group in the process of developing its own identity with its own mores, traditions, and values can be a tremendous source of gratification to the individuals that comprise it,[12] thus contributing to their ongoing growth and development. It is the tremendous power of the group that makes it such a powerful therapeutic medium.

Within the social work literature, there are few situations and personality types that have not been suggested as being amenable to group treatment.[13] In addition, there has been a dramatic change in the perceived desirable structures of groups. For example, for a long time, the group literature seemed to stress the necessity of having similarities in groups. Today there is a marked change in thinking about the need for homogeneity in such things as age, sex, problems, or level of functioning. To a growing extent, skilled therapists find that they can accomodate wide differences in groups and that homogeneity is desirable only in particular situations.[14] Thus, if a group is formed to help mothers of brain-damaged children learn to accept and later utilize the situation, clearly a similarity of problem is desired. But in other situations the very differences among the group members can be sources of strength, growth, and support for the individuals.

There is currently much enthusiasm about groups. As indicated above, the professional literature contains articles that support the use of groups for virtually every presenting situation and factor.[15] Nevertheless, groups are not always the treatment method of choice. Certainly, their use as a primary modality is counterindicated in situations where an individual client may be a severe threat to others because of extremely strong and rigidly held attitudes, or in situations where the personality structure of a particular client manifests serious levels of hostility that could be turned against other members of the group. Groups are also counterindicated in situations where the individual client is judged to be unable to tolerate the prospect of exposure to several individuals. For example, a person's attitudes that some particular component of his behavior may be so shattering to him that the prospect of having other persons know about it or be in a position to comment about it would be very anxiety-provoking. Thus any benefits that could be gained by utilizing a group approach would be canceled out.

A third counterindication of the use of groups is with clients who exhibit some particular form of difference with which other members of the group could not deal comfortably, thus preventing the person from becoming a part of the group. An example would be a debilitating physical condition or a difference in attitudes, values, or viewpoint on some fundamental issue.

From the viewpoint of values, there is another consideration in the use of groups; indeed, it is a consideration for all modalities of treatment. The client's perception of groups might in itself be a counterindication. For example, there are persons whose sense of self and desire for privacy could cause them to be under particular stress in sharing or exposing themselves in a group. Their perception of their problem and how to manage it may include the idea of sharing it with a therapist, but not with other clients. To insist that such a client become a member of the group could create additional stresses that would be counterproductive. This point is underscored again to point out the danger of selecting a treatment modality on the basis of the therapist's preference or values about the model way of practicing. This does not mean that we should not try to interpret to a client who is uncomfortable about starting in a group the advantages of this method or even indicate that our preference would be for him to try a group. Nevertheless it is important that we be careful not to inflict a particular modality of practice on a client when he is not ready for it or interested in it. This caution of course relates to all types of treatment; all things being equal, the choice should be based on the client's situation rather than on the therapist's preference.

But apart from the situations mentioned above, groups are the treatment of choice for many clients. In groups clients can learn to understand and accept differences in others as well as finding support in the commonality of thought and perceptions. Groups are also useful for a person who is fearful of the intensity of the one-to-one interview and who can thus find security in a group as well as the opportunity to learn about himself, his problems and perceptions through hearing others struggle with similar issues.

Presuming an adequate diagnosis of the client's ability to benefit from a group experience, the type of group to be used must also be considered. From the rapid growth in group treatment of the last decade, a rich spectrum of types of groups has emerged.[16]

Thus in the same agency groups can be found with a variety of goals. One might be an activity group with several isolated single mothers. There the goal would be to help them improve their sense of adequacy by meeting together and jointly planning and carrying out enjoyable tasks. There may also be a group of clients meeting to examine their common experiences around a particular life situation, such as a group of recently bereaved women, and to help each other through their accumulated experiences and knowledge. A third group may be structured to help the individual members look at themselves, their attitudes and behavior, both conscious and unconscious, as well as their impact on others and others' impact on them, with the goal of altering some components of their personality. Groups can be short-term or long-term; they can be closed or open; they can work toward clearly specified objectives or take the search for goals itself as their goal.

The role of the therapist as a group leader is a complex one. The principal objective of any type of group is to enable the group process to operate in a healthy, nondestructive way that permits the members to achieve the defined goal or goals. The therapist as group leader has responsibility for selecting group members, orienting them to the group process, getting the group started and moving it through the beginning stages. In addition the leader must foster the group process, help the members deal with unexpected developments within the group, facilitate the achievement of group objectives as well as deal with the termination phase.[17] Throughout this process, the therapist has two goals; enabling, fostering and assessing the group process, and insuring that the needs and goals of the individuals within the group are being respected and not overlooked. In seeking the goals of each individual within the group as well as the goals of the group, it is essential that the worker utilize the group processes as the medium in which the therapy is provided and not fall into a situation where individual or joint therapy is provided within the group.[18]

However, on occasion the therapist will work directly with an individual or a dyad within the group around some particular part of the group process. But when this is done, the entire group process must be kept in mind and the individual work done in such a way that the group can benefit from it.[19] The role of the leader is to move the group to look at itself, to understand itself and to build on its own peculiar identity and strength. Within this process, the group will develop its own traditions, its own mores, its own individual styles of leadership and will assign various roles to different members of the group so as to deal with different components of the group phenomenon at different times.

In attempting to describe the various kinds of interaction that take place in the group, the Hollis sixfold classification discussed in the previous chapter is a useful tool for the therapist. From this approach the worker will support and encourage, will use the influence of his authority as leader and professional, will encourage the members of the group to share in a relevant way, and will lead the group and its constituent parts to reflective thinking about themselves, others, their past and present.

There is a particular kind of reflective thinking that takes place within group therapy that is different from the one-to-one modality. This takes place when the group members are helped to reflect on their own behavior in the group and on the process of the group itself. This ability to utilize the strong loyalties and sense of identification that can develop so quickly in a group strengthens its effectiveness. The group provides an opportunity for members to observe other human beings in interaction with each other and with themselves and to benefit from the opinions of the others about their own behavior and functioning within the group.

However, there is a particular difficulty for the therapist in a group setting that comes from the complex relationship patterns that develop within any functioning group. The number of possible subgroups and interrelationships in even the smallest group is immense and can seriously restrict or diminish the positive and growth-producing components of the total group. Complex as the relationship patterns are among members, the worker's own relationship patterns and responses must be watched.

There are several things that can happen to the group leader from the viewpoint of the group relationships. The leader can be cut off by the group and leadership assumed by someone else in an unplanned way. He can become involved in his own counter-transference reactions to a part of the group. Often a result of such transference reactions is that the group leader begins to look to the group for assurance and reassurance or even for protection from the reactions of portions of the group, if in his opinion the group is not doing well. Also, the group leader can align himself with some members of the group to preserve his own identity, to find support or to find protection from the negative reactions of some person in the group which he does not know how to handle.

Certainly one of the marks of North American society in the late 1960s and early 1970s was the increasing emphasis placed on group phenomena in a wide range of human situations, including the therapeutic one. Out of this interest in groups and in group therapy several approaches to group therapy emerged such as sensitivity groups, weekend marathon groups and intensive confrontation groups. Because of this broad diversity, there is no way as yet to talk about a specific form of group practice peculiar to psychosocial theory. If there is a difference it would revolve around the same comments that were made in talking about one-to-one therapy—that is, the direct and conscious use of the external world of the members of the group as a component of a group process. Thus the psychosocial therapist will make much use of activity groups in which select individuals will be helped to discover new components of their significant life in a way they had not experienced.[20] For example, a group of adolescents might be helped to find a variety of hitherto unknown entertainment resources existing within a community. On the other hand the psychosocial therapist may help the group make use of its strengths and identity to cope with a portion of their reality that has been stress-producing, such as problems with a landlord, with the neighborhood[21] or with a service or an organized system within their lives.

This does not mean that psychosocial therapists do not make use of a more therapeutically oriented type of group in which the members plan to look at themselves and try to bring about desirable changes in their personality structures within the medium of the group. Certainly personality change is frequently the goal for members of groups that we will establish. But direct personality change is not the only objective. In addition there will be a wide range of objectives dealing with various components of the psychosocial reality of the individuals involved.

Two additional comments about groups are relevant. For a few years some advocates adopted an economical viewpoint, arguing that more persons could be seen by fewer people with a resulting financial saving. Anyone practicing in a group format knows that this is not so, except perhaps in those situations where the purpose of a group is to give information rather than interpret the same material on a one-to-one basis, over and over again. Thus some agencies might use a group structure to give some general information to a group of persons interested in becoming foster parents.[22]

Groups provide a particular kind of treatment for a particular range of problems. The decision to use a group process should involve the nature of the client, assessment of the persons involved, the goals to which they are aspiring and their perception of the helping process.[23] That is, the choice to use groups should not be based on an attempt to get more productivity out of a therapist. However, if the decision to use groups is a correct one from the standpoint of finding the best way to help a client achieve his specified goals, then the use of groups can be economical. It is not economical in itself from the standpoint of saving worker time.

An additional comment needs to be made about the assumption that groups are started after the client has been in some form of individual or joint therapy. Although this still tends to be true in most cases, it is important not to overlook natural or pre-existing groups that may be the focus of first involvement. With a psychosocial understanding of the powerful influence of groups in normal healthy living, a rich medium is available in which to practice. Within the group work literature, many examples can be found of effective work with neighborhood groups, teenage groups, play groups, school groups, patient or inmate groups and a wide range of groups that have come together or been brought together for some societal purpose. In these instances the worker starts with the pre-existing group rather than working from a viewpoint that all groups have to be brought together in a special way in order to be considered therapeutic or helpful. Just as individuals can have problems in psychosocial functioning, so can groups. Thus a part of effective psychosocial practice includes working directly with such groups. In these instances the worker starts, as in all therapy, from an assessment of the strengths and limitations of the group, its objectives, its problems, its commitment to work on problems, and the resources available to achieve its goals.

In addition to working with pre-existing groups there are practice situations when a group process is used from the beginning of a case.[24] The assumption is made that the group is the modality of choice and the use of any other form of intervention would be seen as a variant to meet the particular needs of a client.

Hence agencies will sometimes utilize a group approach as part of the intake process or indeed as the intake process.[25] Here it is presumed that there are commonalities in the concerns, interests and processes around the beginning phases of the treatment process that are best dealt with in a group situation. For example, some child welfare agencies have utilized the group process to handle applications to foster or to give information to people interested in adopting or to train volunteers on how to function within a particular setting.[26] Certainly, where there is a commonality of requests for a particular service, a strong case can be made for using groups as the beginning format of service. The idea is that one can build on the strengths and common interests within the helping medium of a directed group. Nevertheless, it is more difficult to make a case for using groups in other settings where a wide range of clients apply for a service and where the intake worker has no knowledge about many of the persons they are to see until after first contact is made.

Families

One of the most significant, influential, and dramatic developments that has taken place in the general field of psychotherapy, particularly within the group of psychosocial therapists, has been the advent and expansion of family therapy over the past fifteen years. It is interesting to speculate on why family therapy developed with such an impact at the time it did. Part of this development seems closely related to psychology's re-identification with the social sciences and the growing understanding of the interconnection between the psyche and the social that was a part of this era.[27]

At the same time, there was growing disappointment with the one-to-one approach, especially in the child and family field, and a related awareness that other members of the family besides the identified clients were also involved in the dynamic process and could be ignored only at the risk of an unsuccessful case. It appears that apart from those few therapists who were practicing in highly selective office-based situations, most social workers of the psychosocial disposition included a wide range of family contacts in their-day-to-day activities with clients. Out of choice or necessity, much direct work with clients was being carried out with other members of the family present under the name of casework. Sometimes this was accidental, as when the worker visited the client in the home. More often, though, the decision to work with several members of the family was deliberate, even though for a long time we tended to refer to this type of activity as "collateral work," designed to assist us in our goals with the identified client, all the while failing to recognize that it was an essential component of the therapeutic process.[28]

Whatever the causes, by the early 1960s, an explosion of interest in family therapy among practitioners in all of the human professions could be observed.[29] An interesting sidelight to this development is that family therapy has not been claimed as the perogative of any one professional group. The leading names in this modality come from a range of professional groups. This phenomenon in turn has had a most important secondary effect on the helping professions in that it has served to greatly diminish the earlier jurisdictional disputes about who does and does not do therapy, about the difference between therapy and counseling, and so on.

In discussing family therapy in a psychosocial framework, an important distinction must be made between family therapy as a modality of practice and family therapy as an orientation to practice.[30] As a modality of practice, family therapy refers to that style of practice in which all the family members are seen together simultaneously in a formal therapeutic setting. The underlying basis of the therapeutic process and the medium of the therapy is the family process itself, the interaction between the various components of the family.

Family therapy as an orientation is of course basic to family therapy as a modality. However, there are some differences. Family therapy as an orientation begins with a psychosocial viewpoint that identifies the family as the most significant determinant of personality development and social behavior.[31] Thus to understand an individual, it is essential to understand the family and the various forms of interaction that have been and may still be taking place between the various segments of the family. The family as a theoretical orientation is not just a basis for understanding families, it is also an important, although not an exclusive, basis of therapy. Hence a family orientation to practice does not necessarily imply that all therapy will be provided in the medium of the family setting. However, whatever clusters of modalities are used, including family interviews, the essential point of orientation for all of them is the impact on the family and its members.[32]

Thus from a psychosocial perspective, the family is a critical source of influence; an influence that can be a source of help and development to family members as well as a cause of stress and malfunction.[33] Like the group, the family is seen as having a life of its own that is separate from and more complex than the lives of the individuals who make it up. Essential to an understanding of this specific identity is a concept from systems theory, homeostasis. Homeostasis means a state of equilibrium that is required by and achieved in a multifaceted system when all the various interacting and interinfluencing components and subsystems find a way of functioning that permits the system to achieve and maintain its identity.[34] Equilibrium is not a static state but a complex balancing of forces and influences. All systems that continue to exist achieve some form of equilibrium. This does not mean, though, that the equilibrium achieved is always the optimum situation. Families frequently achieve their homeostasis at the expense of the individuals who comprise the family structure.[35]

Related to the concept of homeostasis in families are two further points that are critical in family therapy. The first is that when a problem exists in one part of the family system, it influences the total family and must be accommodated by other parts of the family. But the converse of this is also true and of importance to therapy. Positive changes in any part of the system also influence and must be accommodated by the rest of the systems. This twofold influence requires that the total family must be kept in perspective in assessing change. It also means, though, that the total family need not always be treated directly.[36] Thus, for example, if therapy can result in a change in the parental system, this in turn can result in a diminishing of stress on the sibling subsystem.

The previous comments suggest that it is basic to the understanding of the family as a diagnostic and therapeutic entity, to see it as a system made up of a series of subsystems. A related set of concepts that also aid in understanding and modifying families comes from role theory. In a family, it is essential that the various roles played by each member be clarified as well as how such roles are enacted, supported, enforced and sanctioned within the family system.[37]

It is important to consider the family from the viewpoint of diagnosis, but it is also possible to view the family as the focus of treatment. With such a focus, the therapist works with the total family present.[38] As in group therapy, the principal goal or emphasis is to make use of the family's own system to bring about change. Initially, the family therapist is much more of an outsider to the family than the group leader is to the group. Thus, one of the first changes that takes place in family therapy is that the family has to accommodate itself to this outside person and decide to what extent he is going to be allowed to view the family and its inner actions. As the family accommodates itself, the therapist can learn much about how it functions or dysfunctions. This in turn can be used to help the family look at itself and begin to consider whether it wishes or is able to modify some of its behavior in a desired direction.[39]

As clients in joint interviews, so families in family therapy quickly begin to see themselves in a different perspective through the medium of the understanding and accepting feedback of the therapist. With an experienced therapist even in the first interview things happen in families that have not happened for years, if at all.

Many things that happen in a family interview are similar to those that happen in a group. Thus not only do individuals within the family learn by participating in the family interaction but they also learn by observing and listening.

The scapegoated or put-upon members in the family can get a hearing and be understood in a way that is often not permitted in the regular life of the family. Various subsystems of the family see and hear each other in a safe and open way that does not happen in the hectic day-to-day life of the family.

As the family gets to understand itself better, to become more comfortable with some of its patterned ways of behavior and increasingly uncomfortable about dysfunctional ways, the therapist can help the family begin to learn new ways of coping with problems, help individuals and systems within the family find new patterns of interaction and get new perceptions of themselves and each other than can help them to find a more satisfying life style.[40]

A surprising question that often arises for novice family

therapists is who is the family. A therapist might have a clear perception of who the family is but find out that this is not the same perception held by the family itself. This different perception can arise from both cultural and perceptual factors. Thus, for example, a family may take it for granted that a long-term boarder must be included in the family if the total family dynamics are to be considered. Or it may be equally clear to another family that an absent member—for example, an older sibling away from home—is not to be included in the family. Or perhaps there is a grandmother who lives distant from the family but who is nonetheless a key person in the family structure, whose functioning and influence need to be kept in mind if the total family is to be included in treatment.

Although for some therapists the question of who the family is may be a puzzling one, from a psychosocial viewpoint this is not difficult to answer. Whether an individual is or is not a part of the family becomes, for the therapist, not a question of the sociological definition of a family but rather a question of the extent of psychosocial influence a particular person exerts on the family. Hence a psychosocial orientation will alert a therapist to a range of significant others who might be considered part of the intimate family group.

In current practice, a new problem is beginning to emerge related to family constitution and definition. This relates to the increasing frequency of reconstituted families resulting from remarriage. To an increasing extent, we are meeting situations where a remarriage has taken place with children from both marriages being brought together into a new marriage. A further complicating factor is that the natural parents of some of the children often continue to have a significant role in the lives of the children, and their existence must be kept very much in view as one attempts to understand the dynamics of the newly constituted family. Clearly, this complicates assessment of the client interaction, and the question of which family is in treatment, who is to be included in the therapeutic process, and who is to be excluded becomes important. At times some therapists have experimented with bringing some of the absent parents into the therapeutic process to meet with those in the currently constituted family.

As even further complicating factor affecting discussions and considerations about family therapy comes from some of the new forms of marriage that came to the fore a few years ago and continue to exist, such as communal living and homosexual families. There has been little formal literature about working with these types of family structures but the same perception of systems, subsystems, interactions, and transactions can be brought to bear to understand the reciprocal effects of groups and individuals in their search for psychosocial maturity within a family structure.[41]

Awareness of the importance of family life for the development of individuals is of course not new to therapy. What is new is an understanding of how families are made up of several subsystems more diverse than the traditional systems of the parents and the children.[42] Such subsystems have to be understood if one is to get a full perception of the family and its dynamic life. Thus family therapy has enriched our understanding of the significance of early familial influences on development. In addition we have been helped to see that the influence of families on the developing individual does not stop in the early years of childhood but continues on through the maturing life of the individual and indeed is taken on into new families once an individual has left home.[43]

Not only has this richer perception of family led us to a more perceptive and precise understanding of individuals, it has helped us also to be more comfortable in risking ourselves in new modalities of treatment. This in turn has enabled us to expand our repertoire of techniques for helping families look at themselves and learn new behaviors to enhance growth and mutually satisfactory living within the values and cultures of the families concerned. The literature of family therapy has developed a vocabulary of its own about various techniques with which families achieve or frustrate their own goals or the goals of individual family members. It is not possible to cover all of this rich literature in this type of work, except to identify the general parameters within which family has been added to the repertoire of the psychosocial therapists and their practices.

In addition to enriching the treatment repertoire of the psychosocial therapist, family therapy and the conceptual basis on which it is built has affected all forms of treatment. As mentioned above, the enriched understanding of the diversity of the transactional effects on family life has added to our understanding of individual development which in turn has enriched one-to-one practice. Further, family therapy both as cause and effect has helped therapists appreciate and make effective use of systems theory, not only in working with families, but more importantly in building a conceptual bridge between other systems and subsystems in which clients function.

An essential outcome of the development that has not been fully appreciated is how this systems orientation has facilitated understanding of the desirability and possibility of therapists working in a variety of treatment formats, a development integral and essential to psychosocial therapy.

Community

The last modality of intervention within the psychosocial tradition is community work. Community work is intervention in which the community or some identified segment of it is the primary focus of treatment. Here, we are making a distinction between direct work with a segment of the community for its own sake and work with some segment of the community on behalf of an individual, family or group. This latter activity will be the subject of the next chapter.

A problem that has bedeviled the helping professions has been the tradition that separated persons within a profession or separated the professions themselves by the modality of the intervention. In social work there has been a tradition that identified some members of the profession as caseworkers, others as group workers, still others as family therapists and even more separate from these groups, those identified as community workers. An important thesis of this book and of psychosocial therapy is that it not only is possible but indeed necessary for individuals to possess multiple competencies to avoid an approach to practice that restricts one to a particular modality. Certainly there are differences between the modalities, but these have been overstressed and should not prohibit an individual from becoming competent in all of them.

In talking about community skills as a part of the armamentarium of the psychosocial therapist, I am not suggesting that a psychotherapist and a community organizer are or should be one and the same person. But neither are the differences between the community organizer and the therapist so vast that one must take a position on either one side or the other.[44] Although historically the clinical social worker always was sensitive to community structures and their effect on individuals, groups and families and attempted to change them, only in recent decades have we begun to see this aspect of society as a clear and distinct responsibility for practice that in itself is an area of concentration for the psychosocial therapist. In this discussion we are taking as given that community development and social action are and always have been integral components of the social worker's mandate. What is being addressed is some of the internal ways in which this mandate was assigned and discharged.[45] Thus we have moved from the point where the effect of the community on the client was a part of our diagnosis, through to the position where we would on occasion intervene in the community for the sake of the client, arriving finally at the place where now we will, when appropriate, actively make the community our client and seek to intervene and bring about change in some component of it.

This interest in community practice is an understandable development in psychosocial theory, with its strong orientation to understanding the interactions between an individual and his significant environments. From this commitment emerges a responsibility to understand communities, their strengths and limitations, their values and attitudes, their resources and lack thereof and their different impacts on various systems and subsystems. Thus the psychosocial therapist frequently identifies in his practice areas in the community structure where he, the agency, or groups of citizens can be helped to take appropriate action for change that will contribute to problem solving or enriched potential for living for particular groups of clients. Usually the deciding point between practitioners whose total practice orientation is to community development and those whose commitment is to individuals, small groups and families is a question of setting and emphasis. That is, the community activities of the clinician will comprise a lesser part of his practice than those of the person whose total commitment is to seek community change.[46]

Whatever the emphasis, whether it stems from a value perspective that puts greater weight on the importance of community change over individual change or from a personal preference, the responsibility for accountable practice remains the same. Thus in approaching the community the same triad of assessment, diagnosis, and treatment is followed. The practitioner must assess the strengths and limitations of the community and its resources. He must define what alternative approaches are available and eventually develop a planned cluster of interventive tactics.

It is essential for the community-oriented therapist to constantly attempt to sort out where the identified problems lie in systems, in the community or in individuals and how they reciprocally interact with each other. Mistakes can be made in either direction. The social worker could tend to see a problem that a client or a group of clients were experiencing as being based in their own inadequacies or personality deficiencies, and fail to take into account the debilitating effects of a pathological community situation. On the other hand, he could fail to see individual pathology if his perspective always tended to see difficulties as stemming from societal deficiencies. Thus having the community as a component of psychosocial practice helps to maintain the necessary balance between environmental and personality influences.

Two different styles of community practice can be identified within the psychosocial orientation. Both relate to the activities of the therapists themselves. If a therapist in his practice becomes aware in one or a series of cases of some facet of a community's structure that is counterproductive to optimal growth and development, he may directly seek to alleviate this situation. This can be brought about by his own efforts, those of his colleagues or by the setting in which he practices. For example, an agency might recognize a serious lack of day-care facilities for working mothers and seek to utilize its knowledge and skills in the community to bring about altered policies to facilitate the establishing of such services.

A second style of community involvement relates to activities on the part of the therapist to help a group of clients identify a problem and to take appropriate action to solve it. Thus a worker might help a group of parents concerned about a dangerous neighborhood situation to seek a solution through a series of social action activities. In such instances, the skill of the worker would be directed principally at fostering a group process toward an action strategy in a manner where the group itself is a source of strength for its members. In such instances the clients can find satisfaction in achieving a desired goal as well as in carrying out a joint process successfully. In the latter approach to community practice it is important that the therapist be most careful not to encourage the group to pursue goals that are not its own. He must avoid utilizing the group to help bring about community changes which he himself seeks.

The comments on community work are directed principally to the clinical practitioner for whom this book is written. In no way are they intended to downplay the importance of our colleagues whose total practice is committed to community work. Rather, a strong case could be made for the position that a psychosocial approach is an ideal theoretical basis from which to develop a full community practice. Indeed, it is this constant insistence that individuals, families and small groups must be understood within the context of their social realities and the various ways in which individuals act and interact with these realities that gives the psychosocial perspective its unique suitability for community work. By the same token, the psychosocial perspective tries not to lose sight of the fact that social situations and social systems are made up of interacting individuals. This concept should serve to remind the community worker of his responsibility to be aware of individuals and to seek to understand the personality dimensions of the social and community systems in which he or she becomes involved. Often in discussions between practitioners from a clinical orientation and those from a community orientation much stress is put on the difference in styles of practice and apparent values between the two professional groups. In these instances the similarity in perspectives and opportunities for mutual help that practitioners can give to each other are missed or understressed.

Summary

Psychosocial therapy is an open system. It is committed to the concept that a prime requisite of responsible intervention is knowledge of the range of change methods available to a practitioner and selection from these methods so as to best suit the exigencies of the presented situation.

It accepts and supports the idea that therapists will be more skilled in some clusters of interventive modalities than others. Nevertheless, it insists that modalities be seen as neutral resources and that the practice approach selected in a particular instance be chosen to fit the client, the assessment that is made of him and the planned objectives set through the life of the case. This chapter and the previous one have discussed very briefly the principal modalities in current practice. Whether these represent all available modalities or whether others will be developed in the future that can be called into use for the psychosocial enhancement of clients is an open question.

In no way do we presume that our discussion of these modalities is exhaustive. Entire books have been and will continue to be written about each modality in itself. Rather, the objective here has been to present an overview to show that the various modalities are indeed interconnected and that we should not attempt to divide therapists according to their skill in a particular modality.

Notes

1. Donald R. Bardill and Joseph J. Bevilacqua, "Family Interiewing by Two Caseworkers," *Social Casework* 45 (May, 1964), pp. 278–282.

2. John C. Sonne and Geraldine Lincoln, "Heterosexual Co-Therapy Team Experiences During Family Therapy," *Family Process* 4 (1965), pp. 117–195.

3. Robert MacGregor, "Progress in Multiple Impact Therapy," Nathan Ackerman, Frances L. Beatman and Sanford N. Sherman, eds. *Exploring the Base for Family Therapy*, (New York: Family Service Association of America, 1961), pp. 47–58.

4. Agnes M. Ritchie, "Multiple Impact Therapy: An Experiment," *Social Work* 5 (July 1960), pp. 16–21.

5. Alfred S. Friedman, "Co-Therapy as a Family Therapy Method and as a Training Method," in Alfred S. Friedman, eds., *Therapy with Families of Sexually Acting-Out Girls*, (New York: Springer Publishing Co., 1971), pp. 28–35.

6. David Rubinstein and Oskar R. Weiner, "Co-Therapy Teamwork Relationships in Family Psychotherapy," in Gerald H. Zuk and Ivan Boszormenyi Nagy, eds., *Family Therapy and Disturbed Families*, (Palo Alto: Science and Behavior Books, 1967), pp. 206–220.

7. Celia B. Mitchell, "The Uses and Abuses of Co-Therapy as a Technique in Family Unit Therapy," *Bulletin Family Mental Health Clinic*, Jewish Family Service," (1969), pp. 8–10.

8. Grace L. Coyle, *Group Work with American Youth: A Guide to the Practice of Leadership*, 1st ed. (New York: Harper and Bros., 1948).

9. Clara A. Kaiser, "The Social Group Work Process," *Social Work* III, 2, (1958), pp. 67–75.

10. Michael S. Olmsted, *The Small Group* (New York: Random House, 1959).

11. Alexander P. Hare, Edgar F. Borgatta and Robert F. Bales, eds., *Small Groups: Studies in Social Interaction* (New York: A. A. Knopf, 1955).

12. Paul Glasser, Rosemary Sarri and Robert Winter, *Individual Change Through Small Groups* (New York: Free Press, 1974).

13. Ann Murphy, Siegfried M. Preschel, and Jane Schneider, "Group Work with Parents of Children with Down's Syndrome," in F. J. Turner, ed., *Differential Diagnosis and Treatment in Social Work,* 2nd ed., (New York: Free Press, 1976), pp. 468–475, reprinted from *Social Casework* 54 (February, 1972), pp. 114–119.

14. Ralph Kolodny, "A Group Work Approach to the Isolated Child," in F. J. Turner, ed., *Differential Diagnosis and Treatment in Social Work,* 2nd ed., (New York: Free Press, 1976), pp. 36–47, reprinted from *Social Work* 6 (July, 1961), pp. 76–84.

15. Marvin Hersko, "Group Psychotherapy with Delinquent Adolescent Girls," in F. J. Turner, ed., *Differential Diagnosis and Treatment in Social Work,* (New York: Free Press, 1968), pp. 89–96, reprinted from *American Journal of Orthopsychiatry* 32 (1962), pp. 169–175.

16. Sheldon D. Rose, "A Behavioral Approach to the Group Treatment of Parents," in F. J. Turner, ed., *Differential Diagnosis and Treatment in Social Work,* 2nd ed. (New York: Free Press, 1976), pp. 119–131, reprinted from *Social Work* 14 (July, 1969), pp. 21–30.

17. Robert F Bales, *Interaction Process Analysis: A Method for the Study of Small Groups* (Chicago: University of Chicago Press, 1950).

18. James A. Garland, Hubert E. Jones and Ralph Kolodny, "A Model for Stages of Development in Social Work Groups," in Saul Bernstein, ed., *Explorations in Group Work,* (Boston: Boston University School of Social Work, 1965).

19. Dorothy R. Freeman, "Counseling Engaged Couples in Small Groups," *Social Work* 10 (October, 1965), pp. 36–42.

20. Helen Northen, *Social Work with Groups* (New York: Columbia University Press, 1969).

21. Gisela Konopka, *Social Group Work: A Helping Process* (Englewood Cliffs: Prentice-Hall, 1963).
22. William Schwartz and Serapio R. Zalba, *The Practice of Group Work* (New York: Columbia University Press, 1971).
23. Grace Ganter and Norman A. Polansky, "Predicting a Child's Verbal Accessibility to Individual Treatment from Diagnostic Groups," *Social Work* 9 (1964), pp. 56–63.
24. Vera Dillon, "Group Intake in a Casework Agency," *Social Casework* 46 (January, 1965), pp. 26–30.
25. Albertina Mabley, "Group Application Interviews in a Family Agency," *Social Casework* 47 (March, 1966), pp. 158–164.
26. Gayle M. Gilchrist, James and Donna M. McFadden, "Group Intake in a Child Guidance Clinic," *The Social Worker* 36 (1968), pp. 236–243.
27. Isabel L. Stamm, "Family Therapy," in Florence Hollis, ed., *Casework: A Psychosocial Therapy*, 2nd ed. (New York: Random House, 1972), pp. 203–227.
28. Sanford N. Sherman, "Family Therapy," in F. J. Turner, ed., *Social Work Treatment*, (New York: Free Press, 1974), pp. 457–494.
29. Ivan Boszormenyi-Nagy and James L. Framo, eds., *Intensive Family Therapy: Theoretical and Practical Aspects* (New York: Harper & Row, 1965).
30. Donald R. Bardill and Francis J. Ryan, *Family Group Casework: A Casework Approach to Family Therapy* (Washington, D.C.: Catholic University of America Press, 1964).
31. Irene M. Josselyn, "The Family as a Psychological Unit," *Social Casework* 34 (October, 1953), pp. 336–343.
32. Ross V. Speck, "Family Therapy in the Home," in Nathan W. Ackerman, Frances L. Beatman and Sanford N. Sherman, eds. *Exploring the Base for Family Therapy*, (New York: Family Service Association of America, 1961), pp. 39–46.
33. Gerald Handel, ed., *The Psychosocial Interior of the Family: A Sourcebook for the Study of Whole Families* (Chicago: Aldine Publishing Co., 1967).
34. Nathan W. Ackerman, *The Psychodynamics of Family Life: Diag-*

nosis and Treatment of Family Relationships (New York: Basic Books, 1958).

35. Nathan W. Ackerman, Frances L. Beatman and Sanford N. Sherman, eds., *Exploring the Base for Family Therapy* (New York: Family Service Association of America, 1961).

36. Group for the Advancement of Psychiatry, *The Field of Family Therapy* (New York: G. A. P., 1970).

37. Norman W. Bell and Ezra F. Vogel, eds., *A Modern Introduction to the Family,* rev. ed. (New York: Free Press, 1968), pp. 628–649.

38. Virginia Satir, *Conjoint Family Therapy: A Guide to Theory & Technique* (Palo Alto: Science and Behavior Books, 1967).

39. Frances H. Scherz, "Theory and Practice in Family Therapy," in Robert W. Roberts and Robert H. Nee, eds., *Theories of Social Casework,* (Chicago: University of Chicago Press, 1970), pp. 219–264.

40. Jay Haley, comp., *Changing Families: A Family Therapy Reader* (New York: Grune and Stratton, 1971).

41. Irene Fast and Albert C. Cain, "The Stepparent Role: Potential for Disturbances in Family Functioning," *American Journal of Orthopsychiatry* 36 (April, 1966), pp. 485–491, reprinted in F. J. Turner, ed., *Differential Diagnosis and Treatment in Social Work,* 2nd ed. (New York: Free Press, 1976), pp. 676–682.

42. Joan W. Stein, *The Family as a Unit of Study and Treatment,* Trova K. Hutchins, et al., eds. (Seattle: University of Washington School of Social Work, 1970).

43. Charles King, "Family Therapy with the Deprived Family," *Social Casework* 48 (April, 1967), pp. 203–208.

44. Charles F. Grosser, *New Directions in Community Organization: From Enabling to Advocacy* (New York: Praeger, 1973).

45. George Brager and Harry Specht, *Community Organizing* (New York: Columbia University Press, 1973).

46. Eileen Younghusband, *Social Work and Social Change* (London: George Allen and Unwin, 1964). David R. Hunter, "Social Action to Influence Institutional Changes," *Social Casework* 51 (April, 1970), pp. 225–231.

Chapter 7

Significant Environments as Components of Treatment

As has been emphasized in the preceding chapters, a key tenet of psychosocial therapy is that the total spectrum of growth-facilitating factors that are part of healthy functioning must be addressed in the therapeutic process. Man's behavior is multi-influenced, and therefore an understanding of man must be mul-tifaceted and a helping process multidimensional. Such an approach to practice results in an open system, one that attempts to engage the interaction of the full range of the stresses and supports in a person's psychosocial reality with a view to drawing on the strengths as a basis for effective intervention. In this multifa-ceted approach the therapeutic relationship is predominant, but there are other influences in a client's life that facilitate change and that can and should be addressed assiduously in the planning and organization of a therapeutic strategy.[1]

Significant Others

Beyond direct work with the client, one of the most important resources of treatment to which the social worker has traditionally turned is the network of significant others in the client's life.

Unfortunately, this reaching out to others is not always viewed as a component of treatment but rather as a source of information and support. The experienced therapist, however, is well aware that even in the process of gathering information, change can take place that can benefit the client. For example, interaction with a significant other may bring about a new perception of the client by the other person that can result in helpful change. Getting to know the significant others in a client's life can help the therapist discover new resources in persons that he can draw upon in a manner that is helpful to the client. The operational word is *significant,* and it is this aspect of significance that makes the process a potentially helpful one. When we are dealing with persons important in a client's life, it is not possible to remain only in an information-gathering role. The very process of engaging a part of the client's personal network in the therapeutic situation can, when properly used, become a component of therapy and not just a further source of information about the client.[2] So intense and interconnected can this process become that at times it is difficult in the life of some cases to answer the question, who is the client?[3]

In previous chapters, the essential influencing nature of the therapeutic relationship has been stressed. In addition, our understanding of the therapeutic process has developed from our awareness of the power and influence of positive human relationships in everyday life. It is important not to forget this. For just as we try to influence clients through the process of the therapeutic relationship, so too is the client being influenced by other relationships. It would be naive not to take into account those powerful influences in a client's life that may be supporting, enhancing, neutralizing or diminishing the influence of our direct therapy.[4] From both a diagnostic and a management viewpoint it is important that we become aware of the client's network of relationships and be prepared to intervene in it when necessary.

From the viewpoint of diagnosis, getting to know some of the persons important to a client can help us to form a clearer perception of the client and to clarify or test out our own impressions as we get to see how he is seen by others. In the same way, we can get a clearer appreciation of the nature and extent of the various influences on the client's life as we see the persons who exist in his day-to-day world. Knowledge and contact with significant others may also give us access to resources in the client's life of which we were unaware.

This component of the client's reality can also be helpful therapeutically. We can utilize the client's significant others not only in knowledge-building but also in a more direct way, by altering the influence of a person or a group of persons on the client in a manner that can be helpful to him.

As was suggested in our discussion of family therapy, it was our experience with the risks involved in leaving other members of the family out of treatment that helped us to appreciate the importance of working with the total family. By extension, these same ideas can be applied to the client's significant network. Thus for some clients it may well be that we are moving to a point where our therapeutic approach will be directed in part to working with a significant component of the client's persons network. This will be a type of therapy somewhere between family and group therapy but drawing on the same theoretical basis and interventive strategies.[5]

Clearly, the decision as to when it is appropriate and necessary to deal with significant others is a difficult one for the therapist. The economics of practice dictate that we take a parsimonious approach. Nevertheless, we know that there are many cases in which it is important that we move in this direction, whether it be with a close friend, a concerned neighbor, a working associate, or a member of a group of special importance to the client. In discussing this component of intervention, there is always a danger that one's comments may be misinterpreted as supporting an approach to practice that would ignore the client's right to participate in these decisions. It is understood that when we choose to move out of the clinical setting into the client's milieu, this is done with the client's involvement and permission insofar as possible. Again, the very process of negotiating this decision and interpreting our recommendation can be a form of growth for the client as he reflects about himself and others.

A further aspect of this decision is the question of confidentiality and the potential risks to the principal client as we engage others in the process. This must always be taken into account, for there is the constant danger that we have misassessed the role of others in the client's life and that engaging them in the process could be detrimental rather than facilitating.

OTHER PROFESSIONALS

Various members of our own or related professions provide another component of a client's persons-network.[6] Here, we are talking about those interactions with others that are a part of the therapeutic process rather than our day-to-day administrative contacts. There are two distinct functions related to this interprofessional aspect of the therapeutic endeavor. The first relates to those instances in which we ask a member of our own or another profession to take over full responsibility for the management of a case. This type of referral is made either because of some particular need of a client or because of a specific skill and competence of the practitioner to whom we refer. Referral can come about in a variety of ways. It may turn out that the original request to us was inappropriate. Having decided this, we steer the client to the appropriate source, as a part of our function of knowing and locating resources. Some area may emerge that requires the specialized knowledge and competence of another professional, be it physician, clergyman, lawyer, teacher, or any of the many other professionals with whom we may work.

In addition, there are any number of reasons why a client may not be able to work with us. Here, professional responsibility requires us to transfer such a case to someone else with whom the client may be more comfortable. This situation is not one that happens frequently in the practice of an experienced therapist, but it can and does occur. Troubling as this may be to our professional self-esteem, it is important that we discuss this openly with the client and follow through with an appropriate referral.

A second group of situations involves those instances where we will still remain the principal therapist but where there is some particular component of the client's bio-psychosocial need that can be best dealt with by someone else. Thus we may ask a psychologist to conduct a psychological assessment for us, a physician to deal with some physical situation, a lawyer for consultation on a legal problem and so on.

The manner in which we work with other professionals will depend on several factors. The first of these is a conceptual one. If we support the idea that improvements in any component of the client's psychosocial reality will contribute to enhanced functioning, then the use of other professions will be seen as an important aspect of therapy. This use of others will also be influenced by the knowledge we have about the skills and competence of our own colleagues and other professionals. This is an area in which we can make serious mistakes if we do not keep an open, inquiring mind about the abilities of other professions and current developments in these fields. We must constantly guard against distorted stereotypes about the competence, attitudes and skills of other professions.[7] Knowledge of our clients and their needs is clearly an important component of our decision. Thus we must understand both the clients and their personality structures as well as their psychosocial situations. Further, we must perceive the interconnections between the many components of their psychosocial reality to assess adequately the importance and necessity of getting help in some of these areas.

An important part of this knowledge of clients is to know their values and attitudes toward particular kinds of help, settings, and professionals. Failing to understand a client's views about a member of the medical profession, for example, can well result in creating stress for a client that need not have been incurred.

There are, of course, risks in this aspect of practice. There is the risk that we can become so busy about the client's significant subsystems that we complicate rather than facilitate his life by involving him with many persons and services. This risk has to be weighed against the counterbalancing therapeutic principle of the interconnectedness of the ways clients function within many subsystems. As improvement takes place in one aspect of the client's life, it frequently has the effect of bringing about a transactional improvement in other aspects of his life; thus he rarely needs direct assistance in all components of his life.

A further consideration of this aspect of practice is a sociological one relating to the professions and their interconnection. We know that patterns of interprofessional referrals vary from setting to setting and probably from one area of the country to another. For some professionals it is more acceptable to refer a client to one profession then another. The decision to refer is not always based on client need but may be complicated by status issues. Without attempting to specify all of these patterns (which indeed would be an interesting area of research), there do seem to be different perceptions of the importance of different professionals to some social workers. For example, there seems to be a tradition in social work supporting referral to a psychiatrist rather than to a psychologist, and both of these are preferred to making a referral to a clergyman. It may well be that we have evidence about the individual merits of different members of a profession, and this will affect our decision. But we must be on guard to ensure that we avoid stereotypic patterns of behavior in this area.

A component of interprofessional interaction is the issue of ego-autonomy. At times it is hard for us to accept the idea that we are not able to help a client in a particular area. We may feel uncomfortable and experience a sense of personal failure if it is necessary to refer the client to another profession. Thus we might underuse a professional resource that the client needs and at the same time lower our standards of professional practice.

Perhaps an even more critical risk for the therapist is the tendency to see all types of referral as essentially administrative activities rather than as therapeutic ones. Certainly, there are some components of the referral aspect that are principally administrative. There are clients who need a specific type of service that is provided elsewhere, and the referral is very routine. It would be naive to argue that every referral is by definition a growth-producing action and hence therapeutic. Indeed, at times the referral process can be a negative one; it can create stress for the client; it can reinforce his sense of being rejected; it can result in his having to share his concerns and problems with many people; it can create unnecessary drains on the client's resources so that the very referral becomes counterproductive. Nevertheless we should not underestimate the extent to which the location of another helping agent or service can be helpful to a client. Properly assessed, appropriately interpreted, and efficiently implemented, referral can be a sign of approval to a client, a support for his search for growth, a testimony to his ability, and in itself a facilitating activity.

PARAPROFESSIONALS AND VOLUNTEERS

In addition to working with members of other professions, the psychosocial therapist draws on the skilled resources and commitment of a group of persons who are not members of an identified profession but nevertheless are close to and identified with the therapeutic endeavor. In the history of social work therapy, there has always been a strong tradition of utilizing volunteers as adjuncts to programs and services. Particularly in the last decade there has been increased understanding and awareness of the therapeutic influence of such persons and many more attempts to enlist their aid in the therapeutic process.[8] This has helped us move to the point where we no longer see such persons as distant helpers who perform only socializing and service roles. Rather, we are now aware that many of these individuals form special relationships with clients of a helping and enabling nature that is frequently beyond the scope of members of a formal profession. The very strength and position of the therapist, which make him effective in the formal therapeutic role, can limit his effectiveness in other roles. With a richer perspective on what elements constitute help, we have seen a wide range of helping roles developed around the skills, interests, and commitments of volunteers and persons without full professional education.

We have seen how such persons can be helpful to clients in crisis and can aid them in dealing with the often overwhelming bureaucratic complexities of completing an application for service. We have seen how they can provide relief to a family, taking over all or part of the household management or reducing anxiety by sitting with a client waiting for service at a clinic. This list, of course, is not exhaustive. It serves only to remind us of the many roles that can be played by others, roles that when properly understood and built upon can not only provide services to clients but provide them in a way that facilitates their sense of autonomy and growth.[9]

No doubt we have at times been overenthusiastic about the contributions such persons can make. Some have suggested that untrained persons are more effective than trained persons and that therefore professionalism is by definition antitherapeutic. They agree that humanity would be better served by letting the indigenous worker or committed volunteer take over.

Our professional responsibility should lead us to find a middle way. Of course it is essential that we not underestimate the extent to which these persons can be of assistance to the therapeutic process, but it is just as essential that we not fail to see the very real limitations of these paraprofessional roles.[10] At times we have asked such persons to take on responsibilities that are far beyond their competence, with detriment both to them and to the clients they are attempting to help.

The most effective use of such persons depends on the diagnostic skill of the therapist. Such a diagnosis must include the needs, strengths, and limitations of the client as well as the strengths and limitations of the volunteer or paraprofessional and, most importantly, the potential fit or lack thereof between them.[11]

A further component of this process is the client's sociocultural reality. For some clients, having a volunteer assist in completing a pre-interview information sheet or sit in on an interview would be seen as helping and facilitating. On the other hand, some clients would see this as an unwarranted intrusion on their privacy. Some clients would want the assistance of a person with whom they can identify, either from the viewpoint of class, ethnicity, or culture to help deal with some component of reality.[12] Others treasure very much the privacy of dealing with problems and situations on their own, without anyone else being involved. This must be understood to make the helping process as effective as possible.[13]

Substitute Care

Psychosocial therapy in social work has a long experience in the use of planned changes in the physical environment in which a person lives as a feature in facilitating growth or dealing with need.[14] As has been suggested, a restricted perception of therapy tends to exclude this aspect of professional service from the therapeutic process and views it more as an adjunct. The expanded view of the past two decades of the interconnectedness of all components of therapy has helped us form a clearer perception of the essential nature of substitute care.

This is a vast area of practice and it is not possible here to describe and analyze all the forms and components of substitute care that are utilized in the helping professions. Nor is it possible to evaluate the assets and risks involved in this type of care for different groups of clients with different needs.[15] For example, all social workers are aware of the terrible dilemmas involved in decisions about such things as fostercare for children versus remaining in the parental home, of hospitalization of the mentally ill or community daycare, of institutionalization of our aged citizens or helping them remain in their own homes. As with so many components of professional practice there have been fads that at times have bordered on fanaticism related to the advantages and disadvantages of different types of substitute care.

There have been times in history when most forms of institutional care were seen as the preferred way of dealing with some types of problems. At other times, any form of institutional care by definition was deemed harmful and thus to be avoided.

With increased understanding of systems and the interconnections of subsystems in the past two decades much progress has been made in understanding the limitations of various forms of substitute care, as well as in making the most beneficial use of these potential resources.[16]

In the past one hundred years vast amounts of wisdom and experience have been accumulated concerning the use of substitute care, particularly in the child welfare field.[17] The use of adoption, of short- and long-term foster care, and the various kinds of institutions for children are well known. In addition there is an extensive network of daycare, overnight, weekend, and long-term rearrangement of a child's living conditions to meet particular needs and goals.[18] Rather than argue the need for various types of care, as was necessary in an earlier day, we are now at a point where we are better prepared to individualize the care required by each client. Hopefully, we are also at a point of maturity where we do not see substitute care of any kind as a resource that by definition is either bad or good. We presume that we will always need a vast network of various types of substitute care that can be used for the enhancement of some clients.[19]

As with other components of practice, the theoretical tenet from which the psychosocial therapist approaches the use of substitute care is that a person's immediate living milieu is a highly significant component of his perception of himself, his ability to function and his ability to make maximum use of his growth and development potential. We also know that any change in an accustomed lifestyle, regardless of the extent to which the change is seen as facilitating growth, is in itself a source of stress and indeed frequently of crisis. Thus all decisions involving alteration of a client's physical milieu must be carefully weighed from the viewpoint of potential gain and anticipated stress and harm. This type of decision creates many dilemmas for the practicing social worker, related to his uncertainity about the impact of the new

living conditions on a client, the availability of the kinds of
settings one would hope for, the compromises one is prepared to
make to meet the wishes of the client and the need to weigh these
factors against risks to the client if he stays in his present situation. There is the concomitant question of the extent of backup
resources that may be required if the decision is that the client
stays where he is.[20]

Very often it is this question of the suitability of a client's
present living arrangement that puts the social worker in conflict
with society. We have all experienced community pressure to
move someone, be it an aged person, a handicapped person or a
child, out of a particular physical environment, which in our view
is adequate and growth producing. We also know that our indi-
cators of a sustaining home environment might not be the same as
society's. We may be prepared to trade off physical inadequacies
for a sustaining psychological environment. We may be prepared
to leave an older person in a less than adequate physical situation rather than expose him or her to the stress of a move and
life in a nonstimulating institutional situation. We also all have viv-
id memories of children moved from their own homes for reasons
that seemed necessary at the time but for whom all we had to offer
was a long series of foster placements that provided little more
than substitute physical care. Such placements frequently added
little to the psychosocial development of the children and may
have permanently damaged their sense of themselves and their
relationship to their own families or caused other repercussions
which may carry on for decades or even generations. But we also
know that there have been many successful placements that have
been able to undo many scars of earlier traumas or that have fostered potential growth and enhanced maturation. In addition, professional scars remain from the decisions we have made to leave
children in a home where they have later been badly abused or even
killed by their parents.

A current phenomenon in practice, especially in urban practice, has been a much more flexible use of substitute care than
that to which we have been accustomed. This includes the idea of

persons moving in and out of various types of substitute care to deal with particular needs. It seems to be a more acceptable and useful approach to this treatment resource than our earlier approach of an either/or situation. For example, many physically and mentally handicapped individuals have been able to remain in their own homes with the availability of occasional temporary care in a community centre either to deal with a crisis in their own lives or to permit families and significant others to be away from them for awhile.

Other Services

Just as other people can be included in the therapeutic process, so too can the skillful use of services. In this context the word "services" is used to describe that wide range of societal resources whose purpose is to make available the various material goods and human know-how of society to persons who do not have easy access to them, either through the marketplace or from personal or familial resources.[21] The existence of a complex of such services has become an integral component of society, essential to its smooth running. Although the social services in general are frequently the target of popular criticism; it is usually only a limited aspect that is being criticized. For the most part, people forget that in society as we know it there are few if any persons who are not the recipients of some type of such services. Even the psychosocial therapist may take such social services for granted and thus underestimate their importance in the therapeutic process.

It will not take much imagination to be reminded of the impact that a lack of such services and goods can have on adequate psychosocial functioning. We know how emotionally crippling it can be when one is unable to find employment or housing, how frightening it can be when we cannot get medical care or adequate food and clothing. We also know, on the other hand, how finding a job can result in an improved self-image; how being able to get access to medical care can help a person be more effective; how having a proper place to live can improve one's security as a person. It is this awareness of the connection between access to goods and services and adequate functioning that motivates the therapist to place heavy emphasis on knowledge of a client's socioeconomic status and the service and resource network available or not available to him.[22]

The therapist will also draw upon the network of goods and services available in the social system as a part of the therapeutic process. For example, anxiety in a client can be reduced through a therapeutic relationship, through a group experience, or through association with a volunteer. But it can also be reduced through medication, through the provision of financial help, or through the location of some needed resource.[23] Which of these methods will be most efficient will depend on the nature and source of the anxiety and on the skill of the therapist in selecting the most efficient and appropriate method of relieving it. No one method is intrinsically of more value or utility than another. Thus, it is just as wrong to provide therapy when the client needs money as it is to provide medication when the client needs a close personal relationship.

This latter point has been mentioned several times in this book. For the psychosocial therapist all methods of influencing clients are considered of equal importance and are used according to the needs of the client as perceived by the therapist. He does not cling rigidly to an a priori ranking of the different kinds of therapies, which leads to the overuse of some and the underuse of others.[24]

Professional Roles

There is a range of roles and skills required to make the most effective use of various features of the client's significant environment. As was mentioned earlier, too often these resources have been seen as of less benefit than direct therapy and thus much less attention has been given to them in the practice literature. This in turn has led to an oversimplification of the skill, knowledge, and diversity of roles required in this aspect of practice. This deficiency has also resulted in less interest being focused upon them. In addition we have made the mistake of oversimplifying the helping system by referring to this whole aspect of practice as "working with the milieu" or "utilizing of social services." Such terms can bring about a tendency to see these systems as unidimensional or uncomplicated. This again has led to a minimization of the complexity of therapy and an underappreciation of the richness of these resources.

Florence Hollis has thoroughly addressed this question and has made a major contribution in identifying the various roles that are played by the social worker in working with the community resources network.[25] In examining the roles listed by Hollis and expanded by further observations from practice, we can see them as dividing into three groups. First, there is the function of the therapist as the *source* or *creator* of resources.

Frequently, the social worker is called upon to serve as a source of the service or resource that is utilized in the helping process. Frequently the worker has direct access to a range of resources and services that can be called upon as needed. The range and extent of these resources will vary depending on the nature of the agency or setting. Thus, for example, an agency might be able to provide direct financial assistance, temporary housing, homemaker services, institutional care, volunteer services, recreational services or various kinds of home or day care services. Few agencies offer only psychotherapeutic services; indeed, almost all settings have some form of resources or services that are directly available to the practitioner to help the agencies better serve its clientele within the objectives of the agency.

There is also another role in which the therapist serves as the source of services, a role that is indeed more demanding. This is the role of the social worker as the creator of resources.

The importance which some practitioners accord to this role and the skill with which they carry it out will vary from worker to worker depending on their need for it and their commitment to it.

In many cases, the perceptive diagnostician will discover a gap in the client's psychosocial armamentarium which cannot be met within the agency or in the existing network of the agencies. The worker is then faced with the challenge of creating or developing the needed resource. We are not talking here about the worker as someone capable of creating things that do not exist. Rather, we are talking about the skillful and perceptive utilization of the therapist's knowledge of persons and situations to helpfully find a needed resource. This might be as simple as arranging to have a neighbor assume the role of a temporary homemaker when this service does not exist, or as complex as finding a source of financial help on a long term basis for someone not eligible for structured or established programs.

The second group of roles performed by the therapist in the provision of goods and services relates to those activities in which the therapist helps the client make use of existing services outside of the agency. This is done in two ways. First, there is the role of the therapist as the *locater* of services. In this role, the worker seeks out needed resources and makes them available to the client. Again, this is a role that has frequently been over-simplified and thus often down-graded. It frequently requires a sensitive appreciation of the client's needs and ability to make use of some services and to match these up most efficiently with available resources. No doubt at times this is an uncomplicated, nondramatic, everyday function as simple as looking up a partic-ular service in a region's directory of services. Uncomplicated as this role is on some occasions, it is often perceived as a most im-portant service by the recipient of the service or by an interested other. I have been surprised in my own practice to discover that some people have tended to see us as miracle workers simply because we have been able to find a service that was well-known to us, but unknown to them. Where I think we have failed clients is in being less than well informed about the diverse existing services in some communities. For too long we have relied on a limited knowledge of services that does not truly reflect the exist-ing situation.

In recent years, the range of available services, both private and public, organized and free-floating, has multiplied. At the same time, such services are frequently changing, so that most directories are outdated before they are even published. One development that originally arose as a service to individuals and communities but has fast become a resource to professionals is existence of community data banks and information services. There is no doubt that this type of service is going to expand and become more sophisticated as time goes on. There is already a complexity of such services which could best be handled by use of computer programs. By using available computer technology, a wide range of information about services, resources and any idiosyncratic or routine data one might need to know could be stored in such manner that data could be instantly available to practitioners through agency-based terminals. Thus the therapist could describe for the computer the cluster of resources needed and any special features that these resources should have and then have a search made by the computer. This type of storage, search and retrieval could easily be updated any time new data became available. The advantage of a computer program is that such updates need to be done only in one place and then would be available to all users. In addition, such a storage system could save many hours of frustrating searching and thus in an indirect way could ensure the availability of highly individualized services to clients on a short-term basis. This in turn provides a new resource that can help clients in their search for optimum functioning.

Important as the therapist's role as locator of appropriate resources is for a client, there is the equally important role for him of *enabler,* or, the one who sees to it that the client can make adequate use of the resource. There are some instances where the client is unable to make use of a community resource because of some deficiency in the service itself. These situations will be discussed below. Here we are talking about those skills required by clients to make use of resources adequate in themselves. Usually included here are the responsibilities of the therapist to know or ascertain the requirements of the service to which a client is being referred. Little comment need be made here except to point out that it is professional irresponsibility not to follow through with the appropriate data or information required by an agency so that a client is thus delayed or unduly deprived of a requisite service. But in informing a client of a service, it is important that a therapist attempt to ascertain the client's attitudes and perceptions about the service that is being considered. Sometimes there is full acceptance of the need and desire for a particular service, at other times there can be a major emotional, perceptual, or cognitive block about this step in the helping process.

Because of the potential complexities of a referral process the enabling task of the therapist may require him to take on a wide range of roles. In some instances the therapist may need only to gently reassure and encourage, while in others he may need to spend time helping the client work out a long-held negative attitude to some form of help or resource. Once again the diagnostic skills of the therapist are essential. Thus, a thing as simple as helping a woman follow through on the need for a medical referral can assume a variety of forms. We may talk to the woman about it, sit with her while she makes a phone call, make a phone call for her, write a referral letter, send along a volunteer with her or even go ourselves and sit and talk for her. Each of these decisions can be important for the autonomy and comfort of the client, and the extent to which we are sensitive to the client's situation will ensure that we find the fine line between being facilitative, overprotective, or insensitive.

The third cluster of helping roles comprises those activities in which the worker intervenes to help the client to use resources from which the client may be excluded for a variety of reasons. There appear to be three separate but related roles to be identified under this heading. The first of these is the role of *mediator*. Under this category would be included those activities of a therapist aimed at using his knowledge, influence, and skill to make a resource available. This may include interpreting the needs of a client to persons in a setting where his situation may not have been fully understood. An example of this would be to contact a family agency to establish the eligibility of a client who has been refused service. This is a not uncommon situation in our complex service networks. In other instances, the social worker may speak for the client when the client is unable to represent himself or cannot cope with the stress of an application, such as a frightened teenager unable to ask for medical help. A worker may use his knowledge or influence to facilitate the availability of the resource by a letter or visit to a setting requesting service for a client.

The second role in this general category involves a more aggressive use of the mediator role. This is a role that was popular in the literature of the late 1960s and early 1970s and has come to be called the *advocate* role. In this role, the therapist deliberately chooses to intervene for the client to obtain access to some denied role or service. In this type of intervention, the tactics of confrontation, challenge, insistent pressure, and demand are combined with diplomacy and knowledge of systems manipulation. As mentioned earlier, a few years ago this role almost took on the nature of a cause. At that time there was a strong commitment to the need for heavy-handed pressures being put on some services, resources, and systems, access to which was being denied to some individuals and groups.[26] This role of active intervener is a complex role and frequently requires collaboration with other disciplines such as the law, politics, journalism, or community activism.[27] It is also a risky role for both the client and the therapist because aggressive activity can of course create or result in counteraggression and when used in an unskillful manner can harm not only the client for whom the worker is advocating but also other clients who may come after them.

A final role in this subcategory is the role of *broker*. This is a role that appears to have been overlooked as a specific role in much of the literature. Frequently, the practitioner in psychotherapy finds that the client is suffering from an overdose of resources in helping persons rather than a lack thereof. Thus we frequently find in our practice, persons who are active within a large network of helping persons and situations. Clearly there are some very complex psychosocial situations that require a network of community persons and agencies to become involved. In such networks each constituent member may well have a clear mandate and be able to offer something to the client. But because of the inevitable possibilities of confusion, conflict and counterproductive activities, there is the need for a planning, coordinating, facilitating role to be assumed by someone to negotiate the spectrum of helping persons and to ensure that the client is not forgotten. It is important that in such situations, the multifaceted efforts are orchestrated for the good of the client. Obviously, this is a complicated and sensitive role because frequently no one person or agency has a clear mandate to be the coordinator or broker and thus to assume this role. In such instances, tact, skill, persistence, diplomacy, maturity, knowledge of systems, persons, and the sociology of the professions is required. Yet when this role is recognized and skillfully implemented, a rich new resource becomes available to clients, that of integrated structures and agencies, rather than the new stress of having to cope with the complexities and at times competing activities of several subsystems.[28]

In this discussion of the spectrum of roles that a therapist may be asked to perform, it is important that they be viewed as possessing equal worth and not be looked at from a hierarchical perspective. The key variable in choosing an appropriate role is the client's need and sought-for resource. Certainly, economy of time and effort is also a factor; the potential impact on the client, the worker, the setting, and other clients must all be taken into account.

Work with the significant environment is a complex and diversified component of psychosocial therapy. As has been suggested several times in this chapter, it has been a component of practice that has been taken for granted, oversimplified, underused, and misused. When properly understood and utilized, it is an aspect of therapy that gives the richness and diversity that is the mark of psychosocial therapists. It is a fullness that can make a therapist a more efficient, resourceful, and diversified helping person.[29] To make adequate use of these resources, the diagnostic skill of the worker is critical. It is that diagnostic skill that leads to the understanding of the needs of the client, the range of available resources, the potential effect of different resources on the client and his needs and objectives. It also leads to a careful selection of a therapeutic role that will best bring the client into contact with the resource system. The worker must constantly work at understanding the client and his personality structure, but at the same time he must aim to expand his knowledge of the client's significant environments and the resources that are included therein in order to draw appropriately on them for the good of the client in his search for psychosocial health.[30]

Notes

1. Richard M. Grinnell, Jr., "Environmental Modification: Casework's Concern or Casework's Neglect," *Social Service Review* 47, 2 (June, 1973), pp. 208–220. Max Siporin, "Situational Assessment and Intervention," *Social Casework* 53 (1972), pp. 91–109.

2. Ross Speck, "Psychotherapy of the Social Network of a Schizophrenic Family," *Family Process* 6 (1967), pp. 208–214.

3. Lydia Rapoport, "Social Casework: An Appraisal and an Affirmation," *Smith College Studies in Social Work* 39 (June, 1969), pp. 213–235.

4. Allen Pincus and Anne Minahan, *Social Work Practice: Model and Method* (Itasca: F. E. Peacock, 1973), chaps. 10 and 11, pp. 194–246.

5. Carol H. Meyer, *Social Work Practice: A Response to the Urban Crisis* (New York: Free Press, 1970).

6. Rita Lindenfield, "Working with Other Professions," *The Social Worker* 35 (1967), pp. 175–181.

7. Margaret M. Heyman, "Collaboration between Doctor and Caseworker in a General Hospital," *Social Casework* 48 (May, 1967), pp. 286–292.

8. Donald H. Schlosser, "How Volunteers Can Strengthen Child Welfare Services," *Child Welfare* 48 (1969), pp. 606–612.

9. Joel S. Bergman and Dilman Doland, "The Effectiveness of College Students as Therapeutic Agents with Chronic Hospitalized Patients," *American Journal of Orthopsychiatry* 44 (January, 1974), pp. 92–101.

10. Lillian D. Cain and Doris Epstein, "The Utilization of Housewives as Volunteer Case Aides," *Social Casework* 48 (May, 1967), pp. 282–285.

11. Dorothy G. Becker, "Exit Lady Bountiful: The Volunteer and the Professional Social Worker," *Social Service Review* 38 (1964), pp. 57–72.

12. Charles F. Grosser, "Local Residents as Mediators between Middle Class Professional Workers and Lower-Class Clients," *Social Service Review* 40 (March, 1966), pp. 56–63.

13. Pauline R. Coggs and Vivian R. Robinson, "Training Indigenous Community Leaders for Employment in Social Work," *Social Casework* 48 (May 1967), pp. 278–281.

14. Catherine Collier, "Fostering—Yesterday, Today and Tomorrow," *The Social Worker* 37 (1969), pp. 221–226.

15. Joan Mannheimer, "A Demonstration of Foster Parents in the Co-worker Role," *Child Welfare* 48 (1964), pp. 104–107.

16. Genevieve M. Thompson, "Foster Grandparents," *Child Welfare,* 48 (1969), pp. 564–568.

17. Virginia Hikel, "Fostering the Troubled Child," *Child Welfare* 48 (1969), pp. 427–431.

18. Marion M. Mitchell, "Transracial Adoptions: Philosophy and Practice," *Child Welfare* 48 (1969), pp. 613–619. Robert M. Chazin, "Day Treatment of Emotionally Disturbed Children," *Child Welfare,* 48 (1969), pp. 212–218.

19. Man Keung Ho, "Problems and Results of a Shift to Heterogeneous Age Groups in Cottages at a Boys Home," *Child Welfare* 50 (November, 1971), pp. 524–527.

20. Ruth Vietes, Rosalyn Cohen, Renee Riens and Ruth Ronall, "Day Treatment Center and School: Seven Years Experience," *American Journal of Orthopsychiatry* 35 (January, 1965), pp. 160–169.

21. Elizabeth Stringer, "Homemaker Service to the Single-Parent Family," *Social Casework* 48 (February 1967), pp. 75–79.

22. Jean M. Grant and Lucille Pancyr, "The Teaching Homemaker Service of a Welfare Department," *The Social Worker* 38 (May, 1970), pp. 19–24.

23. Shirley Bean, "The Parents' Center Project: A Multiservice Approach to the Prevention of Child Abuse," *Child Welfare* 50 (May, 1971), pp. 277–282.

24. Max Siporin, "Social Treatment: A New-Old Helping Method," *Social Work* 15 (July, 1970), pp. 13–25.

25. Florence Hollis, *Casework: A Psychosocial Therapy*, 2nd ed. (New York: Random House, 1972), pp. 139–163.

26. Robert Sunley, "Family Advocacy from Case to Cause," *Social Casework* 51 (June, 1970), pp. 347–357.

27. National Association of Social Workers, Ad Hoc Committee on Advocacy, "The Social Worker as Advocate: Champion of Social Victims," *Social Work* 14 (April, 1969), pp. 16–22.

28. Fortune Mannino and Milton F. Shore, "Ecologically Oriented Family Intervention," *Family Process* 11 (1972), pp. 499–505.

29. James K. Whittaker, *Social Treatment: An Approach to Interpersonal Helping*. (Chicago: Aldine Publishing Co., 1974), pp. 5–22.

30. John Cumming and Elaine Cumming, *Ego and Milieu: Theory and Practice of Environmental Therapy* (New York: Atherton Press, 1962).

Chapter 8

The Setting and the Sponsor as Components of Practice

Because the psychosocial model of practice stresses the importance of the interaction of people and environments as a critical determinant of human behavior, it is understandable that the place in which the therapeutic process is enacted is a subject of interest. In a general way, this component of psychotherapy has always been understood to be important. But the specific nature and extent of the influence have been considered only occasionally in detail, in part, no doubt, because of the previously mentioned tendency to overemphasize the therapist–client interaction and the concomitant overgeneralizing and underplaying of other aspects of practice.

The importance of the place in which therapy is provided received careful scrutiny from Helen Harris Perlman in her 1957 book, as it did from the functional school in an earlier day.[1] The growing acceptance of social systems theory in the 1960s also provided a framework out of which new interest, awareness and understanding of setting as a component of practice developed.

Among therapists, attitudes about the importance of the setting of therapy range along a continuum. At one extreme is the viewpoint that holds that the process is the critical variable, while the setting is a necessary but noninfluencing factor. Such a viewpoint of course emphasizes the competence of the therapist and the essential importance of the relationship. At the other extreme is the viewpoint that the setting is far from a neutral factor and cannot be ignored, that all of us are influenced by the settings in which we discharge our various social roles and that therefore the setting in which therapy takes place must be viewed as an important part of the therapeutic process and hence should be examined, evaluated, and utilized in a planned way. The latter viewpoint is inherent in the psychosocial tradition.

Evidently there are role implications inherent in the setting that can influence the therapeutic process, as for example when the therapist is a probation officer, a representative of a child protection agency, or a member of a mental health team. In a similar way systems theory helps us to understand more precisely the impact of the setting on treatment. For example, interdepartmental conflicts, status struggles, or professional rivalries can dramatically influence the impact of setting on treatment. But in addition to these there are historical factors that give the setting of practice a specific emphasis. Unlike some other professional activities such as medicine and law which originated in an entrepreneurial mode, social work emerged from a tradition of social commitment. It was out of the social concern of different groups in society that the original concept of professional help in psychosocial matters emerged. Hence, the various activities of helping persons were made available to individuals and groups through the medium of organizations rather than individual entrepreneurs. Even though the direct provision of the service was in the person-to-person mode, the helping person was functioning as the agent of a group or an organization operating with a mandate from at least a segment of society. The settings in which services were offered became known as agencies, meaning the place where society's agents operated. This term is still used and still retains elements of its original meaning. This same phenomenon influenced the development of some health services and the consequent emergence of the term clinic, although the history of the health service delivery system is more complex since it includes the strong intervening component of the autonomous fee-for-service practitioners.

The very existence of agencies where some form of help or service is available manifests a form of societal commitment. We are taking as given that the establishment of such services was positively motivated, even though from today's perspective we might not support or approve of the motives. Social service agencies thus emerged out of society's commitment to be available at some times and in some situations to at least some of society's members. By definition such agencies exist at least as symbols of society's desire to help and at best as potential agents of help.

But this type of agency-administered social commitment to society's members was clearly not universal or all-encompassing. The sponsorship, nature, extent, and focus of the help reflected a variety of interests, motivations and reasons whereby some constituents of society wanted to help some other constituents. Thus resulted over the decades the overwhelmingly complex network of persons, places, services, settings, programs, and sponsorship that make up the psychosocial service system of most urban-based societies.

This diversity, it has been claimed, results in overlap, duplication, gaps, and inefficient and uneconomical use of resources and personnel. In a pluralistic society, efficiency is not always a prime value or even a desirable one. Indeed, diversity and duplication are more often a virtue than a fault. This is not to suggest that society and its members should not attempt to increase efficiency, reduce unnecessary or undesirable duplication and make a richer use of its resources. But in so doing, attention must be given to the advantages of the diversity and the nature and format of the helping network. Too often, this question gets translated too quickly into a value issue before a full examination of the possible advantages that diversity may bring to the therapeutic process.[2]

Earlier, it was mentioned that the existence of visible helping agencies is in itself symbolic of a societal helping orientation. Individuals and groups in society find security and comfort in the fact that resources exist even if they themselves do not make use of them. Most social workers have seen many examples of how the very existence of health plans or unemployment insurance programs has been of tremendous support to marginally employed parents for whom the spectre of heavy medical expenses or unemployment could have been in itself debilitating and stress-producing, resulting in restrictive and inhibited behavior that in time could have been the source of further problems. Clearly, as mentioned earlier, before overstressing this point, further data are required. At this time, the assertion being made is that the diversity of visible services is an important component of society's helping milieu.

In examining the impact of the setting on therapy, there is a danger of overgeneralizing by presuming that all settings are the same. This is obviously not so. The aforementioned historical comments that identify the multi-origins of agencies attest to such differences. The reality and magnitude of the differences and the absence of data make it difficult to discuss the topic in anything but an impressionistic way. What is certain is that settings are different, that they thus have different influences on the therapeutic process, and that responsible practice demands that this factor be critically examined and further studied.

There are seven general areas related to the service setting that have a potential influence on the therapeutic process. Each of these will be discussed separately for convenience. In reality they are interconnected, both in fact and in the way they are perceived by the client.

Legitimacy

An important component of any therapeutic endeavor is the client's perception of both the need for help and the acceptability of seeking help in a particular format or setting. In a society such as ours, where similar kinds of help are given in different places, the nature of setting is an important influencing factor for many clients. For example, a client can receive marriage counseling in a mental health setting, a court, a family agency or a church-sponsored service. In some cases each of these settings may influence the client's involvement in treatment.

Sponsorship

One of the principal factors related to service difference is the sponsorship under which a service operates. Until recently it has been customary in discussing sponsorship to divide agencies into one of two major categories, private or voluntary agencies and public agencies. The basis for this dichotomy is related principally to the source of funding and the nature of the agency's mandate. In recent years, the funding of agencies has become much more diversified and the distinction between the two types based on funding source is much less clear, even though the nature of the mandate is still important. But even if this dichotomy is now less discrete, the diversity of agency sponsorship remains wide. Agencies are sponsored by all levels of government, local, state or provincial, federal, and international; by specialized branches of government; by industry, churches, foundations, and voluntary organizations of many kinds; by special interest groups; by groups representing particular segments of society; and lastly, by private practitioners. This range reflects the pluralistic nature of society and is interesting from this viewpoint alone, but it also reflects different preferential and attitudinal responses of society that in turn affect the presumed legitimization of some services for some groups. Thus, some clients in particular regions in a country may be much more comfortable in using an existing service knowing it is sponsored by the federal government; in other parts of the country or in other countries, this sponsorship would make the service suspect by definition. Some clients can comfortably approach an agency that is church-sponsored where they could not go to a public agency. For example, a Catholic client concerned about an unwanted pregnancy may prefer to receive help from a setting with a clear position on abortion. A veteran of the armed services may only be comfortable in seeking financial assistance from a department of government related to former servicemen and shun all other services as unacceptable forms of welfare. In each case where sponsorship differs we can assume that the sponsorship itself will have different impacts on various groups of clients. This in turn undoubtedly affects the availability and utility of services to some societal groups.[3] What we do not know except in an impressionistic and fragmentary way is the extent and variation of these influences.

Primary and Secondary Agencies

Earlier in the social work literature a distinction used to be made between primary and secondary settings. With the growing diversification of funding, programs, and staffing this distinction has become less relevant. Nevertheless, there is a range of variation in settings for services that extends from agencies that exist on their own to those that exist as a part of some other institutional setting. Among the former are family agencies or children's aid societies; among the latter, social work departments that are part of a court, a hospital or an industrial setting.[4] Once again, experienced practitioners know that this aspect of setting affects some clients' perception of the legitimacy of the service. For some groups, for example, the hospital and its clinics are a legitimate place to seek help for a child exhibiting some problem of functioning because it can be seen as health-related. For others, a child welfare agency or family agency would be preferred. The court in some segments of society is a place to be feared and shunned while in others it is a place to which one can turn for help in solving various family problems.

Location

Over the years, agencies have learned that frequently it is important to house services in a particular geographic location to enhance their perceived legitimacy for some groups. Thus, the fact that a service is located in a particular neighborhood or that it operates from a recognized structure, such as a church basement or a school, affects the way it is perceived. The location can give a message of concern and interest to some groups, just as it can give a message of distance and rejection to others.[5] In recent years, this sensitivity to location has been reflected in the establishment of mobile clinics, storefront agencies, street workers, and other neighborhood-based services.[6] These shifts in location give tacit recognition to the reluctance of some societal groups to make use of existing services perceived as unacceptable to them when operated outside their immediate milieu.

Values

From a psychosocial perspective, one of the principal arguments for a rich diversity of helping settings is the fact that individuals in society have different perceptions about the acceptability of some kinds of problems and the range and source of their solution. This stems principally from differences in values and attitudes, a key concept in psychosocial understanding.

Several times in these pages emphasis has been placed on this question of the value orientations of clients. It has been mentioned that values affect how persons perceive the world and others in it, how they view the nature of man and his destiny and how they come to terms with the the need to face and solve problems.[7] Knowledge of values in the therapeutic process itself is important; it is also a key variable in understanding the effect of the setting on therapy. Because of these value differences, some clients will be able to relate to certain settings more easily than others, depending upon their view of significant others and their perception of and comfort with the process of seeking help outside their own significant network.

This perception of the helping process can be a critical component in therapy and must be respected in clients. Thus sectarian agencies, ethnic agencies and neighborhood services, and public and private agencies all seek to respond to the particular needs of particular people at particular times. This does not mean that all clients are motivated or influenced by the setting or sponsorship of a service. There are many clients who are not unduly upset when a desired characteristic of a helping system is not present, and there are others who are equally comfortable in any setting as long as competent help is received. But the planners of service must be sensitive to the value orientations of particular groups of clients. They must also assess the strengths and flexibility of these needs and when appropriate respond to them. These comments are not meant to imply that diversity by definition enhances the therapeutic quality of service. This would be naive. We must not let our own value perceptions of how services should be structured interfere with tested experience and accumulated data.[8]

This latter point is raised to remind ourselves that we too as a professional group have value sets that may influence our perception of how services are to be offered. Traditionally, many therapists have believed that services that were voluntary in nature, community-supported and free from government identification were preferable and more acceptable to clients. This attitude may well reflect some of the inherent values of professionals more than it reflects a generalized analysis of what different groups of clients think.

In a similar way, there is a current value within society that stresses austerity, reduction of duplications, efficiency and demonstrated effectiveness as being the highest priorities. Clearly, these are laudable goals to which most responsible practitioners would commit themselves. Where mistakes may be made is in the method used to translate such commitment into practice. An example may be the risk of overstressing the importance of reducing duplication and overlap. Here an important yet frequently omitted distinction is to be made between duplication and unnecessary duplication. Certainly, all agencies do some things in common and thus to some extent duplicate some services and resources. But over and above this inevitable duplication of staff, equipment, resources, and personnel there is the possibility of unnecessary duplication of service. This is a much more sensitive question not easily answered and certainly not answered by exhortations only. Part of the answer lies in a careful and sensitive understanding of the perception of clients, actual and potential, as to where services can appropriately be sought. It is not the purpose of this work to attempt to define what is or is not unnecessary duplication. It is sufficient to underscore the complexities of this question since it involves perceptions, attitudes, and mores of clients, professionals, and community groups, funding bodies, and available resources.

Private Practice

There is a final point to be made about the sponsorship of services as a component of therapy that has become of increasing importance in the past decades. This is the development of private practice, a new phenomenon for social work with its deep-rooted tradition in societally mandated services.[9] Growing numbers of therapists are setting themselves up either alone or in small groups to provide their services in an entrepreneurial mode. This provides a new alternative to individuals seeking psychotherapy. Although there were strong criticisms made a few years ago of social work colleagues who chose to practice in this way, this has now passed. Such groups as the International Council for the advancement of Private Practice made a major contribution in bringing acceptance to this type of practice.[10] Although there are still serious problems related to the funding of private practice through public or private insurance programs, these eventually will be solved, as well as the more complex ones of setting, maintaining, and enforcing standards of competence and ethical behavior.

This development, especially in North America, is of relevance to the psychosocial tradition. The ideas expressed in the first part of this chapter about the necessity of the setting being amenable to the attitudes, values and perceptions of the client are equally relevant here.[11]

There are groups in our society for whom it is particularly important that therapists exist who are not attached to any formal agency, be it private or public. Such persons rightly expect that this type of help will be available in a setting that is acceptable to them. One of the earlier criticisms of private practice related to its alleged elitism.[12] That is, it was posited that the movement would draw off senior colleagues to serve the more affluent members of society. This was considered to be a denial of our commitment to the disadvantaged. This certainly has not happened. Not every member of the profession is interested in or capable of the loneliness and solitary autonomy of private practice. In addition, private practitioners find that even given the higher fees of private practice, their clients cover a wide portion of the socioeconomic spectrum. This phenomenon has been a surprise both to practitioners and critics of private practice.

An interesting secondary function served by private practitioners has been to provide useful service to agencies. That is, many agencies have found it most helpful to take on private practitioners on a fee-for-service basis to carry a segment of the agency's services. In addition to providing direct service to clients, who otherwise might have had to be placed on waiting lists, agencies have found that the productivity and effectiveness of private practitioners have been high and indeed an economical way of providing services. Some agencies have even found that the interview count of part-time practitioners and full-time colleagues is not all that different. This phenomenon may well give indications of a different structure for many agencies of the future. Thus a system could be imagined where there would be a core staff of resident therapists and a much larger contingent of private consultants with different responsibilities to the agencies.

Accessibility

A second area related to the effect of setting on therapy is accessibility. A particular service may be effective and resourceful but it is of diminished utility if it is not accessible to the clients in fact or in perception. There are three aspects to the question of accessibility.

PHYSICAL

A particular problem facing many services in current society is the question of their actual location in a community. We know all too well that the geographic location of any community resource will influence who will or will not use it. Thus the section of a city in which a service is offered will attract some clients and deter others. The variables that are operative here relate to such things as neighborhood reputations, transportation, parking, security, and convenience. We judge the community resources and services that we use partially from the perspective of their location in the community. Commercial enterprises spend large amounts of time and resources in the search for a location that will best achieve the objects of the enterprise and attract the persons they hope to serve. Certainly it is not being suggested that agencies embrace the same values that motivate commercial activities. Rather, the point is that much time and effort need to be put into analyzing the psychosocial impact on the client of the location of services. Frequently, it seems that decisions about location are made on the basis of economics, rather than on an understanding of a neighborhood and the effect of location on the helping process.[13]

TIME

A second component of the helping process that is related to accessibility is time. This can be viewed in two ways. First, there is the question of when services are available. Too often, services have been planned to suit the convenience of the agency rather than the needs of clients. A frequently stated position is that if a client "really" wants help he will find a way to get to the agency during its regular hours. Hopefully, this viewpoint is changing. Society itself is becoming more open, the concept of the work week more varied, and criticism is growing of the simplistic notions that have been held about motivation and the ability to conform to a 9–5 working day. All of us have learned that many clients can make much better use of community resource when it is available at a time that fits their life schedule, where they can be free from concerns about an irate boss, lost time on the job, children coming home from school, baby-sitting fees, and daily tasks left unattended. In our own lives we know how difficult it is to function in some roles when we are under other pressures. So, too, with our clients. Agencies are responding to this, although complaints are still heard in many communities that it is extremely difficult to find a social worker after five and even more difficult to find one on a weekend.

Much has been learned from the crisis theoreticians about the importance of making the right kind of help available at the right time. This has had a dramatic impact on the increased availability of services at other than regular office hours. Again, it is not being suggested that all services must be available at all times to all people but rather that optimum use be made of time as a component of psychosocial reality.

There is a second component of time related to accessibility of services. This refers to the interval between a request for service and the actual availability of service. Here, the point is to provide service when the client can make best use of it. Having a client wait for an appointment has often been justified on the basis of testing motivation. Also, a long waiting list is seen as proof of an agency's reputation. Crisis theory and related experiments in short-term treatment have demonstrated that for some clients a critical factor related to their ability to move effectively into a therapeutic situation is the timing of the process. We know from systems theory and the concept of homeostasis that individuals find ways of dealing with problems one way or another, even if in a detrimental manner. If they must find them without treatment, they may then be more comfortable in living with the compromise than in facing the new disequilibrium required to invest in a helping process at a later date. Certainly, there are situations met in practice that need not, and indeed should not be responded to immediately. Similarly, others require such immediacy. But the therapist's decision about timing must be a diagnostic one rather than an attitudinal one. For example, I have frequently found it useful to wait a few days before seeing clients who wish to discuss what appears to be a momentous life decision. Often when I see them on the scheduled day they have changed their mind. This is a common occurrence with university students who have decided to terminate their studies. On the other hand there are those critical situations related to such things as imminent suicide attempts or risks of child abuse that require immediate intervention at any time of day or night.

CLIENTELE

The third factor related to the impact of accessibility on therapy is the question of whom a particular agency or setting serves or who is perceived as being served. There are two components to this question. The first relates to the target group or groups an agency may wish to serve and the second to whether a particular service is perceived as being available to all who appropriately may wish to use it.

The history of the helping professions in our society is the history of a dramatic attempt to recognize the particular needs of various societal groups and to shape services in a manner that appears to accommodate and serve such groups. Thus we have agencies that aim at various ages of clients, others whose clientele is made up of people with particular ethnic or racial origins. There are agencies set up to serve a particular religious group and others to serve clients who have a particular status in society, such as that of veteran, immigrant or ex-offender. Lastly, we have agencies whose services are set up to deal with clients in a particular geographic area or a particular part of the community.

It is not our purpose here to argue the merits of targeting by client type but only to point out that there are indeed clients who are more able to involve themselves in a helping process when the service is aimed specifically at them and because of this factor an additional variable is added to the therapeutic perspective.

Secondly, we have agencies that focus on a particular kind of service or methodology rather than on a particular kind of client. For example, there are agencies that provide group services, individually based counseling services, homemaker services, recreational services, daycare services or referral services, to name only a few of the many ways in which agencies have chosen to restrict what they do. In so restricting itself, an agency is recognizing that the range of psychosocial problems experienced by clients varies as does the particular cluster of helping resources needed for such clients. In the ongoing search for the most efficient and effective way of bringing services to people, some agencies have found it useful to provide a restricted package of services. Implied in this pattern of planning is the belief that there is an advantage in bringing together in one center the accumulated expertise, wisdom, and resources needed to provide a particular service.

There is no doubt that when the particular kind of service required by a client is identical with the services offered by an agency, this is an effective manner of providing a high quality service.

Thirdly, some agencies provide services to persons with a specific diagnostic problem. This is a more common basis of differentiating service than the focus on a particular activity or expertise on the part of the agency. There is a long-standing tradition of this type of service delivery, for it is closely related to the historical origins of the profession. As mentioned earlier, helping systems in our society emerged from a variety of interests, values, commitments and concerns from different segments of society. And so at varying times in our history, there have been groups committed to the importance of family life, others more concerned with the protection of children, still others concerned that the problems of alcohol received specific attention and on and on through the many different identified problems and clusters of problems that have resulted in the development of specific agencies and the provision of services to a particular group of clients.

Certainly over the decades, various interconnections have developed as new problems have been identified and the interest and need for services in other areas have lessened or disappeared. Nevertheless, this range indicates the interest and ability of society to respond to particular problems overlooked by other groups or to problems which required a special kind of focus or service. Here again, it can be emphasized that when a group is recognized as having a particular problem and society shows itself ready to respond to it, the very existence of the agency manifests concern to a client and can provide help in a manner that is efficient and sensitive.

But in addition to setting up services targeted to specific groups or problems, there is the aforementioned question of perceived accessibility. This is a complex issue, replete with values, biases, rhetoric, and strong emotions. In recent years, the network of helping services has been frequently accused of prejudice against certain societal groups. Without presuming to exhaust the list of grievances, services have been said to be middle-class oriented, racially biased, religiously biased, ethnically biased, and politically biased. Agencies have been accused of being against long-haired youths, homosexuals, draft evaders, the aged, the physically handicapped and drug users. Undoubtedly, some of these alleged barriers to agency access did and do exist, but more often they are misperceptions rather than facts. Nevertheless, whether valid or not, these very misperceptions keep some individuals from getting the help they need and make others uncomfortable or untrusting in seeking help. Because this reluctance does exist, attention must be paid to what kinds of persons do not use a particular service, as well as to those who use it.[14]

Policies and Programs

The third area in which the setting affects therapy relates to the actual policies and programs an agency provides. Hopefully, services that are provided to society are helpful and enabling to the people served. But to achieve this the planners of services must be sensitive to the needs of particular groups of the community in order to assess the strengths and flexibility of these needs and when appropriate to respond to them. An equally important responsibility is to be aware when needs have changed so that appropriate alternative programs can be introduced. Thus, some immigrant groups have needed specially planned services at different times in history. Often, such needs are temporary and service can be terminated once the process of community identification has taken place. In a similar way, the highly visible youth movement of a few years ago required special attention. At that time, it was necessary to set up programs that provided services to youths unwilling to trust or make use of services offered in a traditional setting. The current demands for certain family planning services and services to women are further examples of perceived special program needs.

Frequently, when a need for change in the service delivery system has been demonstrated, it does not necessarily follow that a new service is required. Often what is required is flexibility in an existing service to permit it to alter its structure or format to accommodate the new need. In recent years, many examples were seen of dramatic efforts to make services more sensitively available to the poor and to minority groups by such things as setting up neighborhood offices, making use of volunteers, training of indigenous workers, and active outreach programs.[15]

Traditionally, voluntary agencies have been considered the type of setting most capable of adjusting their services and structures. These agencies have indeed responded quickly to new needs by changing their location, personnel, boards, staff policies, programs and even their names. But it is incorrect to think that only the private agency is flexible. In recent years, some public agencies at all levels have been equally able to innovate in an imaginative and highly flexible way.

But this is not always so. At times, the oft-repeated maxim that therapy must "start where the client is" comes into conflict with agency functioning. Earlier, it was argued that a rich diversity of specifically targeted services in a community is in itself a facilitating factor, communicating concern and interest. But often this very diversity can be antitherapeutic, especially if the client does not get directly to the agency or clinic that can serve him most appropriately. Instead, a client may get caught up in a wearisome and at times hurting referral network. It requires a reasonably well-integrated person to invest the time and energy required to move through several intake interviews or applications before he finds the setting or service that is needed. Most practitioners do seem to be sensitive to the potential dangers of an inefficient, complex and poorly managed referral process. But we know that not infrequently clients do give up or withdraw from seeking the help in which they have been ready originally to invest themselves.

At times, with the best of intentions, agency policies and practices can operate against the client in other ways. Earlier mention was made of the fact that services are not always provided at a time when a client can make best use of them. Similarly, agency policies may require detailed histories to be taken before service can be given, a referral from another profession, or various lengths of waiting periods; they may refuse to make home visits, or agree to see people only in groups, or only if the husband or wife or parent is present, or only for a set number of interviews, and so on through the many components of agency practice that can influence the ability of some would-be clients to receive the therapeutic help they need and want. Obviously, it is easy to criticize agency practices; this we all do well, often without fully appreciating the basis on which some policies have been developed. But on the other hand, it is clearly evident that not everything an agency does is necessarily for the therapeutic good of the client it purports to serve. Often, policies are adopted for the convenience of staff or formulated out of enthusiasm for some new and un-tested approach to practice. Often such policies have not been assessed from the client's perspective. A psychosocial orientation to practice stresses the importance of the setting and is strongly committed to the necessity of always including this component of a client's reality in the diagnostic process.[16]

Resources

No agency or clinic has unlimited resources and this limits in a general way the quality of psychosocial help that can be given. Indeed, many agencies have only minimal resources with which to function. Surely, one of the unrecognized triumphs of our society is the way many helping agencies have been able to offer excellent services from a minimum of resources. But over and above this reality of our non-Utopian existence, there are aspects of an agency's resources that can have important implications for the effectiveness of the services that are provided. The extent to which resources as adjuncts to therapy are seen as either impor-tant or as unnecessary frills will stem from a perception of the potential effect on psychosocial functioning of man's material world.[17]

Obviously, the kinds of facilitating resources that can be utilized will vary widely depending on the nature of the setting and the services that are offered. For example, many agencies have made exciting and imaginative use of volunteers, who in addition to providing much needed services can also convey to clients concern and interest. Volunteer drivers, persons to assist with application forms or sit in on interviews, home visitors and baby sitters can also be facilitative.

Another important resource often underused in some settings is the cadre of administrative and maintenance staff. One only needs to sit for awhile in the waiting room of some agencies to observe the amount of interaction that takes place between the agency receptionist and waiting clients. Usually, it is one of the secretarial staff to whom a client first speaks. If indeed the helping process does begin at this point, then it is essential that this first contact be a facilitative one. I have often thought that some of our most effective crisis managers have been our unrecognized receptionists and switch-board operators. But the reverse is often true.

In addition to the resources of personnel an agency can provide, there are material resources that can assist the therapeutic task. Again, this varies from setting to setting but a few examples will suffice. Several times in this book, reference has been made to information as a component of healthy functioning. Many of our community agencies could greatly assist their clientele by making information about the agency available in pamphlet form or providing answers to frequently asked questions or giving information about other community resources. There is a myriad of information available about many community services that could easily be provided to clients in as simple a way as a pamphlet rack in a waiting room. More imaginative ways could and have been devised, once this is seen as an important resource.

Other facilitating resources that can be important are such things as an easily accessible telephone for clients, parking facilities, play space for children, washrooms, interesting reading and also writing materials in the waiting room and food services when appropriate. These are just a few of the ways in which an agency can convey interest, concern, respect and encouragement to assist its clientele in their involvement in the therapeutic process.

Professional Competence

An essential component of the helping process is the quality of the professionals who are providing, planning, and administering the service. Throughout these pages, it is presumed that the therapist is a fully trained, broadly educated, highly skilled, well-integrated, ethically responsible person. Nevertheless, because of the history of our profession and current community practices, some additional comments seem appropriate. In an earlier chapter reference was made to the use of adjunctive personnel as a component of service. A psychosocial orientation stresses that we are all differently influenced by the significant others in our lives. Applying this to a therapeutic process underscores the advantage of using a wide spectrum of persons with varying kinds and levels of skills in achieving the client's psychosocial goals. Most professions have accepted this and in the last two decades there has been a dramatic increase in both levels of training within professions and a whole host of new professions, paraprofessions and occupations in the helping services. It is not relevant to this work to discuss the complex, sociological, professional, political, and administrative challenges this diversity creates. Here, it will suffice to underline the dual responsibility we have as therapists in this matter. On the one hand, we must not disparage the tremendous resources that people who are not fully trained professionals can provide; on the other hand, we must not fall into the trap of giving them responsibilities and setting expectations that they cannot meet. Apart from the stress this creates for them, the risk to clients is immense and not to be minimized.

Further, a strong responsibility of all therapists in current practice is to engage in a continuous process of professional development. A client coming for help should expect that he will receive the best that the current state of professional development can realistically provide.

A further question that must be addressed is the client's part in choosing a therapist. Although professional norms support the concept that similarity of competence is related to similarity of training, we know that wide variations exist among professionals related to levels and types of competence as well as to individual differences. We know there are colleagues more skilled in one practice method than another. We know there are therapists able to work better with one age group of clients than another. We know also that there are therapists who are effective with some types of problems or cases and ineffective with others.

Given the reality that some therapists can work more effectively with some clients, it follows that some clients will relate more effectively to some therapists. This raises the important question of matching in the provision of therapy. That is, to what extent is it important that both clients and therapists have some say about the process of matching? The concept of matching does not necessarily imply a commitment to similarity between client and worker but rather a shared perception of being able to work together effectively. It is interesting that we often accommodate in a covert manner to therapists' wishes and perceptions about the types of case with which they feel they are most effective, although rarely has the reality of this been tested. We frequently make decisions about the kind of therapist that is best for a client. Hence, we decide that there are times when for either diagnostic, sociological, political, or value reasons, a female therapist, a black therapist, an Italian therapist, a Catholic therapist or a physically handicapped therapist is best for a client.

But rarely does the client have a say in choosing his therapist except when he seeks out a particular therapist as a private practitioner. Occasionally at intake, some clients mention a particular preference for a man or woman therapist or a black or white therapist and at times we are able to accommodate them. One of the factors influencing the relative lack of choice has been our tradition of offering services as agents of society's objectives and values, usually in a format where fees are not involved. Thus, there has been less commitment on the part of the services to address the question of matching and less perceived legitimacy in the client raising the question. In a situation involving a private client-practitioner contract, this would be more significant.

From a psychosocial perspective, the question of matching is seen as critical, yet it is one on which few data are currently available. At best, we are now comfortable in raising it as a question of great significance to the therapeutic endeavor.

Physical Characteristics of Agencies

The physical qualities of the setting are the final attribute seen to be significant in psychosocial practice. Even though, conceptually and historically, emphasis has been placed on the effects of physical settings on psychosical behavior, it is remarkable that the literature on this critical topic is almost nonexistent. This absence of data is even more interesting when it is known that there are indeed many data available from other fields, such as industry.[18] Here, the location and appearance of store, office or plant is considered of great importance and hence large sums are expanded to insure that the proper setting is provided to create a particular mood or to convey a particular message. While corporations spend more on physical setting than our profession would be able or want to, we may be overinfluenced by a long tradition which dictates that in providing services to clients, we should do so in a style that also conveys need and limited resources. Even today, it appears that we are still uncomfortable in providing physical amenities to our clients and concomitantly in locating, decorating, and furnishing agencies in a manner that reflects comfort, concern, and competence.

Although the following remarks will be critical for the most part, it is first important to pay tribute to those agencies and clinics who indeed have striven consciously to plan and equip the settings in which therapy is provided in a way that makes use of the available knowledge of how physical settings and surroundings can affect behavior. The principal point here is that such settings are still very much in the minority.

In addition to the geographical location mentioned earlier, the actual appearance of the psychotherapeutic center is important. Does the setting give a first appearance of concern, competence, comfort, of a place where an individual, family, or group will find the kind of understanding and wise help that is sought? Or does the setting give the message of incompetence, lack of respect, lack of privacy, lack of comfort that could well deter persons? Clearly, it is not being argued that agencies have to be opulent or dramatic in their appearance. Rather, it is essential that they should manifest a concern for appearance related to their nature and function.

It is more often the interior of an agency that can be legitimately criticized. So often the waiting rooms of agencies are uncomfortable, harshly furnished, cold in appearance and completely devoid of anything but the most basic of amenities. A particular failing of many waiting rooms is the lack of privacy. Over and over again, agencies can be found where conversations can be overheard, be they those of the receptionist receiving phone calls or taking information at a reception desk or those of persons talking in other parts of the agency.

Within the actual office where the therapeutic process takes place, attention must also be given to the physical setting. The office should be adequate in size, well-illuminated and comfortably furnished in a manner that permits some flexibility for both the clients and the therapist to conduct the interview in a variety of ways. It is especially important that offices be sound proof and appear so to clients. The therapist, insofar as possible, should be free from distractions such as interruptions by telephone or other staff or colleagues.

The function, the color, the decoration and the equipment in the office all should convey to the client those qualities of respect and concern that are the hallmark of responsible therapy. Certainly, there is a wide range of variations possible and indeed desirable in the therapeutic office that will differ according to the tastes of the therapist and the needs of the agency. These factors will also vary according to the nature of the setting, the type of therapy provided and the groups of clients being served. As a general rule, offices should provide a range of flexibility, along with being comfortably and tastefully appointed.

There are few therapists who would deny the importance of these factors. However, it is often difficult to assess objectively the message that the appearance of our offices conveys to clients. It is so easy to be comfortable with the familiar that we fail to appreciate how our setting is seen by others or how it affects them. Secondly, we often fail to make use of the information available from others on the effects of color, lighting, furniture arrangement, and amenities on providing the kind of setting that is desired. It appears that too often we are prepared to overestimate our ability to develop and maintain a therapeutic relationship and to underestimate the usefulness, knowledge, and expertise of skillful interior decorators. Once again, the value of parsimony seems to be operative. Somehow, we feel that our stewardship to the public should not include a concern for how clients will respond to the physical setting of our agencies. It would be interesting to do research on the impact of the physical settings on a client and the totality of the therapeutic process.

It is surprising that therapists who are so sensitive to the emotional reactions of clients, to every nuance of gesture and speech, are frequently so insensitive to their physical and sociological needs. Items as obvious yet as important as the type of chair or chairs we provide for our clients are often overlooked. A chair can be comfortable or uncomfortable, freeing or restraining, formidable or secure, friendly or imposing, yet we often fail to consider our own furniture from this standpoint. I have been in interviewing rooms where the therapist's chair was higher than the client's and conveyed the impression of the therapist looking down on the client.

In addition to furniture, there are other amenities that can help a client feel welcome, respected, and understood. For example, having our name in a visible place can be helpful, especially in first interviews. Just as we can forget clients' names, so too can they forget ours and be too uncomfortable to ask. Having a clock visible to the client can be a helpful reminder of busy schedules, parking limitations, or domestic responsibilities. Just as we must program our time carefully to meet our obligations, so must many of our clients. The increase in tension toward the end of an interview may be related to significant psychodynamic material, but it may just as well be related to worry about missing a bus.

Clients should know where the agency washrooms are and

have easy access to them. This seems obvious, yet frequently clients are placed in the uncomfortable situation of not having this information and being uncertain about asking. Paper and pencil, paper handkerchiefs, an ashtray, a coat rack and a mirror in which to check one's appearance after a difficult interview, all are items that can be helpful and facilitating. It would be difficult to argue that the outcome of therapy depends on the availability of some of these items. Nevertheless, there is evidence that these things can increase the trust, security, and comfort a person experiences in the process and thus should be ignored if we really believe in the enhancement of client functioning.[19]

A recurring problem in many agency settings is the phenomenon of the unplanned termination. Undoubtedly, there are many reasons for such terminations. Among these may well be the possibility that the client's perception of the value of the help available has been affected negatively by the impact of the physical aspects of the agency. Because of this possibility, it is of great importance that this component of the therapeutic process be much more rigorously examined than has been done to the present.[20]

Informal Setting

Up to here, we have been talking about the formal therapeutic setting. It is essential that some comment also be made about the "nonsetting." Most therapists in psychosocial practice have found that at times it is helpful and indeed essential that the therapeutic process be conducted outside the formal clinical setting. Thus, we have many examples of people who have interviewed persons on park benches or while taking a walk. Others have set up interviews in restaurants and places of work or in cars while traveling. And of course, there is the whole tradition of the home visit. Without dealing with each of these matters in detail, this tradition itself is one that supports and reflects a psychosocial commitment.

No doubt, there are people who are able to deal with problematic components of their life situation better in an informal setting than in a formal one. Some people feel more secure and more trusting when they are in either a neutral setting or a social situation in which they are, as it were, in their own territory. Obviously, many distractions to the therapeutic process exist outside of a formal setting and one of the skills of the competent therapist is to constantly attempt to weigh the gains and losses involved in utilizing a less formal setting. It is interesting that frequently we are more comfortable in dealing with children and adolescents in informal settings and indeed there are many psychological and sociological reasons why this is so. I suggest, though, that there are clients other than adolescents and children who can also benefit from a less formal approach to therapy in some situations. I think frequently of those highly deprived adults for whom very little of a positive nature has ever been done. The skillful use of informal approaches can strengthen the client's sense of being accepted and respected in a manner that can be particularly helpful in the total situation.

Once again, there is the inevitable question of values versus facts. In recent years, we went through a very strong wave of anti-establishment and antiformal therapy attitudes. Some of our colleagues took up the cause of getting everyone out from behind their desks, indeed, out of their offices altogether in order to make the therapeutic process more informal.

It would be wrong to ignore the possibility that many of us have become too office-bound in the provision of some of our services. It would be just as remiss to accept such a postulation without question. The mark of the responsible therapist today is not in espousing fads but rather in carefully translating new ideas into practical experience and concomitantly in continuing the process of evaluating such changes. We are not speaking against enthusiasm or against new ideas. What we are against is the tendency, that at times has seemed to mark our profession, of moving too quickly into new ideas and in so doing scrapping all that we have learned from the past as we launch into a new panacea of therapy.

Notes

1. Helen Harris Perlman, "The Place," *Social Casework* (Chicago: University of Chicago Press, 1957), pp. 40–52.

2. A. J. Kahn, "Perspectives on Access to Social Services," *Social Work* (U.K.) 26, 3 (July, 1969), pp. 3–9.

3. Beatrice Werble, Charlotte S. Henry and Margaret W. Millar, "Motivation, or Using Casework Services," *Social Caework* 39 (February–March, 1958), pp. 124–137.

4. Paul R. Brooks, "Industry–Agency Program for Employee Counseling," *Social Casework* 56 (July, 1975), pp. 404–410.

5. Henry Freeman, et al., "Can A Family Agency Be Relevant to the Inner Urban Scene?" *Social Casework* 51 (January, 1970), pp. 12–21.

6. Renee Pellman, Rory McDonald and Susan Anson, "The Van: A Mobile Approach to Services for Adolescents," *Social Casework* 58 (May, 1977), pp. 268–275.

7. Francis J. Turner, "Effect of Value Reevaluation on Current Practice," *Social Casework* 56 (May, 1975), pp. 285–291.

8. Florence Hollis, "Casework and Social Class," *Social Casework* 46 (October, 1965), pp. 463–471.

9. *Handbook on the Private Practice of Social Work* (New York: National Association of Social Workers, 1967).

10. Margaret A. Golton, "Analysis of Private Practice in Casework," *Social Work* 8 (January, 1963), pp. 72–78.

11. Sidney Levenstein, *Private Practice in Social Casework* (New York: Columbia University Press, 1964).

12. Sherman Merle, "Some Arguments Against Private Practice," *Social Work* 7 (January, 1962), pp. 12–17.

13. Ruth Ellen Lindenberg, "Hard to Reach: Client or Casework Agency?" *Social Work* 3, 4 (1958), pp. 23–29.

14. Morton Chethik, Elizabeth Fleming, Morris F. Mayer, and John N. McCoy, "A Quest for Identity: Treatment of Disturbed Negro Children in a Predominantly White Treatment Center," *American Journal of Orthopsychiatry* 37 (January, 1967), pp. 71–77.

15. Ellen Handler, "Comparative Effectiveness of Four Preschool Pro-

grams: A Sociological Approach," *Child Welfare* 51 (January, 1972), pp. 550–561.

16. Beth L. McCutcheon and Karen S. Calhoun, "Social and Emotional Adjustment of Infants and Toddlers to a Day Care Setting," *American Journal of Orthopsychiatry* 46 (January, 1976), pp. 104–108.

17. Linda R. Hoffman, Virginia Lehman and Eli D. Zer, "A Group Home-Hospital Treatment Model for Severely Disturbed Adolescents," *Child Welfare* 54 (1975), pp. 283–289.

18. Brett A. Seabury, "The Arrangement of Physical Space in Social Work Settings: A New Perspective in Practice," *Social Work* 16 (October, 1971), pp. 43–49.

19. Donald W. Clemens, "Functional Design in Building a Residential Treatment Facility," *Child Welfare* 50 (November, 1971), pp. 512–518.

20. Richard A. Cloward, "Agency Structure as a Variable in Services to Groups," in Group Work and Community Organization, 1956 *Selected Papers, 83rd Annual Forum,* National Conference on Social Welfare (New York: Columbia University Press, 1956).

Chapter 9

Psychosocial Therapy and Research

A Contemporary Overview

As long as the psychosocial therapist has aspired to a responsible, knowledge-based form of intervention, there has been both implicit and actual commitment to the values and methods of the social scientist and hence to research and experimentation. Yet, in spite of this long-standing commitment, the actual output of research in the psychosocial tradition has not been extensive. One of the most popular parlor games of the current therapeutic tradition has been to be ultracritical about both the quantity and the quality of research efforts related to social work clinical practice.

Certainly, it was hardly respectable in the past decade to give a professional paper without exorting one's colleagues to increase their skills and commitment to research. I have long been a part of this ongoing polemic, and in beginning this chapter I had intended to add one further item to the extensive list of critical comments on our activities. But further thought, resulting from recent examination of the literature for other purposes, has led me to pause. Our long efforts to expand our colleagues' interest in research surely has had some effect. The myriad of research courses, the ever increasing number of highly trained doctoral candidates, the vastly improved availability of research funds, the ongoing efforts of journal editors to encourage research-based articles, the establishment of new research-based journals, all attest to dramatically expanded research efforts by social workers and other psychotherapists, especially those in the psychosocial tradition. The word "especially" is used in regard to psychosocial therapists for a special reason. The psychosocial tradition has been strongly influenced by the social sciences, principally psychology and sociology and to a lesser extent political science and economics. These related disciplines have also greatly expanded their interest and activities in research. Inevitably, psychosocial therapists have been further reinforced in their research interest by their close associations with other disciplines.

A specific payoff of these relationships is that the psychosocial therapist has had available a wide diversity of research methodologies, designs, strategies, and skills upon which to draw in attempting to address the vast array of untouched research questions. In addition to expanded activity in research, there have been two concomitant developments. The first relates to the scope of research thrusts and the second to quantity and diversity. It appears that in the late 1970s we finally reached a clear awareness that efforts to engage in the vast, all-encompassing research questions are in vain. Without retelling an oft-told tale, it has now been sufficiently demonstrated that research projects that deal with such questions as "is casework effective" or "does psychotherapy help" or "is marriage counseling useful" are in vain. By now we have aptly demonstrated that such efforts to deal with these large questions will usually be inconclusive or at best give some minor supporting evidence. The risk of these kinds of projects is that findings are quickly politicized and used to bolster or weaken various arguments engaged in for other than disinterested motives.

We seem now to have learned something that our colleagues in other disciplines have long known; knowledge is advanced by very minute steps. The payoffs from research on a study-by-study basis are very minuscule. What does succeed is the accumulated interconnected knowledge that comes from a number of small, well-developed, and implemented programs of research.

This then is the second observation. We are now seeing much greater comfort with and support for the small, highly focused project that deals with some very restricted or detailed component of practice.

Some Examples of Research

As is so often the case in professions, practice is already ahead of the current perception of many colleagues, who continue to decry the lack of research without being fully aware of what the reality is. To help increase this awareness, the remainder of the chapter will describe a series of research activities on topics closely related to the theory and practice of psychosocial therapy. This list is not to be considered as exhaustive; the projects have been selected to demonstrate the richness and variety of research activities of recent years. I do not suggest that these projects are models of perfect research, free from weaknesses that can be criticized. Rather, they were selected as being of general interest to social workers and of sufficiently good quality to merit special mention.

CONTINUANCE AND DISCONTINUANCE IN TREATMENT

In discussions of research in the psychosocial tradition an important place has to be given to the group of studies that emerged out of the work of Florence Hollis at Columbia University.[1] In the early 1960s Hollis began to experiment with a typology of casework treatment that provided a method of classifying the range of worker–client verbal exchanges in interviews in a manner that permitted quantitative comparisons between interviews. This typology proved to be a useful instrument for some formal research by Hollis herself as well as by a group of doctoral students at Columbia.

In one of these projects Hollis compared a group of cases from the caseloads of several family agencies. These caseloads were divided into two subgroups. The first contained those cases in which the client continued in treatment according to plan; the second, clients who discontinued treatment before a planned conclusion. Both groups of clients had sought help with marital problems and all were seen in individual interviews.

By means of the typology, the profile of client–worker communication used in each group of case was identified and compared. Differences were found between the two groups. Among the findings in the study was the observation that the therapists in the discontinued cases were generally more active in the early interviews.

The importance of this study is twofold; first, it indicated the possibility of gathering and examining data about worker–client verbal exchange, which is of course the heart of the psychosocial interventive process. Secondly, it supplied some sound data to support the viewpoint that workers' styles are related to client performance. This in turn provided a basis for further examination of strategies aimed at reducing the amount of unplanned discontinuance, a problem that has long plagued social work practice. This study and others like it also demonstrate that this type of research is expensive and time-consuming, but with important although not dramatic outcome.

JOINT INTERVIEWING WITH MARITAL CASES

The Hollis work focused principally on work with individuals. At about the same time, Shirley Erinkrantz experimented with the possibility of collecting and analyzing similar data from joint interviews in cases involving husbands and wives with marital problems.[2] It was hoped that such data could in turn be compared with data from interviews where a one-to-one modality of treatment was used. Again, cases from family agencies were gathered and compared, utilizing the Hollis typology. Statistically significant differences were found between the individual and the joint styles of interviews. Such a finding was of course as expected. What was particularly important, though, was the demonstration that it was possible to collect quantitative data that permitted comparisons between different modalities of treatment. An important aspect of the Erinkrantz studies was the finding that it was possible to demonstrate patterned mistakes by the worker. This was especially noted in the failure to make use of the special advantages of the joint interview.

This study is important for the ongoing development of psychosocial practice in that it shows that it is possible to compare treatment methodologies in a manner that permits differential evaluation of such methodologies against several variables. Within the literature there have been and continue to be many articles that argue the various advantages and disadvatages of different treatment modalities. For the most part, these arguments have been based on the impressionistic perceptions of therapists concerning the differences between modalities. The type of research done by Erinkrantz indicates that patterned differences do exist between modalities and that it is possible to measure such differences. It is only in this way that we can begin to gather data that demonstrate in a replicable manner the different impacts of various modalities.

VALUE ORIENTATIONS AS A COMPONENT OF TREATMENT

Two projects conducted by the present author also utilized the Hollis typology as a basis and presented data that supported further components of psychosocial therapy related to the sociocultural aspects of clients' behavior. Both projects addressed the question of value differences and their effect on the therapeutic process. In the first,[3] a comparison was made between two groups of clients with different value orientations, as manifested through the Kluckhohn Value Orientation Instrument. The clients were all drawn from family agencies and were controlled for socioeconomic class, presenting problem, and length of treatment. The research question concerned the effect of value differences on the content of interviews.

When the recorded content of the two groups of interviews was examined, it was observed that there was a range of significant patterns and differences related to value differences. For example, it was observed that the social workers used sustaining procedures more often with individualistically oriented clients than with collaterally oriented clients. In addition, individualistic clients tended to ventilate more than their collaterally oriented counterparts.

Client values have always been considered an important part of treatment. The findings of this study indicated the possibility of locating and identifying value differences in a manner that permitted the worker to specifically address this issue. This is something that had long been considered important but the precise data have been hard to obtain.

ETHNIC DIFFERENCES AS A COMPONENT OF TREATMENT

The same theme was developed further in a second study that again looked at value differences, but introduced the further variable of ethnic difference.[4] In this study, a comparison was made between French-speaking and English-speaking clients and social workers. Several variables were controlled in the sample selection and interview contents as well as case outcomes were examined. In this study, unlike in the previous one, tape recordings of the interviews were used. This helped to minimize the problem of the validity of workers' reports on the therapeutic process. As in the previous study, patterned differences were observed in the value differences, interview contents and outcomes in the two groups. In addition, the value profile of the two groups of ethnically different therapists was found to be different.

In psychosocial therapy a client's ethnic identity has always been considered an important variable that affects both the client's ability to function in a therapeutic situation and the outcome of that process for him. These two studies provided data that further support this concept and added precision to it.

SOCIOECONOMIC CLASS AS A VARIABLE IN TREATMENT

A study carried out by Edward Mullen has indicated that there are identifiable and measurable patterns in the worker–client therapeutic process.[5] In a content analysis of the client-worker interactions of a group of lower middle-class urban clients in a community agency, Mullens was able to demonstrate that experienced, trained workers have an identifiable style of practice in which the client is first helped to talk about his situation and then to engage in a reflective consideration of current interpersonal and situational matters.

There were two important research findings in this project. The first is that experienced workers have a similar therapeutic style, allowing of course for differences according to the particular needs of the case. Secondly, and what is more important, Mullen found that in keeping with the tenets of psychosocial therapy, the majority of our work with clients is present-oriented and focused on the conscious mind. These findings are of particular importance because of the long-standing belief by both the public and the profession that social workers of this persuasion spend much time looking at past history and its impact on the client's unconscious.

SEXUAL ROLE PERCEPTIONS AS A DIAGNOSTIC VARIABLE

An important component of psychosocial theory relates to a person's self-concept and how it is formed, developed, maintained, and altered. To this end much attention has been given to class and cultural values and how they are reinforced and transmitted. Of particular interest in recent years has been our deepened understanding of the factors that influence the development of sex roles and expectations, especially as we have become aware that much of our knowledge in this area is influenced by our preconceptions rather than being based on data. Thus studies such as that carried out by Luther Balen are important.[6] In this study a group of thirty-eight never-married women and a matched group of married women were compared on personal and social adjustment by means of a California test of personality. Further data about individual life styles were gathered by means of individual interviews.

The findings of the study supported the view that a sense of adequacy and fulfillment is not related to marriage and motherhood. Rather, a creative sense of societal contribution could equally result in an experience of personal fullfilment. Again, this study emphasizes the necessity and possibility of testing assumptions that frequently influence intervention and treatment goals to the detriment of a full understanding of a client.

In a more general way, this type of project underscores the psychosocial commitment to individualization as a key interventive focal point. This is based on the understanding that there are many routes to satisfaction, growth and maturity beyond those sanctioned by social tradition.

CLIENT EVALUATION OF THERAPEUTIC IMPACT

A key and as yet unanswered question in evaluating the effects of psychosocial intervention relates to who should decide if a particular process is helpful or not. Should it be the therapist, other therapists, significant others in the client's life, the client himself, or all of these? There is an agreement that all these persons have a stake in the therapeutic process, although the criteria by which decisions about it are made are disputed. Nevertheless, the impact on clients of the various processes in which we involve them is important. A project by Paula Eastman represents a useful examination of these questions.[7] It is also an example of research in which the researcher's attention focused on a type of group intervention.

In this project, a consciousness-raising group was observed and its impact on the individuals involved was assessed by means of individual interviews. A group of eleven women who participated in most of the twenty-five group sessions were selected, and a structured interview was administered to explore their expectations at the beginning of the process and whether these expectations had been fulfilled at the end of it. The general findings were that the individuals had had a positive experience and that shifts in identity, self-awareness and world view had occurred.

Clearly, there are methodological problems in conducting this type of research, especially when efforts are made to draw comparisons between different interventions, as for example between groups. Nevertheless, this project adds support to the importance of the structured gathering of data from persons who have experienced a common interventive process—in this case, in a group experience. These types of data help us to work backward to identify which components of the process have been effective and which ineffective. This project is also useful in adding further understanding of how a person's identity can be altered in a positive direction.

THE EFFECTS OF GRIEF ON THE AGING

The different ways of understanding growth and development is stressed in psychosocial therapy. In understanding individuals it is important to comprehend how they are like all other human beings, how they are like some other human beings and how they are like no other human beings. To this end tremendous amounts of work still need to be done to compare how similar phenomena affect different groups. Barbara Shelski's project asked whether grief in the elderly differs from that of other age groups in terms of symptomatology, management, and resolution of the mourning process.[8] The methodology involved a study of the residents in an apartment building for the aged who had lost a spouse in the previous three years and who were over sixty-five when this occurred.

Three instruments were used to gather data: unstructured interviews, an activities and attitudes schedule, and a checklist of grief phenomena. The findings of this study indicated that indeed the grieving process and its resolution in people of this age are different from the typical picture of grief described in the literature. The grieving process is of course intense and painful. To cope with this suffering the persons studied utilized a series of defensive maneuvers which seemed to allow them to continue to function but did not permit them to freely engage in the mourning process and thus prolonged their suffering. In itself, this is an important finding that could be of benefit in therapy with the elderly. In such cases we frequently underestimate the impact of death in the belief that death must be so much a part of their lives that they must have gotten used to it.

More generally and perhaps more importantly, the study reinforces the necessity of continued examination of the various life stages and the particular challenges and risks of each stage. At this point we understand the major aspects of each stage, but are just beginning to comprehend the subtleties and minor patterns and differences within each stage that are essential to sensitive and effective therapy.

THE EFFECTS OF DIFFERING THERAPIES

As has been mentioned before, psychosocial therapy is committed to the utilization of a broad range of interventive strategies and to the ongoing assessment of their effectiveness. With the wide range of thought systems currently influencing practice and with the tendency in the helping professions to rely more on enthusiasm than on data as the basis for adopting certain strategies, studies that examine this question are important. Christoph Heinicke drew on the conceptual basis of psycho-analytic social work, a strongly influential body of thought on psychosocial therapy, as the basis for an interesting research proj-ect.[9] In this project, 115 preschool children in two cities were compared. Three interventive approaches were considered: open-ended interpretative, supportive therapy, problem-oriented ther-apy, problem-oriented therapy, and consultation. The people stud-ied were children and their families who had been identified as being in "risk situations." The families were measured at several specific points in the life of the case by IQ scores, child develop-ment ratings, and parent-child ratings conducted by a social worker.

It was observed that parents who received the therapy based on open-ended intervention changed in a more positive direction, both as persons and in their parent–child functioning, than par-ents in the other two groups. Follow-up assessment of these families in kindergarten indicated that this group continued to improve and those in the no-treatment group to decline.

Two observations can be made from this project. First, the data support a type of intervention that stresses the inclusion of the whole family situation in the therapy. This seems especially true in therapy that stresses early intervention with a preventative objective. Secondly, this project underscores the advantages of using a multiple approach to measurement as a way of correlating findings as well as of getting different perspectives on the impact of intervention.

A particular challenge for psychosocial therapy has been to accurately specify the locus of the impact of intervention. All therapists have had experiences that convince them that clients are adjusting better. However, it has been difficult to identify the precise areas of psychosocial makeup in which the changes are occurring. For example, a surprising finding in the study just described was that improvements in a child's IQ were found in the open-ended treatment group. IQ has not been a variable that has been frequently looked at in studies on the impact of therapy. This reminds us of the need to be sensitive to all the possible areas in a client's life that may be affected or, of equal importance, not affected by treatment.

The Psychosocial Effects of Home Care Following Hospital Discharge

Work on a client's significant environment has been stressed in the earlier chapters as a key component of psychosocial therapy. This is not an area that has been given prime attention by researchers. Thus a study by L. W. Gerson and A. F. E. Berry conducted in Newfoundland is noteworthy.[10] In this study, a randomized controlled test was carried out to evaluate the efficacy of the early transfer of hospital in-patients to home care. Several categories of surgical intervention were identified and patients were divided into three groups: homecare patients, non-homecare patients, and a control group. In all cases, psychosocial functioning was measured at two points in time. The first measurement, conducted at the time of hospital admission, established a baseline. The second was carried out three weeks after discharge. These interviews were conducted by social workers.

Several areas of statistical difference were found in the rates of adjustment between homecare and hospital patients, particularly in the area of household task performances. No significant differences were found in the rates of adjustment to other life areas, such as the return to work or the resumption of leisure activities. In addition, differences were found in the rate of adjustment in patients in the after-care program which related to the nature of the surgery.

Once again this type of project demonstrates the impact of significant environments and persons in role transition. It also underscores the importance of understanding the physical functioning of our clients. Thus, clients who were considered to be equally ready for discharge were not able to readjust at a similar note to post-hospital living, and these differences were patterned rather than random.

Psychosocial therapy has long stressed the connection between a person's physical endowment and functioning and his ability to function adequately and productively in society. Yet we are still lacking a precise understanding of the relationship between different kinds of physical limitations and growth-enhancing functioning. Only with precise data on these areas can we begin to make more effective use of the different resources and modalities of treatment, as for example in deciding on the relative effectiveness of home care versus hospital care, the implementation of which has tremendous therapeutic and economic implications.

ROLE SATISFACTION AND PSYCHOSOCIAL FUNCTIONING

A second study also carried out in Newfoundland again stresses the interconnection between the somatic condition of man and his psychosocial adjustment. The *Kedward Self Study* compared the social functioning and adjustment of fifty female patients suffering from nonpsychotic psychiatric illness with a demographically similar group of fifty psychiatrically symptom-free women.[11] Both were screened by means of standardized psychiatric and social work tests. In the social work assessment three areas were examined: material conditions, social functioning, and satisfaction. Differences were observed between the two groups in all areas measured by the social work component of the project. In summary, the symptom group was less well off materially, functioned less well, and was markedly less satisfied with its lot.

The findings of this study are important from a theoretical viewpoint in several ways. First, there were significant cultural factors bearing on the role satisfactions of the women in the geographical area in which the study was conducted. In addition, the study once again brings into perspective the relationship between self-satisfaction and physical and mental health, and the need to address these two essential components of a total person concomitantly in any planned intervention.

The most important aspect of this and similar types of research concerns its implications for service delivery. As discussed earlier, a key feature of psychosocial therapy is the planned use of the resources, knowledge and skills of other disciplines. This commitment to interprofessional collaboration is far removed from the discipline-based isolation approach to practice that has long marked some components of the helping professions' history.

No one profession and no one member of a profession can begin to be expert in all the kinds of help and resources required by clients. Interdisciplinary services are an important and ongoing part of current practice. Many more projects of an interdisciplinary nature are required before we can accurately identify those areas where an impact can be made on significant components of the functioning of designated groups of clients.

FAMILY ADJUSTMENT TO THE DEATH OF A MEMBER

An area of psychosocial reality that has recently been given considerable attention by social workers, although long avoided, has been the reality of death. Increased awareness and acceptance of these influencing phenomena have also contributed to a better understanding of the management of crisis at a time of loss or perceived loss by the persons involved and by those close to them.

The effect of death on the family of the dead person and the way in which the adjustment to death is made are of particular interest. Since many persons are met in practice who have not dealt successfully with the experience of death, it is critical that this process be studied so that we can be of more help to clients experiencing it.

A study carried out in Cincinnati by P. Cohen and her associates examined the adaptation of families to the terminal illness and death of a parent.[12] A group of forty-two middle-class families who had received service from a cancer unit family service were studied. Of these, twenty-nine agreed to participate fully. One goal of the study was to conduct an interview with each family, and this was done in most of the population studied.

Four instruments were devised for use in the study to gather medical information, demographic data, and family functioning data from the family and from individual members over eight years of age. The first instrument dealt with demographic and medical information, the second with family functioning, the third, completed by family members, gathered information about their reactions, and the fourth was a clinical description of the family written by the interviewer. The findings of the study identified several essential components of the process; a communications flow between family members, the use of external support networks, and the ability to pool and share information. All of these were seen as necessary to achieve a successful adjustment to death.

Additional findings demonstrated that different adjustment patterns in families existed depending on whether the mother or the father had died. Also it was found that families hesitated in sharing information with the children about the impending death. Finally, different patterns of the use of external resources were observed in families according to their tendency to be either inward- or outward-looking.

The desire for a better understanding of the death process and the adjustments of the survivors was of course the crucial issue in this project. What was also important were two methological issues. The first relates to the ethical issues involved in subjecting persons under severe stress to a type of probing whose principal function is to elicit information on which to develop theory and compare practice. This is a critically important question for social workers, one we have to face and not avoid by hiding behind a rationalization based on the sensitivity of our clients.

We must never cease to be aware of and be sensitive to clients' needs. But we must also discharge our responsibilities to better understand the phenomena with which we deal and thus to intervene more effectively. This research and others like it have shown that it is possible to gather data even in the most sensitive areas in a way that is both dignified and humane.

But this type of research also raises another methodological difficulty, that of locating and involving respondents for study. Serious sampling problems can arise in areas of high sensitivity due to refusals or the inability to participate. This kind of problem obviously affects our ability to generalize in a definitive way. Nevertheless, even with imperfect samples we can still strengthen our structured experience with particular groups of clients. Although such approaches do not have the certitude of hard research, they do serve us better than untried impressions.

There are many more projects that could be mentioned. In selecting only a few, others not quoted are not being evaluated. An effort has been made to give an overview of the kinds of projects that are being conducted in the helping professions to advance our understanding of psychosocial man. The essential theme is that research is going on. A review of eleven years of clinical social work literature in ten journals showed that 945 articles have been written based on clinical research. Of these, eighty-eight were written from either a psychosocial or an ego-psychological viewpoint.

Many of these projects have several things in common, a factor that is both their strength and their weakness. The first of these is their limited data base. Over and over again in the critical literature of social work research, the inadequacy of samples has been mentioned as a major weakness in our evaluative activities. With samples lacking the quality of randomness, obviously there is little or no possibility of generalizing appropriately beyond the group that was studied. This has resulted in an obsessive-like determination to dismiss such research as of little consequence.[13]

This is not the place to reopen the great controversy about the effectiveness of psychotherapeutic intervention[14] based on analysis or reanalysis of published projects. What is being strongly argued here is the need for a value shift in favor of the importance of the small well-designed project of limited generalizability as mentioned above. There are still too many problems involved in the large study design because of the vast numbers of variables that need to be considered. Thus there is little hope in asking large research questions. It would follow then that projects which attempt to measure "whether case work is effective" or "whether families get better" or whether "therapy reduces juvenile delinquency" will do little to advance the development of theory. They may be essential projects from the standpoint of social policy or advancing political goals at many levels. But they do little to advance the search for theory development. The building of detailed knowledge and the refining of skills so necessary for sensitive practice are only going to take place when we humbly accept the importance of the small and carefully selected sample in which only a small component of the therapeutic process is examined.

Knowledge can be developed and improved by the small experiment conducted with limited populations. Only when we have detailed knowledge can we move to the development and testing of theory. Nonrandom samples do not constitute bad research in themselves. If they are chosen carefully and studied with precision they can be valid sources of new knowledge. Certainly, scientists learned much about the moon through the study of a few pounds of hastily gathered rocks, and just as certainly the limited sample of moon rocks raised many new questions, as does all good research. But in no way can we conclude that we know all there is to know about the moon. More precision, detail and rigor are needed and a concomitant comfort in solid, small and nondramatic results. Extending an alcoholic's dry period by a few days or lessening the intensity of depression by a few degrees may be dramatic gains in practice if we can identify how we brought such an event about, how it can be repeated in other cases, and how to teach others to do this.

The twelve studies mentioned above all addressed only selected components of the therapeutic process. But in each case change was observed in a direction predicted by theory. All were able to base their conclusions on statistical evidence. None could generalize to larger populations. Melvin N. Brunner talks about ministudies as a viable approach to research in the social services.[15] He gives this term a specific meaning related to some prepared research kits. Taking his ideas further, it is suggested that we must also get comfortable with minisamples as a strategy in research. Too often large components of research resources have been expended in attempts to expand the number of clients to be included in a particular study. Frequently, to do so require compromises in sample characteristics or much time being lost waiting for new cases to appear. It is my belief that we might better spend our efforts on a more rigorous examination of fewer cases.

But acceptance of the ministudy and minisample is not enough. A further requirement is the establishment of better linkages between research projects. Now that we are heavily committed to and involved in many research activities, a desirable next goal should be to find ways of developing linkages between projects and establishing families of projects. As a teacher, each year I see student projects completed that naturally lead to other projects. Unfortunately, though, these next phases of projects do not often happen. We do not seem to have established a tradition of building on the work of one another. The Hollis research is an example of how interconnections can be built and a family of research projects evolved. Out of the original research by Hollis,[16] fifteen to twenty related doctoral projects were completed, which as a group made a considerable impact on the advancement of the understanding of client–worker communication patterns. Similarly, there was a rich array of research completed around the concept of crisis intervention stemming from the original work by Lindemann. Examples are the work of Lydia Rapoport and

Naomi Golan. Again, important as each of the individual projects was in itself, as a group they have made a tremendous impact on the professional understanding and management of crisis reactions.

The original work of Reid and Shyne on brief and extended treatment[17] that later moved to task-oriented therapy[18] was a further example of the efficacy of the interconnected thematic kind of research. If we could find a way of fostering more of this, we would do much to continue to improve our effectiveness as therapists.

As we continue to search for ways of improving our understanding of the therapeutic process and its overwhelming complexities we must be sure that we make use of all available resources. Certainly the computer with its tremendous capacity to deal with large amounts of data is increasingly a part of the armamentarium of the helping professions. This is a tremendous resource for the kind of research required in our field. The challenge of dealing with large numbers of variables has been mentioned, as well as the corresponding difficulty in specifying the details of change in the therapeutic process. It is already evident that the computer can be of assistance to us, especially in its ability to store large amounts of detailed information about many cases and to retrieve it in patterned ways. This can be done in a manner not possible with the methods available in the recent past.

Earlier in this chapter the case was made for the need for miniprojects and minisamples. There is also a need in our field for the examination of large numbers of cases and clients. These two ideas are not contradictory; the small study can help us identify and isolate components of change that appeared to influence practice in general. Access to large amounts of data about many cases can help us look for similar observations in a way that can permit us to then generalize to practice.

The search for new knowledge is humbling, nondramatic, difficult, frequently disappointing, but everlastingly important. To seek to understand man is presumptuous; to seek to understand his interaction with significant environments borders on folly. Yet this is the goal to which the psychosocial therapist addresses himself. It is an approach to helping human beings achieve their potential that has a rich, glorious, and noble history; but it is a task that the complexities of modern science have made even more difficult. The easy solution to the challenge is a flight into cynicism; the more difficult task is a commitment to search. It is this commitment that will continue to be the hallmark of the psychosocial practitioner.

Notes

1. Florence Hollis, "Development of a Casework Treatment Typology," *Final Report NIMH Grant MH-00513* (1966).
2. Shirley Ehrenkranz, "A Study of Joint Interviewing in the Treatment of Marital Problems," *Social Casework* 48 (October and November, 1967), pp. 498–502 and 570–574.
3. Francis Turner, "A Comparison of Procedures in the Treatment of Clients with Two Different Value Orientations," *Social Casework* 45 (May, 1964), pp. 273–277.
4. Francis Turner, "Ethnic Difference and Client Performance," *Social Service Review* 44 (March, 1970), pp. 1–10.
5. Edward J. Mullen, "Casework Communication," *Social Casework* 49 (November, 1968), pp. 546–551.
6. Luther G. Baker, "The Personal and Social Adjustment of the Never-Married Women," *Journal of Marriage and the Family* 30 (1968), pp. 473–479.
7. Paula Costa Eastman, "Consciousness-Raising as a Resocialization Process for Women," *Smith College Studies in Social Work* 43–44 (June, 1973), pp. 153–183.
8. Barbara E. Skelskie, "An Exploratory Study of Grief in Old Age," *Smith College Studies in Social Work* 45 (February, 1975), pp. 159–182.
9. Christoph Heinicke, "Aiding 'At Risk' Children Through Psychoanalytic Social Work with Patients," *American Journal of Orthopsychiatry* 46 (1976), pp. 89–103.

10. L. W. Gerson and A. F. E. Berry, "Psycho-Social Effects of Home Care: Results of a Randomized Controlled Trial," *International Journal of Epidemiology* 5 (1976), pp. 159–165.

11. H. B. Kedward and Judith Sylph, "The Social Correlates of Chronic Neurotic Disorder," *Social Psychiatry* 9 (1974), pp. 91–98.

12. Pauline Cohen, Israel M. Dizenhuz and Carolyn Winget, "Family Adaptation to Terminal Illness and Death of a Parent," *Social Casework* 58 (April, 1977), pp. 223–228.

13. Joel Fischer, *The Effectiveness of Social Casework* (Springfield: Charles C. Thomas, 1976).

14. Edward J. Mullen and J. R. Dumpson, *Evaluation of Social Intervention* (San Francisco: Jossey Bass, 1972).

15. Melvin N. Brenner, "The Quest for Viable Research in Social Services: Development of the Ministudy," *Social Service Review* 50 (September, 1956), pp. 426–444.

16. Florence Hollis, "The Coding and Application of a Typology of Casework Treatment," *Social Casework* 48 (July, 1967), pp. 489–497. Florence Hollis, "A Profile of Early Interviews in Marital Counseling," *Social Casework* 49 (January, 1968), pp. 35–43. Florence Hollis, "Explorations in the Development of a Typology of Casework Treatment," *Social Casework* 48 (June, 1967), pp. 335–341.

17. William J. Reid and Ann W. Shyne, *Brief and Extended Casework* (New York: Columbia University Press, 1969).

18. William J. Reid and Laura Epstein, *Task-Centered Casework* (New York: Columbia University Press, 1972).

Bibliography

ABERLE, DAVID F., "The Psycho-Social Analysis of a Hopi Life History," *Comparative 4 Monographs* 121, 1, ser. 107. Berkeley: University of California Press, 1951.

ACKERMAN, NATHAN., "Emergence of Family Psychotherapy on the Present Scene," *Contemporary Psychotherapies,* Morris I. Stein, ed. New York: Free Press of Glencoe, 1961.

――――. *The Psychodynamics of Family Life: Diagnosis and Treatment of Family Relationships.* New York: Basic Books, 1958.

ACKERMAN, NATHAN W., BEATMAN, FRANCES L., and SHERMAN, SANFORD N., eds. *Exploring the Base for Family Therapy.* New York: Family Service Association of America, 1961.

ACKOFF, RUSSELL L. *Redesigning the Future: A Systems Approach to Societal Programs.* New York: John Wiley, 1974.

ALGER, IAN, and HOGAN, PETER, "Enduring Effects of Videotape Playback Experience on Family and Marital Relationships," *American Journal of Orthopsychiatry* 39 (January, 1969), pp. 86–94.

ALLAN, EUNICE F., "Psycho-Analytic Theory," *Social Work Treatment,* Francis J. Turner, ed. New York: Free Press, 1974.

APPEL, GERALD, "Some Aspects of Transference and Counter-Transference in Marital Counseling," *Social Casework* 47 (May, 1966), pp. 307–312.

AUSTIN, LUCILLE N., "Supervision of the Experienced Caseworker," reprinted from *The Family* (January, 1942), in *Principles and Tech-*

niques in Social Casework, 2nd ed., Cora Kasius, ed. New York: Family Service Association of America, 1950.

BAHN, ANITA K., "A Multi-Disciplinary Psychosocial Classification Scheme," *American Journal of Orthopsychiatry* 41 (October, 1971), pp. 830–845.

BAKER, LUTHER G., "The Personal and Social Adjustment of the Never-Married Women," *Journal of Marriage and the Family* 30 (August, 1968), pp. 473–479.

BAKER, R., "Client Appointment Preferences in a Child Guidance Centre: An Exploratory Study," *British Journal of Social Work* 2 (Spring, 1972), pp. 47–56.

BALES, ROBERT F. *Interaction Process Analysis: A Method for the Study of Small Groups.* Chicago: University of Chicago Press, 1950.

BARDILL, DONALD R., and BEVILACQUA, JOSEPH J., "Family Interviewing by Two Caseworkers," *Social Casework* 45 (May, 1964), pp. 278–282.

BARDILL, DONALD R., and RYAN, FRANCIS J. *Family Group Casework: A Casework Approach to Family Therapy.* Washington D.C.: Catholic University of America Press, 1964.

BARRETT-LENNARD, G. T., "Significant Aspects of a Helping Relationship," *Mental Hygiene* 47 (April, 1963), pp. 223–227; and in *Canada's Mental Health* 13 (July-August, 1965), supplement no. 47.

———, "The Client-Centered System: A Developmental Perspective." in *Social Work Treatment,* Francis J. Turner, ed. New York: Free Press, 1974.

BARTLETT, HARRIETT M. *The Common Base of Social Work Practice.* New York: National Association of Social Workers, 1970.

BEAN, SHIRLEY L., "The Parents' Center Project: A Multiservice Approach to the Prevention of Child Abuse," *Child Welfare* 50 (May, 1971), pp. 277–282.

BEATMAN, FRANCES, SHERMAN, SANFORD, and LEADER, ARTHUR, "Current Issues in Family Treatment," *Social Casework* 47 (February, 1966), pp. 75–81.

BECKER, DOROTHY G., "Exit Lady Bountiful: The Volunteer and the Professional Social Worker" *Social Service Review* 38 (1964), pp. 57–72.

BEHRENS, MARJORIE L., and ACKERMAN, NATHAN, "The Home Visit

as an Aid in Family Diagnosis and Therapy,'' *Social Casework* 37 (January, 1956), pp. 11–19.

BELL, JOHN E. *Family Group Therapy,* Public Health Monograph no. 64. Washington, D.C.: Government Printing Office, 1961.

BELL, NORMAN W., and VOGEL, EZRA F., eds. *A Modern Introduction to the Family,* revised ed. New York: Free Press, 1968.

BERGMAN, JOEL S., and DOLAND, DILMAN J., ''The Effectiveness of College Students as Therapeutic Agents with Chronic Hospitalized Patients,'' *American Journal of Orthopsychiatry* 44 (January, 1974), pp. 92–101.

BERKOWITZ, SIDNEY, ''Some Specific Techniques of Psychosocial Diagnosis and Treatment in Family Casework,'' *Social Casework* 36 (November, 1955), pp. 399–406.

BETTELHEIM, BRUNO, and SYLVESTER, EMILY, ''A Therapeutic Milieu,'' *American Journal of Orthopsychiatry* 48 (April, 1948), pp. 191–206.

BIESTEK, FELIX. *The Casework Relationship.* Chicago: Loyola University Press, 1957.

BIBRING, GRETE, ''Psychiatry and Social Work,'' *Journal of Social Casework* 28 (June, 1947), pp. 203–211.

BLANCK, RUBIN. ''The Case for Individual Treatment,'' *Social Casework* 47 (February, 1965), pp. 70–74.

BLOOM, MARY LARKIN, ''Usefulness of the Home Visit for Diagnosis and Treatment,'' *Social Casework* 54 (February, 1973), pp. 67–75.

BOEHM, WERNER. *Social Work Practice.* New York: Columbia University Press, 1962.

BOLEN, JANE K., ''Easing the Pain of Termination for Adolescents,'' *Social Casework* 53 (November, 1971), pp. 519–527.

BOSZORMEYI-NAGY, IVAN, and FRAMO, JAMES L., eds. *Intensive Family Therapy: Theoretical and Practical Aspects.* New York: Harper & Row, 1965.

BOWERS, SWITHUN, ''The Nature and Definition of Social Casework,'' reprinted from *The Journal of Social Casework* (October, November, December, 1949) in *Principles and Techniques in Social Casework,* Cora Kasius, ed. New York: Family Service Association of America, 1950.

222   PSYCHOSOCIAL THERAPY

BOWLBY, JOHN. *Maternal Care and Mental Health,* 2nd ed. ("World Health Organization Monograph Series," no. 2). Geneva: World Health Organization, 1952.

BRAGER, GEORGE and SPECHT, HARRY. *Community Organizing.* New York: Columbia University Press, 1973.

BRENNER, MELVIN N. "The Quest for Viable Research in Social Services: Development of the Ministudy," *Social Service Review* 50 (September, 1956), pp. 426–444.

BRIGG, ELVIRA HUGHES, "The Application Problem: A Study of Why People Fail to Keep First Appointments," *Social Work* 10 (April, 1965), pp. 71–78.

BROOKS, PAUL R., "Industry-Agency Program for Employee Counseling," Social Casework 56 (July, 1975), pp. 404–410.

BROWN, SELMA B., "Time, Content and Worker as Factors in Discontinuity," *Smith College Studies in Social Work* 36 (February, 1966), pp. 210–233.

BURNS, MARY E., and GLASSER, PAUL H., "Similarities and Differences in Casework and Group Work Practice," *Social Service Review* 37 (1963), pp. 416–428.

CAIN, LILLIAN PIKE, and EPSTEIN, DORIS W. "The Utilization of Housewives as Volunteer Case Aides," *Social Casework* 48 (May, 1967), pp. 282–285.

CAMERON, NORMAN A. *Personality Development and Psychopathology: A Dynamic Approach.* Boston: Houghton Mifflin, 1963.

———. *The Psychology of Behavior Disorders: A Biosocial Interpretation.* New York: Houghton Mifflin, 1947.

CHAZIN, ROBERT M. "Day Treatment of Emotionally Disturbed Children," *Child Welfare* 48 (April, 1969), pp. 212–218.

CHEA, MARY WONG. "Research on Recording," Social Casework 53 (March, 1972), pp. 177–180.

CHETHIK, MORTON, FLEMING, ELIZABETH, MAYER, MORRIS F., and McCOY, JOHN N., "A Quest for Identity: Treatment of Distrubed Negro Children in a Predominantly White Treatment Center," *American Journal of Orthopsychiatry* 37 (January, 1967), pp. 71–77.

CLARKE, F. G., "Termination: The Forgotten Phase?," *The Social Worker* 35 (November, 1967), pp. 265–272.

CLAUSEN, JOHN A. "Psycho-Social Diagnosis: What and Why," *American Journal of Orthopsychiatry* 41 (October, 1971), pp. 847–848.

CLEMENS, DONALD W. "Functional Design in Building a Residential Treatment Facility," *Child Welfare* 50 (November, 1971), pp. 512–518.

CLIFFORD, GLEN, and ODIN, KATHERINE, "Young Adulthood: A Developmental Phase," *Smith College Studies in Social Work* 44 (February, 1974), pp. 125–142.

CLOWARD, RICHARD A., "Agency Structure as a Variable in Services to Groups," in *Group Work and Community Organization, 1956 Selected Papers, 83rd Annual Forum,* National Conference on Social Welfare. New York: Columbia University Press, 1956.

COGGS, PAULINE R., and ROBINSON, VIVIAN R. "Training Indigenous Community Leaders for Employment in Social Work," *Social Casework* 48 (May, 1967), pp. 278–281.

COHEN, PAULINE, DIZENHUZ, ISRAEL M., and WINGET, CAROLYN, "Family Adaptation to Terminal Illness and Death of a Parent," *Social Casework* 58 (April, 1977), pp. 223–228.

COLLIER, CATHERINE, "Fostering—Yesterday, Today and Tomorrow," *The Social Worker* 37 (November, 1969), pp. 221–226.

CORINNELL, RICHARD M. JR., "Environmental Modification: Caseworker's Concern or Caseworker's Neglect?," *Social Service Review* 47 (1973), pp. 208–220.

COUCH, ELIZABETH H. *Joint and Family Interviews in the Treatment of Marital Partners.* New York: Family Service Association of American, 1969.

COWAN, BARBARA, DASTYK, ROSE, and WICKHAM, EDCIL R., "Group Supervision as a Teaching Learning Modality in Social Work," *The Social Worker* 40 (December, 1972), pp. 256–261.

COYLE, GRACE L. *Group Work with American Youth: A Guide to the Practice of Leadership,* 1st ed. New York: Harper and Bros., 1948.

CUMMING, JOHN, and CUMMING, ELAINE. *Ego and Milieu: Theory and Practice of Environmental Therapy.* New York: Atherton Press, 1962.

CUNNINGHAM, JAMES M., "Psychiatric Case Work as an Epidemiological Tool,'' *American Journal of Orthopsychiatry* 18 (October, 1948), pp. 659–669.

DEIKUSS, RUDOLF, "The Adlerian Approach to Psychodynamics," *Contemporary Psychotherapies,* Morris I. Stein, ed. New York: Free Press, 1961.

DILLON, VERA, "Group Intake in a Casework Agency," *Social Casework* 46 (January, 1965), pp. 26–30.

DOHRENWEND, BRUCE P., "Notes on Psychosocial Diagnosis," *American Journal of Orthopsychiatry* 41 (October, 1971), p. 846.

EASTMAN, PAULA COSTA, "Consciousness-Raising as a Resocialization Process for Women," *Smith College Studies in Social Work* 43 (June, 1973), pp. 153–183.

EGGLESTON, SARAH, "Supportive Casework: Its Theoretical and Practical Meaning to Caseworkers," *Smith College Studies in Social Work* 38 (June, 1968), pp. 185–201.

EHRENKRANZ, SHIRLEY, "A Study of Joint Interviewing in the Treatment of Marital Problems" *Social Casework* 48 (October and November, 1967), pp. 498–502 and 570–574.

EINSTEIN, GERTRUDE, and MOSS, MIRIAM, "Some Thoughts on Sibling Relationships," *Social Casework* 48 (November, 1967), pp. 549–555.

EMPEY, LA MAR T., "Sociological Perspectives and Small-Group Work with Socially Deprived Youth," *Social Service Review* 62 (1968), pp. 448–463.

EPSTEIN, LAURA, "Is Autonomous Practice Possible?," *Social Work* 18 (March, 1973), pp. 5–12.

ERIKSON, ERIK H. *Childhood and Society,* 2nd ed., revised and enlarged. New York: W. W. Norton, 1963.

FANTL, BERTA, "Integrating Psychological, Social and Cultural Factors in Assertive Casework," *Social Work* 3 (October, 1958), pp. 30–37.

FAST, IRENE, and CAIN, ALBERT C., "The Stepparent Role: Potential for Disturbances in Family Functioning," *American Journal of Orthopsychiatry* 36 (April, 1966), pp. 485–491; and in *Differential Diagnosis and Treatment in Social Work,* 2nd ed., Francis J. Turner, ed. New York: Free Press, 1974.

FINCK, GEORGE H., REINER, BEATRICE SIMCOX, and SMITH, BRADY O., "Group Counseling with Unmarried Mothers," *Journal of Marriage and the Family* 27 (1965), pp. 224–229.

FINESTONE, SAMUEL, "Issues Involved in Developing Diagnostic Classifications for Casework," *Casework Papers*. New York: Family Service Association of America, 1960.

FISCHER, JOEL. *The Effectiveness of Social Casework*. Springfield: Charles C. Thomas, 1976.

FRANK, LAWRENCE. *Society as the Patient: Essays on Culture and Personality*. New Brunswick: Rutgers University Press, 1948.

FREEMAN, DOROTHY R. "Counseling Engaged Couples in Small Groups," *Social Work* 10 (October, 1965), pp. 36–42.

FREEMAN, HENRY, HOFFMAN, MARY ELLEN, SMITH, WINIFRED, and PRUNTY, HOWARD, "Can a Family Agency Be Relevant to the Inner Urban Scene?," *Social Casework* 55 (January, 1970), pp. 12–21.

FRIEDMAN, ALFRED S. "Co-Therapy as a Family Therapy Method and as a Training Method," *Therapy with Families of Sexually Acting-Out Girls*, A. S. Friedman *et al.*, eds. New York: Springer Publishing Co., 1971.

FRIEND, MAURICE R., and POLLAK, OTTO, "Psychosocial Aspects in the Preparation for Treatment of an Allergic Child," *American Journal of Orthopsychiatry* 24 (January, 1954), pp. 63–72.

FREUD, SIGMUND. "The Unconscious," in *Collected Papers*, vol. 4. London: Hogarth Press, 1949.

GANTER, GRACE, and POLANSKY, NORMAN A. "Predicting a Child's Accessibility to Individual Treatment from Diagnostic Groups," *Social Work* 9 (July, 1964), pp. 36–53.

GARLAND, JAMES A., JONES, HUBERT E., and KOLODNY, RALPH. "A Model for Stages of Development in Social Work Groups," *Exploration in Group Work*, Saul Bernstein, ed. Boston: Boston University School of Social Work, 1965.

GARRETT, ANNETTE, "Transference in Casework," reprinted from *The Family* (April, 1941) in *Principles and Techniques in Social Casework*, Cora Kasius, ed. New York: Family Service Association of America, 1950.

———, "Historical Survey of the Evolution of Casework," reprinted from *The Journal of Social Casework* (June, 1949) in *Principles and Techniques in Social Casework,* Cora Kasius, ed. New York: Family Service Association of America, 1950.

GEIST, JOANNE, and GERBER, NORMAN M., "Joint Interviewing: A Treatment Technique with Marital Partners," *Social Casework* 41 (February, 1960), pp. 76–83.

GERMAIN, CAREL B., "Time: An Ecological Variable in Social Work Practice," *Social Casework* 57 (July, 1976), pp. 419–426.

GERSON, L. W., and BERRY, A. F. E., "Psycho-Social Effects of Home Care: Results of a Randomized Controlled Trial," *International Journal of Epidemiology* 5 (1976), pp. 159–165.

GESELL, ARNOLD. *The First Five Years of Life: A Guide to the Study of the Preschool Child,* 9th ed. New York: Harper and Row, 1940.

GLASSER, PAUL, SARRI, ROSEMARY, and WINTER, ROBERT. *Individual Change Through Small Groups.* New York: Free Press, 1974.

GOLAN, NAOMI, "Crisis Theory," in *Social Work Treatment,* Francis J. Turner, ed. New York: Free Press, 1974.

GOLDBERG GALE, "Breaking the Communication Barrier: The Initial Interview with an Abusing Parent," *Child Welfare* 54 (1975), pp. 274–282.

GOLTON, MARGARET A., " Analysis of Private Practice in Casework," *Social Work* 8 (January, 1963), pp. 72–78.

GOTTLICK, WERNER, and STANLEY, JOE H., "Mutual Goals and Goal Setting in Casework," *Social Casework* 48 (October, 1967), pp. 471–481.

GRANT, JEAN M., and PANCYR, LUCILLE, "The Teaching Homemaker Service of a Welfare Department," *The Social Worker* 38 (May, 1970), pp. 19–24.

GREEN, ROSE, "Terminating the Relationship in Social Casework: A Working Paper," *Annual Institute on Corrections,* University of Southern California (April), 1962.

GRINKER, ROY. *Psychiatry in Broad Perspective.* New York: Behavioral Publications Inc., 1975.

GRINNELL, RICHARD M., "Environmental Modification: Casework's Concern or Casework's Neglect?," *Social Service Review* 47 (June, 1973), pp. 208–220.

GROSSER, CHARLES F. *New Directions in Community Organization: From Enabling to Advocacy.* New York: Praeger, 1973.

_____, "Local Residents as Mediators between Middle-Class Professional Workers and Lower-Class Clients," *Social Service Review* 40 (March, 1966), pp. 56–63.

GROUP FOR THE ADVANCEMENT OF PSYCHIATRY. *The Field of Family Therapy.* New York: G.A.P., 1970.

HALEY, JAY, comp. *Changing Families: A Family Therapy Reader.* New York: Grune and Stratton, 1971.

HALL, BERNARD H., and WHEELER, WINIFRED. "The Patient and His Relatives: Initial Joint Interview," *Social Work* 2 (January, 1957), pp. 75–80.

HALL, GALVIN S., and LINDZEY, GARDNER. *Theories of Personality.* 2nd ed. New York: John Wiley and Sons, 1970.

HALLOWITZ, DAVID, "Individual Treatment of the Child in the Context of Family Therapy," *Social Casework* 47 (February, 1966), pp. 82–86.

_____, "Problem Solving Theory." In *Social Work Treatment,* Francis J. Turner, ed. New York: Free Press, 1974.

HAMILTON, GORDON, "Basic Concepts in Social Casework," *The Family* 18 (July, 1937), pp. 147–156.

_____, "The Underlying Philosophy of Social Case Work," *The Family* 23 (July, 1941), pp. 139–147.

_____. *Theory and Practice of Social Casework,* 2nd ed., revised. New York: Columbia University Press, 1951.

Handbook on the Private Practice of Social Work. New York: National Association of Social Workers, 1967.

HANDEL, GERALD, ed. *The Psychosocial Interior of the Family: A Sourcebook for the Study of Whole Families.* London: George Allen and Unwin, 1968.

HANDLER, ELLEN, "Comparative Effectiveness of Four Preschool Programs: A Sociological Approach," *Child Welfare* 51 (January, 1972), pp. 550–561.

HANKINS, FRANK, "The Contributions of Sociology to the Practice of Social Work" *Proceedings of the National Conference of Social Work,* 1930. Chicago: University of Chicago Press, 1931.

HANSEN, CONSTANCE C., "An Extended Home Visit With Conjoint Family Therapy," *Family Process* 7 (March, 1968), pp. 67–87.

HARE, ALEXANDER PAUL, BORGATTA, EDGAR F., and BALES, ROBERT F., eds. *Small Groups: Studies in Social Interaction.* New York: A. A. Knopf, 1955.

HARTMANN, HEINZ. *Ego Psychology and the Problem of Adaptation,* translated by D. Rapaport. New York: International Universities Press, 1958.

HEARN, GORDON. "General Systems Theory and Social Work." In *Social Work Treatment,* Francis J. Turner, ed. New York: Free Press, 1974.

HEINICKE, CHRISTOPH, "Aiding 'At Risk' Children Through Psychoanalytic Social Work with Parents," *American Journal of Orthopsychiatry* 46 (1976), pp. 89–103.

HENDERSHOT, GERRY E., "Familial Satisfaction, Birth, Order and Fertility Values," *Journal of Marriage and the Family* 31 (February, 1969), pp. 27–33.

HENRY, JULES, "Environmental and Sympton Formation," *American Journal of Orthopsychiatry* 17 (October, 1947), pp. 628–632.

HERSKO, MARVIN, "Group Psychotherapy with Delinquent Adolescent Girls," reprinted from *American Journal of Orthopsychiatry* 32 (January, 1962), pp. 169–175, in *Differential Diagnosis and Treatment in Social Work,* 1st ed., F. J. Turner, ed. New York: Free Press, 1968.

HERZOG, ELIZABETH, and LEWIS, HYLAN, "Children in Poor Families: Myths and Realities," *American Journal of Orthopsychiatry* 40 (April, 1970), pp. 375–387.

HEYMAN, MARGARET M., "Collaboration Between Doctor and Caseworker in a General Hospital," *Social Casework* 48 (May, 1967), pp. 286–292.

HIKEL, VIRGINIA, "Fostering the Troubled Child," *Child Welfare* 48 (November, 1969), pp. 427–431.

HO, MAN KEUNG, "Problems and Results of a Shift to Heterogeneous Age Groups in Cottages at a Boys Home," *Child Welfare* 50 (November, 1971), pp. 524–527.

HOFFMAN, LINDA R., LEHMAN, VIRGINIA L., and ZEV, ELI D., "A

Group Home-Hospital Treatment Model for Severely Disturbed Adolescents," *Child Welfare* 54 (1975), pp. 283–289.

HOGARTY, GERARD, "Discharge Readiness: The Components of Casework Judgement," *Social Casework* 47 (March, 1966), pp. 165–171.

HOLLIS, FLORENCE. *Casework: A Psychosocial Therapy*, New York: Random House, 1964 (1st ed.) and 1972 (2nd ed.)

———, "Casework and Social Class," *Social Casework* 46 (October, 1965), pp. 463–471.

———, "The Coding and Application of a Typology of Casework Treatment," *Social Casework* 48 (October, 1967), pp. 489–497.

———, "Development of a Casework Treatment Typology," *Final Report NIMH Grant MH-00513, 1966.*

———, "Explorations in the Development of a Typology of Casework Treatment," *Social Casework* 48 (June, 1967), pp. 335–341.

———, "Personality Diagnosis in Casework," *Ego Psychology and Dynamic Casework,* H. Parad, ed. New York: Family Service Association of America, 1958.

———, "A Profile of Early Interviews in Marital Counseling," *Social Casework* 49 (January, 1968), pp. 35–43.

———, "Social Casework: The Psychosocial Approach," *Encyclopedia of Social Work* 2. New York: National Association of Social Workers, 1971.

———, *Social Casework in Practice: Six Case Studies.* New York: Family Welfare Association of America, 1939.

HORNEY, KAREN. *New Ways in Psychoanalysis.* New York: W. W. Norton and Co., 1939.

HUNTER, DAVID R., "Social Action to Influence Institutional Change," *Social Casework* 51 (April, 1970), pp. 225–231.

HUSBAND, DIANE, and SCHEUNEMANN, Henry R., "The Use of Group Process in Teaching Termination," *Child Welfare* 51 (October, 1972), pp. 505–513.

HUXLEY, JULIAN, "The Evolutionary Vision," *Evolution After Darwin, Vol. 3, Issues in Evoltion,* Sol Fax and Charles Cullinder, eds. Chicago: University of Chicago Press, 1960.

JAMES, GAYLE, GILCHRIST, M., and MCFADDEN, DONNA M. "Group Intake in a Child Guidance Clinic," *The Social Worker,* 36 (November, 1968), pp. 236–243.

JEHU, DEREK. *Learning Theory and Social Work.* London: Routledge & Kegan Paul, 1967.

JOSSELYN, IRENE M. *Psychosocial Development of Children.* New York: Family Service Association of America, 1948.

———, "The Family as a Psychological Unit," *Social Casework* 34 (October, 1953), pp. 336–343.

KADUSHIN, ALFRED, "Testing Diagnostic Competence: A Problem for Social Work Research," *Social Casework* 44 (July, 1963), pp. 397–405.

KAHN, A. J. "Perspectives on Access to Social Services," *Social Work* (U.K.) 26 (July, 1969), pp. 3–9.

KAISER, CLARA A., "The Social Group Work Process," *Social Work* 3 (April, 1958), pp. 67–75.

KAMMEYER, KENNETH, "Sibling Position and the Feminine Role," *Journal of Marriage and the Family* 29 (August, 1967), pp. 494–499.

KANE, ROSALIE A., "Look to the Record," *Social Work* 19 (August, 1974), pp. 412–419.

KASIUS, Cora, ed. *A Comparison of Diagnostic and Functional Casework Concepts,* Report of the Family Service Association of America to Study Basic Concepts in Casework Practice. New York: Family Service Association of America, 1950.

KATZ, ALFRED H. "Some Psychosocial Problems in Hemophilia," *Social Casework* 40 (January, 1959), pp. 321–326.

KEDWARD, H. B., and SYLPH, JUDITH, "The Social Correlates of Chronic Neurotic Disorder," *Social Psychiatry* 9 (1974), pp. 91–98.

KEMPER, THEODORE D., "Mate Selection and Marital Satisfaction According to Sibling Type of Husband and Wife," *Journal of Marriage and the Family* 28 (August, 1966), pp. 346–349.

KING, CHARLES H., "Family Therapy with the Deprived Family," *Social Casework* 48 (April, 1967), pp. 203–208.

KLUCKHOHN, FLORENCE R., and STRODTBECK, FRED L. *Variations in Value Orientations.* Evanston: Row, Peterson and Co., 1961.

KLUCKHOLM, C., and MURRAY, H. *Personality in Nature, Society and Culture*. New York: Alfred A. Knopf, 1953.

KOLODNY, RALPH, "A Group Work Approach to the Isolated Child," reprinted from *Social Work* 6 (July, 1961), pp. 76–84, in *Differential Diagnosis and Treatment in Social Work,* 2nd ed., F. J. Turner, ed. New York: Free Press, 1976.

KONOPKA, GISELA. *Social Group Work: A Helping Process*. Englewood Cliffs: Prentice-Hall, 1963.

KOUNIN, JACOB, POLANSKY, NORMAN, *et al.* "Experimental Studies of Clients' Reactions to Initial Interviews," *Human Relations* 9 (1956), pp. 265–293.

KRILL, DONALD F., "Existential Social Work," *Social Work Treatment*, Francis J. Turner, ed. New York: Free Press, 1974.

LEVENSTEIN, SIDNEY. *Private Practice in Social Casework*. New York: Columbia University Press, 1964.

LIDZ, THEODORE. *The Person: His Development Throughout the Life Cycle*. New York: Basic Books, 1968.

LINDENBERG, RUTH ELLEN, "Hard to Reach: Client or Casework Agency?," *Social Work* 3 (October, 1958), pp. 23–29.

LINDENFIELD, RITA, "Working with Other Professions," *The Social Worker* 35 (September, 1967), pp. 175–181.

LITTNER, NES, "The Impact of the Client's Unconscious on the Caseworker's Reactions," *Ego Psychology and Dynamic Casework,* Howard J. Parad, ed. New York: Family Service Association of America, 1958.

——. *Some Traumatic Effects of Separation and Placement*. New York: Child Welfare League of America, 1956.

LONG, NICHOLAS, "Information and Referral Services: A Short History and Some Recommendations," *Social Service Review* 47 (1973), pp. 49–62.

LOWE, GORDON R. *The Growth of Personality from Infancy to Old Age*. London: Harmondsworth, Penguin Books, 1972.

LUTZ, WERNER A. *Concepts and Principles Underlying Social Casework Practice,* Monograph III, Social Work Practice in Medical Care and Rehabilitation Settings. Washington, D. C.: National Association of Social Workers, 1956.

MACGREGOR, ROBERT. "Progress in Multiple Impact Therapy," *Exploring the Base for Family Therapy,* Nathan Ackerman, Frances L.

Beatman and Sanford N. Sherman, eds. New York: Family Service Association of America, 1961.

MCCUTCHEON, BETH, and CALHOUN, KAREN S., "Social and Emotional Adjustment of Infants and Toddlers to a Day Care Setting," *American Journal of Orthopsychiatry* 46 (January, 1976), pp. 104–108.

MCGRIFF, DOROTHY, "A Co-Ordinated Approach to Discharge Planning," *Social Work* 10 (January, 1965), pp. 45–50.

MCKANE, MAUREEN, "Case-Record Writing with Reader Empathy," *Child Welfare* 54 (1975), pp. 593–597.

MABLEY, ALBERTINA, "Group Application Interviews in a Family Agency," *Social Casework* 47 (March, 1966), pp. 158–164.

MALONEY, SARA E., AND MUDGETT, MARGARET H., "Group Work—Group Casework: Are They the Same?," *Social Work* 4 (April, 1959), pp. 29–36.

MANNHEIMER, JOAN, "A Demonstration of Foster Parents in the Co-worker Role," *Child Welfare* 48 (February, 1964), pp. 104–107.

MANNINO, FORTUNE V., AND SHORE, MILTON F. "Ecologically Oriented Family Intervention," *Family Process* 2 (December, 1972), pp. 499–505.

MARCUS, LOTTE, "Communication Concepts and Principles," in *Social Work Treatment,* Francis J. Turner, ed. New York: Free Press, 1974.

MASON, MARY E., "The Contribution of the Social History in the Diagnosis of Child Disturbances," *British Journal of Psychiatric Social Work* 9 (Autumn, 1968), pp. 180–187.

MASSERMAN, JULES H., ed. *Psychoanalysis and Social Process.* New York: Grune and Stratton, 1961.

MEIER, ELIZABETH, "Interactions Between the Person and his Operational Situations: A Basis for Classification in Casework," *Social Casework* 46 (November, 1965), pp. 542–549.

MERLE, SHERMAN, "Some Arguments Against Private Practice," *Social Work* 7 (January, 1962), pp. 12–17.

MEYER, CAROL H. *Social Work Practice: A Response to the Urban Crisis.* New York: Free Press, 1970.

MITCHELL, MARION M. "Transracial Adoptions: Philosophy and Practice," *Child Welfare* 48 (December, 1969), pp. 613–619.

MORSE, JOAN, "Making Hospitalization a Growth Experience for Arthritic Children," *Social Casework* 46 (November, 1965), pp. 550–556.

MULLEN, EDWARD J., AND DUMPSON, J. R. *Evaluation of Social Intervention.* San Francisco: Jossey-Bass, 1972.

———, "Casework Communication," *Social Casework* 49 (November, 1968), pp. 546–551.

MURPHY, ANN, PEUSCHEL, SIEGFRIED M., and SCHNEIDER, JANE, "Group Work with Parents of Children with Down's Syndrome," reprinted from *Social Casework* 54 (February, 1973), pp. 114–119, in *Differential Diagnosis and Treatment in Social Work,* 2nd ed., F. J. Turner, ed. New York: Free Press, 1976.

NATIONAL ASSOCIATION OF SOCIAL WORKERS, AD HOC COMMITTEE ON ADVOCACY. "The Social Worker as Advocate: Champion of Social Victims, *Social Work* 14 (April, 1969), pp. 16–22.

NESSER, WILLIAM B., AND SUDDERTH, GRACE B., "Genetics and Casework," *Social Casework* 46 (January, 1965), pp. 22–25.

NICHOLS, JR., WILLIAM C., AND RUTLEDGE, AARON L., "Psychotherapy with Teenagers," *Journal of Marriage and the Family* 27 (1965), pp. 166–170.

NORTHEN, HELEN, *Social Work with Groups.* New York: Columbia University Press, 1969.

OBERMAN, EDNA, "The Use of Time-Limited Relationship Therapy with Borderline Patients," *Smith College Studies in Social Work* 37 (February, 1967), pp. 127–141.

OLMSTED, MICHAEL S. *The Small Group.* New York: Random House, 1959.

PARSLOE, PHYLLIDA, "Presenting Reality—The Choice of a Casework Method," *British Journal of Psychiatric Social Work* 8 (1965–1966), pp. 6–10.

PELLMAN, RENEE, MCDONALD, RORY, AND ANSON, SUSAN, "The Van: A Mobile Approach to Services for Adolescents," *Social Casework* 58 (May, 1977), pp. 268–275.

PERLMAN, HELEN H., ed. *Charlotte Towle on Social Work and Social Casework.* Chicago: University of Chicago Press, 1969.

———, "Diagnosis Anyone?," *Psychiatry and Social Sciences Review* 3 (8:1969–1970), pp. 12–17.

_____, "Intake and Some Role Considerations," *Social Casework* 41 (December, 1960), pp. 171–177, reprinted in *Persona: Social Role and Personality,* H. H. Perlman, ed. Chicago: University of Chicago Press, 1968, pp. 162–176.

_____, *Social Casework: A Problem Solving Process.* Chicago: University of Chicago Press, 1957.

PHILLIPS, DORIS CAMPBELL, "Of Plums and Thistles: The Search for Diagnosis," *Social Work* 5 (January, 1960), pp. 84–90.

PIAGET, JEAN, *The Origins of Intelligence in Children.* Translated by M. Cook. New York: International Universities Press, 1952.

PINCUS, ALLEN, AND MINAHAN, ANNE, *Social Work Practice: Model and Method.* Ithaca: F. E. Peacock, 1973.

POLLITT, ERNESTO, EICHLER, AVIVA, AND CHAN, CHEE-KHOON, "Psychosocial Development and Behavior of Mothers of Failure-To-Thrive Children," *American Journal of Orthopsychiatry* 45 (July, 1975), pp. 525–537.

RAPOPORT, LYDIA, "Social Casework: An Appraisal and an Affirmation," *Smith College Studies in Social Work* 34 (June, 1969), pp. 213–235.

_____, "Crisis Intervention as a Mode of Brief Treatment," *Theories of Social Casework,* R. W. Roberts and R. H. Nee, eds. Chicago: University of Chicago Press, 1970.

REID, WILLIAM J., AND SHYNE, ANN W., *Brief and Extended Casework.* New York: Columbia University Press, 1969.

REID, WILLIAM J., AND EPSTEIN, LAURA, *Task-Centered Casework.* New York: Columbia University Press, 1972.

REINER, BEATRICE SIMCOX, AND KAUFMAN, IRVING, *Character Disorders in Parents of Delinquents.* New York: Family Service Association of America, 1959.

REYNOLDS, BERTHA, "Is Diagnosis an Imposition?," *Social Work and Social Living.* New York: Citadel Press, 1951.

RHIM, BONNIE C., "The Use of Videotapes in Social Work Agencies," *Social Casework* 57 (December, 1976), pp. 644–650.

RICHMOND, MARY E., *Social Diagnosis.* New York: Russell Sage Foundation, 1917.

_____, *What is Social Case Work? An Introductory Description.* Social Work Series. New York: Russell Sage Foundation, 1922.

RIPPLE, LILLIAN, ALEXANDER, ERNESTINA, AND POLEMIS, BERNICE W., *Motivation Capacity and Opportunity*. Social Service Monographs. Chicago: University of Chicago Press, 1964.

RITCHIE, AGNES M., "Multiple Impact Therapy: An Experiment," *Social Work* 5 (July, 1960), pp. 16–21.

ROBERTS, R., AND NEE R., EDS. *Theories of Social Casework*. Chicago: University of Chicago Press, 1970.

RODGERS, DAVID A., ZIEGLER, FREDERICK J., ALTROCCHI, JOHN, AND LEVY, NISSIM, "A Longitudinal Study of the Psychosocial Effects of Vasectomy," *Journal of Marriage and the Family* 27 (1965), pp. 59–64.

ROGERS, CARL R., "Characteristics of a Helping Relationship," *Canada's Mental Health*, Supplement 27. Ottawa: Department of National Health and Welfare, March, 1962.

ROKEACH, MILTON. *The Nature of Human Values*. New York: Free Press, 1973.

ROSE, SHELDON D., "A Behavioral Approach to the Group Treatment of Parents," reprinted from *Social Work* 14 (July, 1969), pp. 21–30, in *Differential Diagnosis and Treatment in Social Work*, 2nd ed., F. J. Turner, ed. New York: Free Press, 1976.

ROSENBLATT, AARON. "The Application of Role Concepts to the Intake Process," *Social Casework* 43 (January, 1962), pp. 8–14.

RUBINSTEIN, DAVID, AND WEINER, OSKAR, R., "Co-Therapy Teamwork Relationships in Family Psychotherapy," *Family Therapy and Disturbed Families*, Gerald H. Zuk and Ivan Boszormenyi Nagi, eds. Palo Alto: Science and Behavior Books, 1967.

RUSSEL, A. "Late Psychosocial Consequences in Concentration Camp Survivor Families," *American Journal of Orthopsychiatry* 44 (July, 1974), pp. 611–619.

SARK, FRANCES B., "Barriers to Client-Worker Communication at Intake," *Social Casework* 40 (1959), pp. 177–183.

SATIR, VIRGINIA. *Conjoint Family Therapy: A Guide to Theory and Technique*. Palo Alto: Science and Behavior Books, 1967.

SCHERZ, FRANCES H., "Casework—A Psychosocial Therapy: An Essay Review," *Social Service Review* 38 (1964), pp. 206–211.

———, "Theory and Practice in Family Therapy," *Theories of Social*

Casework, Robert W. Roberts and Robert H. Nee, eds. Chicago: University of Chicago Press, 1970.

SCHIFF, SHELDON K. "Termination of Therapy: Problems in a Community Psychiatric Outpatient Clinic," *Archives of General Psychiatry* 6 (1962), pp. 93–98.

SCHILD, SYLVIA. "The Challenging Opportunity for Social Workers in Genetics, *Social Work* 2 (April, 1966), pp. 22–28.

SCHLOSSER, DONALD H. "How Volunteers Can Strengthen Child Welfare Services," *Child Welfare* 48 (December, 1969), pp. 606–612.

SCHOENBERG, B., ET AL. Psychosocial Aspects of Terminal Care. New York: Columbia University Press, 1972.

SCHOENBERG, BERNARD, CARR, ARTHUR C., PERETZ, DAVID, KUTSCHER, AUSTIN H., KUTSCHER, LILLIAN, EDS. *Teaching Psychosocial Aspects of Patient Care.* New York: Columbia University Press, 1972.

SCHULTZ, AMELIA L., "The Impact of Genetic Disorders," *Social Work* 2 (April, 1966), pp. 29–34.

SCHULTZ, AMELIA L. AND MOTULSKY, ARNO G. "Medical Genetics and Adoption," *Child Welfare* 50 (January, 1971), pp. 4–17.

SCHWARTZ, WILLIAM, AND ZALBA, SERAPIO R. *The Practice of Group Work.* New York: Columbia University Press, 1971.

SEABERG, JAMES R., "Case Recording by Code," *Social Work* 10 (October, 1965), pp. 92–98.

SEABURY, BRETT A., "Arrangement of Physical Space in Social Work Settings," *Social Work* 16 (October, 1971), pp. 43–49.

SHALINSKY, WILLIAM., "Group Composition as an Element of Social Group Work Practice," *Social Service Review* 43 (1969), pp. 42–49.

SHAPIRO, RODNEY J., AND BUDMAN, SIMON H. "Defection, Termination and Continuation in Family and Individual Therapy," *Family Process* 12 (1973), pp. 55–67.

SHERESHEFSKY, PAULINE, "Pregnancy and its Outcome: Psychosocial Aspects: An Essay Review," *Social Service Review* 43 (1969), pp. 194–200.

SHERMAN, SANFORD N. "Family Therapy," in *Social Work Treatment,* Francis J. Turner, ed. New York: Free Press, 1974.

———, "Joint Interviews in Casework Practice," *Social Work* 4 (April, 1959), pp. 20–28.

SHYNE, ANN W., "The Contribution of Alfred Adler to the Development of Dynamic Psychology," *American Journal of Orthopsychiatry* 12 (April, 1942), pp. 352–359.

SILVERMAN, PHYLISS R., "A re-examination of the Intake Procedure," *Social Casework* 51 (December, 1970), pp. 625–634.

SIPORIN, MAX, "Situational Assessment and Intervention," *Social Casework* 53 (February, 1972), pp. 91–109.

———, "Social Treatment: A New-Old Helping Method." *Social Work* 15 (July, 1970), pp. 13–25.

SKELSKIE, BARBARA E., "An Exploratory Study of Grief in Old Age," *Smith College Studies in Social Work* 45 (February, 1975), pp. 159–182.

SMALLEY, RUTH E. *Theory for Social Work Practice.* New York: Columbia University Press, 1967.

SONNE, JOHN C., AND LINCOLN, GERALDINE, "Heterosexual Co-Therapy Team Experiences During Family Therapy," *Family Process* 4 (September, 1965), pp. 177–195.

SPECK, ROSS V. "Family Therapy in the Home," *Exploring the Base for Family Therapy,* Nathan W. Ackerman, F. L. Beatman, and Sanford N. Sherman, eds. New York: Family Service Association of America, 1961.

———, "Psychotherapy of the Social Network of a Schizophrenic Family," *Family Process* 6 (September, 1967), pp. 208–214.

STAMM, ISABEL L., "Family Therapy," *Casework: A Psychosocial Therapy,* 2nd ed., Florence Hollis, ed. New York: Random House, 1972.

STEIN, HERMAN D., AND CLOWARD, RICHARD A., EDS. *Social Perspectives on Behavior.* New York: Free Press, 1958.

STEIN, JOAN W. *The Family as a Unit of Study and Treatment.* Trova K. Hutchins *et al.,* eds. Seattle: University of Washington School of Social Work, 1970.

STEIN, MORRIS I. *Contemporary Psychotherapies.* New York: Free Press, 1961.

STREAN, HERBERT S. "Application of the 'Life Model' to Casework," *Social Work* 17 (September, 1972), pp. 46–53.

———, "Role Theory," *Social Work Treatment,* Francis J. Turner, ed. New York: Free Press, 1974.

238   PSYCHOSOCIAL THERAPY

STRINGER, ELIZABETH A., "Homemaker Service to the Single-Parent Family," *Social Casework,* 48 (February, 1967), pp. 75–79.

STROUP, ATLEE L., AND HUNTER, KATHERINE J. "Sibling Position in the Family and Personality of Offspring," *Journal of Marriage and the Family* 27 (February, 1965), pp. 65–68.

STUART, RICHARD B., "Behavior Modification: A Technology of Social Change," *Social Work Treatment,* Francis J. Turner, ed. New York: Free Press, 1974.

SULLIVAN, HARRY S. *The Interpersonal Theory of Psychiatry.* New York: W. W. Norton and Co., 1953.

SUNLEY, ROBERT, "Family Advocacy from Case to Cause," *Social Casework* 51 (June, 1970), pp. 347–357.

TAYLOR, RONALD, "Psychosocial Development among Black Children and Youth," *American Journal of Orthopsychiatry* 46 (January, 1976), pp. 4–19.

THOMAS, EDWIN J., ED. *Behavioral Science for Social Workers.* New York: Free Press, 1967.

THOMPSON, GENEVIEVE M. "Foster Grandparents," *Child Welfare* 48 (1969), pp. 564–568.

TOBIN, M. DORSEY, "Diagnostic Use of the Home Visit in Child Guidance," *Smith College Studies in Social Work* 38 (June, 1968), pp. 202–213.

TOFFLER, ALVIN. *Future Shock.* New York: Bantam Books, 1971.

TURNER, FRANCIS J., ED. *Differential Diagnosis and Treatment in Social Work,* New York: The Free Press, 1968 (1st ed.) and 1976 (2nd ed.).

———, "A Comparison of Procedures in the Treatment of Clients with Two Different Value Orientations," *Social Casework* 45 (May, 1964), pp. 273–277.

———, "Effect of Value Reevaluation on Current Practice," *Social Casework* 56 (May, 1975), pp. 285–291.

———, "Ethnic Difference and Client Performance," *Social Service Review* 44 (March, 1970), pp. 1–10.

———, "Psychosocial Therapy," *Social Work Treatment,* Francis J. Turner, ed. New York: Free Press, 1974.

_____, "The Search for Diagnostic Categories in Social Work Treatment." Unpublished paper given at Learned Societies of Canada, University of York, Toronto, 1969.

_____, "Values and the Social Worker," *Reflections on Values Education*, J. R. Meyer, ed. Waterloo: Wilfrid Laurier University Press, 1976.

VIETES, RUTH, COHEN, ROSALYN, RIENS, RUTH, AND RONALL, RUTH, "Day Treatment Center and School: Seven Years Experience," *American Journal of Orthopsychiatry* 35 (January, 1965), pp. 160–169.

WASSER, EDNA, "Family Casework Focus on the Older Person," *Social Casework* 47 (July, 1966), pp. 423–431.

WASSERMAN, SIDNEY L., "Ego Psychology," in *Social Work Treatment*, Francis J. Turner, ed. New York: Free Press, 1974.

WATSON, ANDREW S., "Reality Testing and Transference in Psychotherapy," *Smith College Studies in Social Work* 36 (June, 1966), pp. 191–209.

WATSON, KENNETH W., "Differential Supervision," *Social Work* 18 (November, 1973), pp. 80–88.

WELINS, ELSA G., "Some Effects of Premature Parental Responsibility on the Older Sibling," *Smith College Studies in Social Work* 35 (October, 1964), pp. 26–40.

WERBEL, BEATRICE, HENRY, CHARLOTTE S., AND MILLAR, MARGARET W., "Motivation for Using Casework Services," *Social Casework* 39 (February-March, 1958), pp. 124–137.

WERNER, HAROLD D., "Cognitive Theory," *Social Work Treatment*, Francis J. Turner, ed. New York: Free Press, 1974.

WHITTAKER, JAMES K. *Social Treatment: An Approach to Interpersonal Helping*. Chicago: Aldine Publishing Company, 1974.

WILLMOTT, PHYLLIS. *Consumers' Guide to the British Social Services*. London: Harmondsworth, Penguin Books. 1967.

WOOD, ALFRED, FRIEDMAN, JACK, AND STEISEL, IRA. "Psychosocial Factors in Phenylketonuira," *American Journal of Orthopsychiatry* 37 (1967), pp. 671–679.

YELAJA, SHANKAR A., "Functional Theory for Social Work Practice,"

Social Work Treatment, Francis J. Turner, ed. New York: Free Press, 1974.

YOUNGHUSBAND, EILEEN. *Social Work and Social Change.* London: George Allen and Unwin, 1967.

ZASTROW, CHARLES, "The Current Status of Community-Wide Social Data Banks," *Social Worker* 40 (May, 1972), pp. 107–112.

Index

Abnormal functioning: *see* Personality
Abnormality, nature of, 37–39; *see also* Normality
Accountability, of therapist, 53
Adjustment, impact of environment on, 209–210
Advocate, therapist as, 165
Agencies:
  barriers to service access, 184
  historical development of, 171
  location of, 175–176
  physical characteristics of, 191–194
    impact on client, 192–194
    and unplanned termination, 194
  primary and secondary, 175
  and private practice, 179
  sponsorship, 174–175
  target groups, 182–184

  see also Setting
American Journal of Orthopsychiatry, 12
Assessment:
  definition of, 77
  elements of, 77–78
  see also Diagnosis
Attitudes: *see* Values
Authority, use of, in therapy, 108

Balen, Luther, 204–205
Beginnings, as component of treatment, 87–88
Benedict, Ruth, 16
Berry, A.F.E., 209
Bettelheim, Bruno, 13
Biological and physical endowment:
  and personality, 25–27

and physical endowment, 26
and physical well-being, 27
unconscious as a component
of, 29
values as a component of, 32
Physical endowment, and relationship to functioning,
25–27, 210
Physical environment, influence
of, 55
Physical well-being, and personality, 27
Policies and programs, 185–187
antitherapeutic aspects of, 186
in response to need, 185
and service delivery system,
185
Pollak, Otto, 13
Practice, risks of:
to the client, 66
development of dependency,
65
issue of diagnostic competence, 67
with significant others, 152
to society, 66–67
to the therapist, 67
Prevention, as a component of
therapy, 208
Privacy, importance of, in
therapy, 102, 111
Private practice:
affiliation with agencies, 179
development of, 178–179
Problem: *see* Psychosocial problem
Professional help:
development of concept, 171
historical development, 182
quality of, 188

use of adjunctive personnel,
189
see also Professionalism and
therapy
Professional roles: *see* Roles, of
professionals
Professionalism and therapy:
effect of value sets, 177
level of competence, 188
need for continuous development, 189
professional training, 53
societal accountability, 53
supervision, 54, 104–105,
108, 122
Professionals:
as adjuncts to therapy, 152–
154, 189
as sources of data, 74
see also Professionalism and
therapy
Psychoanalytic school, influence
of, 56, 103–104
*Psychosocial Interior of the
Family, The,* 12
Psychosocial problem, nature of,
39
Psychosocial theory:
conceptual history of, 13
definition of, 5
definition of diagnosis, 78–79
emergence of, 4
and group therapy, 125,
130–131
and group work, 11
historical origins, 5–17
influence of casework on, 100
influence of the social sciences on, 198
and the medical tradition, 42

definition of, 43
diagnostic competence of, 67
difficulties as a group leader, 129–130
emotional and legal risks for, 67
influence of worker style on client, 201
and multimodality approach, 101
as a person, 53
and professional training, 53
roles of, 160–167
  in community intervention, 141–142
  family therapy, 136–138
  in individual therapy, 103, 108–111
  in referrals, 164
and societal accountability, 53
supervision, purposes of, 53–54, 104–105, 108, 122
see also Roles, of professional; Social worker
Therapy:
changes resulting from, 45–49
components and structure of, 7, 71
effect of different approaches, 207–209
empirical study and evaluation of, 70, 205–206
feelings in, 46–47
goal of, 44
importance of values in, 152, 202–203
as an individualized process, 70, 205

knowledge and understanding in, 45–46
learning theory, implications for, 48
legal risks in, 67
length and spacing of interviews, 57
matching process in, 190
multifaceted approach, 148
present orientation, 204
preventative, 208
provision of information in, 111
psychoanalytic school, influence of, 56
a rational process, 71–72
role of maturational process in, 58
setting, 54, 170, 171, 173–180
as a technical process, 70
use of conscious and unconscious in, 105–108, 204
use of other professionals, 151–154
use of other services, 54, 159–160
use of paraprofessionals and volunteers, 154–156
use of significant others, 150
see also Agencies; Change; Data gathering; Diagnosis; Goal setting; Modalities of treatment; Referral; Setting; Short-term treatment; Significant others; Therapeutic relationship; Therapist